BARRON'S

Pass Key to the

GED TEST®

2ND EDITION

Christopher M. Sharpe

Joseph S. Reddy

Kelly A. Battles

W9-BRF-629

ABOUT THE AUTHORS

Christopher M. Sharpe is the Director of the English Language Arts and English Language Learners Department at a career and technical education charter school in New York City, and he is the CEO of Sharpe Consulting Group, LLC. Throughout his professional career, he has worked to prepare students for success on the GED® test and in college at a variety of organizations, including Columbia University. He has also worked at the regional and state level as a provider of professional development to teachers and administrators of adult education programs.

Joseph S. Reddy has been a professional test preparation teacher and tutor for over 20 years, and is the founder of JSR Learning, a test preparation services company. He has also helped hundreds of students prepare for the GED® test through the Community Impact GED program at Columbia University.

Kelly A. Battles is an English teacher, published author, and freelance editor. For the past 21 years, she has taught and tutored high school and college students, as well as professional adults. She has provided TOEFL test preparation for foreign students and private GED tutoring for adults. In addition to working on *Barron's How to Prepare for the GED® Test* and *Barron's Pass Key to the GED® Test*, she is one of three authors on the updated *Barron's GED® Test Flash Cards*. She has also edited several books for emerging authors.

Acknowledgments

A special thank you goes out to Robbie Johnson and Alisha Pelligrini for their writing contributions. They are not only my talented students, but they are both gifted writers with a great future ahead of them!—Kelly Battles

GED® is a registered trademark of the American Council on Education (ACE) and is administered exclusively by GED Testing Service LLC under license. This material is not endorsed or approved by ACE or GED Testing Service.

All inquiries should be addressed to:
Barron's Educational Series, Inc.
250 Wireless Boulevard
Hauppauge, New York 11788
www.barronseduc.com

ISBN: 978-1-4380-0801-1

Library of Congress Control Number: 2016961435

PRINTED IN CANADA
9 8 7 6 5 4 3 2 1

10%
POST-CONSUMER
WASTE
Paper contains a minimum
of 10% post-consumer
waste (PCW). Paper used
in this book was derived
from certified, sustainable
forestlands.

Contents

UNIT 2: MATHEMATICAL REASONING

UNIT 4: SCIENCE

Introduction

Congratulations! You've decided to pursue your GED® test credential, which is a very important and positive decision. Taking this exam is usually the first major step on the path to continuing education or career development. Many students who have moved on to college, graduate school, or career-level employment point to passing this test and receiving their diplomas as the first part of a life-changing process. You've made a very positive choice, and we congratulate you for it!

The GED® test is intended to show that a person has the skills and knowledge necessary to pursue post-secondary education, which means college and graduate school, or to pursue professional employment, which means a career path. Post-secondary means "after high school." Since the GED® test is testing at a high school level, you need to reach a high school level of skill and knowledge to pass the exam. If you have some gaps in your prior education, you may need to do some extra studying to fill them. You won't need to learn *everything* that's currently being taught in high school. However, you will want to be well prepared in the material that makes up the core of a high school education.

This book will help you learn or review some of the most important things you'll need to know to pass the exam. It will also help you make the most of what you know when you take the exam. It will even help you identify the gaps you need to fill.

What this book will NOT do is replace a secondary-level education. Depending on your strengths and weaknesses when you start preparing, you might need to budget some additional time to study certain subjects.

STEPS TO SUCCESS

Relax!

This is very important. Most students build up a lot of stress worrying about the GED® test. Some students just really don't like to take tests. Plus the fact that they have to take a test to get their diplomas is stressful.

Just relax. This exam is not nearly as hard or as scary as you might think. Most of the stress (and yes, even fear) that you may feel is just worry about the unknown. Just remember that worrying has never increased an exam score. All worrying does is make it more difficult to learn and remember. That's the bad news.

The good news is that fear of the unknown has a simple cure: **knowledge**. When you learn about the GED® test, you will find that you don't have much to worry about. When you have a plan to prepare for and a strategy to take the test, you can stop being so scared. You will develop confidence and good study habits, which always raise exam scores.

Learn About the Test

To succeed on any test, you need to learn more than just the material on the test. You also need to learn about the test itself. The more you know about what the test measures, how it is designed, and what will be expected of you, the more likely you will be to pass. By the time we're done with you, you will be an expert about the test's contents.

Follow a Plan

The GED® test is a big exam. It covers a wide range of content across multiple subjects. To be ready, you'll need to study and practice a lot of material. If you tried to prepare for everything at once, you would quickly find yourself overwhelmed. The only way to complete a process this large successfully is to break it down into smaller, more manageable pieces. As you complete each piece, you'll feel a sense of accomplishment. You'll also see yourself making progress.

Prepare Every Day

Creating an individual study plan is the easy part. The more difficult part for most people is consistently using a study plan. The best plan ever created will do you no good if you don't have the self-discipline to follow it. You might need to make a real effort to continue working through your plan, so be ready to push yourself a little. The effort will definitely pay off.

Plan to spend some time preparing **every day** between today and the day you take the test. This may sound extremely difficult or even impossible, but it really isn't. The amount of time you spend each day doesn't always have to be the same. You can spend an hour or 2 one day and then you can spend 20 minutes the next day. You can study 5 or 10 minutes at a time 3 times in a day. The important thing is to spend some time each and every day. This will keep your knowledge fresh, your skills sharp, and your forward progress nice and steady.

You can prepare in lots of ways, even when you don't have time to spend an hour with this book. Having a strong knowledge of vocabulary is important. You can learn a few words at a time by working with a list or from flash cards. Your mental math skills need to be sharp. You can practice calculations when you buy things or pay bills. Your reading skills are critical. You can develop them by reading a book, newspaper, or magazine a few pages at a time. Later on, we will discuss a number of easy ways to make test preparation a part of every day.

Strengthen Core Skills

Successful GED® test preparation requires you to have a strong foundation. The mental attitudes and habits we've just described form the first layer of this foundation. The next layer is made up of several very important and fundamental skills. Every student and test taker needs these skills because they are essential for understanding and learning new things. Without these skills, your chances of success on the GED® test will be much worse. Carefully read the following information about these 7 core skills.

READING Much of what we learn is written down, so having strong reading skills is essential. To succeed on the GED® test, you will need to read comfortably and actively. You will need to read at the correct pace, not too fast and not too slowly.

WRITING The ability to communicate clearly in writing is another essential skill. Succeeding in educational or professional settings is impossible if you don't have strong writing skills. A good command of grammar and mechanics is required, as is the ability to organize information clearly and efficiently.

VOCABULARY The common link between the first two skills on this list, reading and writing, is that they both involve words. Even though you can often figure out the meaning of a word, there is just no substitute for knowing what a word actually means. If you learn more words, your reading and writing will be more effective.

INTERPRETING GRAPHIC INFORMATION In addition to the written word, a lot of what we learn is presented in visual or graphic forms. These include charts, graphs, models (diagrams), pictures, maps, illustrations, and other nontext formats. As the popularity of television, the Internet, and mobile wireless technology increases, more and more information will be presented to us in these graphic forms. The ability to interpret data presented in these forms is another essential skill.

USING A COMPUTER The updated GED® test is computer based. This move from paper-based to computer-based testing reflects the transition that has taken place in our society as a whole. Computers are everywhere. They are here to stay. In fact, they are a part of virtually every professional and academic role. Most areas of the workforce require that employees have high levels of computer literacy. Postsecondary education and academic research now involve an almost constant reliance on computers and related information technology. Your computer skills must be strong, and this includes the ability to type comfortably.

USING A CALCULATOR The updated GED® test provides you with an online scientific calculator. Although you may not need to use all features of the calculator, you should definitely learn the basics of how to use one so that you can take advantage of it during the test.

TAKING TESTS EFFECTIVELY Advancement in education or along a career path usually involves taking tests. Certain commonsense habits can help to increase test performance. Knowing how to approach passages, graphics, and test questions strategically will help you make the most of what you know.

THE GENERAL EDUCATION DEVELOPMENT (GED®) TEST

The General Education Development (GED®) test is an assessment of high school equivalency. It compares the skills of those who take the test with the skills of recent high school graduates. For more than 70 years, adults have been taking the test as a first step to entering the workforce or pursuing higher education.

Throughout its history, the GED® test has focused on fundamental skills and subjects: language arts (reading and writing), math, science, and social studies. This makes sense since these subjects have long been the foundation of an American high school education. They still are today. The updated GED® test covers these four subjects:

→ **REASONING THROUGH LANGUAGE ARTS (RLA)**
→ **MATHEMATICAL REASONING**
→ **SOCIAL STUDIES**
→ **SCIENCE**

Although the subjects covered on the GED® test have not changed much over the years, a number of other things about the test have changed. Since the standards for high school equivalency and workforce readiness have changed, the test has changed and evolved in order to match those changing standards. The updated GED® test is the newest step in this evolution.

For example, when the exam was first established, the majority of jobs did not require the applicant to have a college education. A high school credential (diploma) was sufficient for most people looking for a good job at a good wage. Today, though, most jobs require applicants to have a postsecondary credential from a college, university, or graduate school. As a result, a growing number of students are seeking a GED® test credential as a way to show that they are ready to enter college. In response to this trend, the updated version of the exam measures both high school equivalency and college/career readiness.

Another big change affecting the exam is the increasing role that technology plays in our society. Seventy years ago, computers and other forms of information technology were barely even imagined by the average person. Today computers, tablets, and smartphones play a major role in everyday life. Very few jobs exist today that do not require the employee to have some level of comfort with technology.

To address this, the updated GED® test introduces one of the biggest changes in the history of the test: computer-based testing. Students will take their test using a computer rather than the paper-and-pencil format used in past versions. Taking a computer-based test allows students to show that they have the fundamental computer skills required for today's careers and colleges.

Perhaps the most important change to the test since it was first introduced in 1942 is the shift from testing recall (remembering memorized facts) to testing reasoning (using evidence to support answers). This shift was made in response to an early effect of technology on our society: rapid innovation. Since at least the 1960s, information technology has been speeding up the rate at which we learn new things, develop new abilities, and overcome new challenges. Landing on the moon was just one early example of revolutionary discovery and accomplishment. Prior to this time, the pace of innovation was slower because the tools available were not as powerful.

This increase in the rate or pace of innovation had a dramatic effect on our definition of high school equivalency and workforce readiness. Prior to this time, if a student in high school memorized a large volume of facts in a given field, like science or social studies, he or she would almost certainly be asked to remember and use those facts in college or in the workforce because new information and new fields of study were slower to develop. In the early 1970s, however, rapid innovation was leading to a growing number of new fields of study and work. It was becoming more important that students know how to learn and apply new information quickly and correctly. The ability to think logically and figure out new things was becoming far more important than the ability to repeat memorized facts. As a result, for the last 40 years, the GED® test has been a test of reasoning skills, or the ability to figure things out using new information. This aspect of the test is probably the most important thing for students to remember. The exam is designed to measure *how you think*, NOT *what you remember*.

Sections of the Test

The exam is made up of four parts, which we call subject tests. Each subject test is focused on one area of subject matter, or content.

1. The **REASONING THROUGH LANGUAGE ARTS (RLA)** subject test measures reading, writing, and grammar skills.
2. The **MATHEMATICAL REASONING** subject test measures fundamental knowledge and problem-solving skills in arithmetic and algebra.
3. The **SOCIAL STUDIES** subject test measures the ability to apply reasoning skills to material that deals with civics and government, U.S. history, economics, geography, and the world.
4. The **SCIENCE** subject test measures the ability to apply reasoning skills to content taken from life science, physical science, earth science, and space science.

Test Sequence and Timing

The GED® test takes around seven and a half hours to complete. Below is a list of approximate timings for each of the subject tests.

Subject Test	Time
Reasoning Through Language Arts (RLA)	Section 1 (All Content): 35 minutes Section 2 (Extended Response): 45 minutes Student Break: 10 minutes Section 3 (All Content): 60 minutes Total = 150 minutes
Mathematical Reasoning	Two parts that total 115 minutes
Social Studies	One 75-minute section
Science	One 90-minute section
Total	Approximately 7 hours and 30 minutes*

*Note that the complete GED® test is not taken in one day. However, some states require students to complete the test in a maximum number of days.

The actual test may include some unscored questions at the end that are presented for field testing.

Focus on Fundamentals

Each subject test assumes that students are familiar with the fundamental concepts in that subject. The RLA subject test assumes that you can read and write carefully and that you know the basic rules of grammar in standard written English. The Mathematical Reasoning subject test assumes that you can perform basic operations in arithmetic and algebra and can work with things like proportions, equations, and geometric figures. The Science and Social Studies subject tests assume you are familiar with the core concepts in these subjects, such as knowing that all living things are made up of cells (life science) or knowing the process by which laws are made (civics and government). To pass the subject tests, students need a strong understanding of the fundamental, big-picture concepts being tested.

The majority of these fundamentals, particularly those related to reading, writing, and math, are covered in this book. Many of the central science and social studies concepts are addressed here as well. Since these two subject tests cover fairly wide areas of content, though, it isn't practical for us to cover all of them in depth, even in a book this large. When you read the content summaries for the Science and Social Studies subject tests, you may find that some subjects are not familiar. If you think you need to spend some time reviewing them, we suggest you go to the following websites:

BARRON'S
www.barronseduc.com/study-guides.html

GED TESTING SERVICE
www.gedtestingservice.com/ged-testing-service

COMPUTER-BASED TESTING

The updated GED® test is computer based. Although taking a test on the computer may be a new experience for many students, the required computer skills are easy to develop. They include basic keyboard (typing) and word-processing (cut, copy, paste) skills plus the ability to use a mouse (point, click, drag, drop). If you use a computer for things like e-mail, Web browsing, or word processing, then you probably already have the skills you need. If your computer skills are not very strong yet, now is the time to start building them.

The computer-based format of the updated GED® test will evaluate your skills in some new ways. It will ask you to perform interactive tasks that can be performed only using a computer. Some of these tasks will feel similar to ones you've seen on paper-and-pencil tests in the past, but some might be a bit new to you. Some questions ask students to choose answers from a list, fill in a short answer, or give an extended written response. These tasks are essentially the same ones found on traditional tests. The main difference is that students click answers instead of filling in bubbles, or they type text instead of writing by hand. New types of questions ask students to point at things on the screen or to move things around on the screen. These questions can be used to test your ability to sort, organize, or sequence pieces of information. You might also be asked to build a graph or point to a relevant piece of information in a chart or diagram. The good news is that even the questions that involve new kinds of tasks are really quite easy to work with. Although you may not have previously used some of the new tasks on the exam, you've probably used point-and-click and drag-and-drop skills on a computer, smartphone, or tablet.

QUESTION TYPES

Multiple-Choice

The multiple-choice question is perhaps the most familiar type of standardized test question. It consists of a text-based prompt followed by a number of possible answer choices. In some cases, the question may refer to a passage or graphic. On the updated computer-based GED® test, these questions will each have four answer choices. Test takers will use a mouse to click the answer they select. Approximately 80% of the questions on the exam will be multiple-choice questions.

Fill-in-the-Blank

A type of fill-in question has been part of more recent paper-based versions of the exam. These questions include a prompt, but do not provide answer choices. Therefore, test takers must work out the answer themselves. On the new test, rather than writing in an answer, test takers will use a keyboard to type a number, word, phrase, or sentence into a text box on the computer screen. These questions may also refer to a stimulus.

Short-Answer

The short-answer question is new for this version of the test. It presents the test taker with a prompt and/or stimulus. The question requires that the student type a brief answer. This answer will often require the student to type more than one sentence.

Drop-Down Items

This is a new type of question that combines multiple-choice and fill-in-the-blank elements. Test takers are presented with a question that includes text with drop-down lists embedded in one or more locations. Each list will contain choices for completing, or filling in, that portion of the text. Test takers must choose the best option.

Interactive Items

These new question types make the most significant use of the new testing technology, specifically the computer mouse.

HOT SPOT

The **hot spot** question type will require test takers to click one or more locations on a graphic based on information in the question.

DRAG-AND-DROP

The **drag-and-drop** question type will require test takers to move words or graphics into target locations on the screen based on information in the question.

Extended-Response

This is another relatively familiar question type. An extended response is just a question that requires students to write a long answer. Test takers will be required to type a well-structured written response to an RLA prompt. The time limit for this question is 45 minutes.

Question Type Summary

	Reasoning Through Language Arts	Mathematical Reasoning	Science	Social Studies
Multiple-Choice	Y	Y	Y	Y
Drop-Down	Y	Y	Y	Y
Fill-in-the-Blank	Y	Y	Y	Y
Drag-and-Drop	Y	Y	Y	Y
Hot Spot		Y	Y	Y
Short-Answer	Y		Y	
Extended-Response	Y			

SCORING

Each section of the GED® test is scored, weighted, and scaled. What does this mean? It means that there is not a pre-determined number of questions you will need to get correct. The number of correct questions needed will vary from test to test. Based on the total value of the raw score, the score will be scaled. That's the number that will determine the type of diploma you get.

GED® College Ready + Credit **175+**
GED® College Ready **165+**
Pass/High School Equivalency **145+**

If you score between 145 and 164, you will have answered 70% to 84% of the questions correctly and will obtain your GED certificate.

If you manage to score between 165 and 174, it shows that you are ready to enter a credit-bearing college. In fact, many colleges will exempt you from their entrance exam.

If you score 175 or more, you will have answered at least 93% of the questions correctly, and you may qualify for up to 10 hours of college credit.

To find out if you are exempt from a college entrance exam, or if you qualify for college credit, please visit the website of the American Council on Education® (*www.acenet.edu*) and confirm with the college of your choosing. Although you can't retake the exam just to improve your score, if you scored below 145, you may be eligible to retake a specific subject test. Note that, at the time of this book's printing, there may be some states that have not yet adopted the new scoring.

FOCUS ON REASONING

The modern-day GED® test is an assessment of reasoning skills. On a reasoning skills test, the way you think is much more important than the list of facts you remember. Some fundamental knowledge of facts and concepts is required. However, the majority of the questions on the test will require you to do more than just recall a fact. They will present you with new facts and ask you to use those facts as evidence to support your answers. This process of thinking about new information and using it as a basis to answer questions is called reasoning. The vast majority of questions on the test will require you to use your reasoning skills, explain your reasoning for an answer, or both.

Standardized tests have a very specific way of testing reasoning skills. They begin by presenting you with new information. On the RLA subject test, this may be a reading passage, a sentence to be edited, or the stated topic (or prompt) for a writing exercise. On the Mathematical Reasoning subject test, you will encounter a word problem, graph, or equation. In the Science and Social Studies subject tests, you may see a passage or other form of text, a visual presentation (graph, chart, diagram, map, cartoon), or both. The information presented is called a **stimulus**. The questions to be answered will be based on the information in the stimulus. The student's job is to read and understand the stimulus, apply the information contained in it to the questions, and then choose or provide answers to the questions. This process is called testing subject matter knowledge in context because students can figure out the meaning of a term, symbol, or concept by using the surrounding information (context) as a guide. People do this every day when they work out the meaning of one unfamiliar word in a sentence using the words around it.

Although it may not seem very important on first glance, the method that the GED® test uses to measure reasoning skills in context is really a very big deal. Let's take a moment to think about what this means. **Almost all of the information you'll need to answer a question on the GED® exam will be provided to you as part of the test.**

The test will never require you to use the definition of an important term without first providing you with enough information in context to figure out the definition. As long as you can read, understand, and use the information provided in the stimulus, you should be able to find most or all of the information you need to answer the questions. For example, you'll never see a question on the Science subject test that asks you to define photosynthesis without providing any background information or a stimulus. That type of question only tests your ability to recall facts, not your ability to use facts. A GED® test question would provide you with a passage or a diagram that provides all the information you need to answer the question.

Before you begin your review, it is important to familiarize yourself with the three types of reasoning questions and the strategies for answering them, as outlined below.

Question–Answer Relationship Strategy

REMEMBER AND REPEAT (R) These questions don't require a lot of thought. They will ask you to find information in the source material and then select an answer choice that matches the information.

ANALYZE AND APPLY (A) These questions require a bit more thought. To answer them, you will need to break down the information in the source material and identify some new relationships or uses for the information.

EXPLAIN AND EXTEND (E) These questions take the most thought and effort because they ask you to explain the reasoning that leads to your answer. To answer them fully, you will need to do more than simply analyze the information in the source material and use it to support an answer. You will also need to explain how the evidence in the source material supports the answer.

Approach every question by looking at the relationship between the question and the answer:

→ What is the question asking you to do? Is it an R, an A, or an E question?
→ What steps should you take to answer it?

QAR and RAE

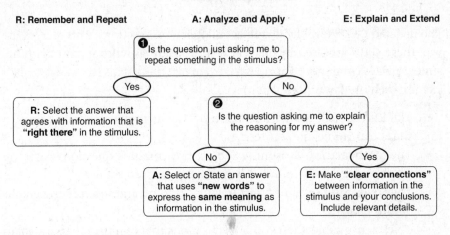

R: Remember and Repeat   A: Analyze and Apply   E: Explain and Extend

❶ Is the question just asking me to repeat something in the stimulus?

Yes

No

R: Select the answer that agrees with information that is **"right there"** in the stimulus.

❷ Is the question asking me to explain the reasoning for my answer?

No

Yes

A: Select or State an answer that uses **"new words"** to express the **same meaning** as information in the stimulus.

E: Make **"clear connections"** between information in the stimulus and your conclusions. Include relevant details.

STEP 1 Is the question just asking you to repeat information as it is presented in the stimulus?

- If Yes, this is a remember and repeat (R) question, and you can expect it to be fairly easy. The answer will be right there in the stimulus. Select or state the answer that agrees with the information in the stimulus.
- If No, go to Step 2.

STEP 2 Is the question asking you to explain your reasoning?

- If No, this is an analyze and apply (A) question. To answer it, you will need to break down the information in the stimulus and work out the relationships among the parts. The correct answer will agree in meaning with the stimulus but will express that meaning in a new or different way. Your job will be to reassemble the parts into an answer that means the same thing as described in the stimulus but uses different words.
- If Yes, this is an explain and extend (E) question. To answer it, you will need to go beyond just the answer and explain your reasoning process. Since all reasoning on the test is based on effective use of evidence, your job will be to make clear connections among what the stimulus says, what the stimulus means, and how that relates to your answer or conclusion. The correct answer will agree in meaning with the stimulus but will express that meaning in a new or different way. Your job will be to reassemble the parts into an answer that means the same thing as described in the stimulus but uses different words.

BLENDED SUBJECTS

The updated GED® test blends subject matter across sections. This reflects the way these skills are used in the real world. Reading, writing, and math are almost always combined. The updated exam test these skills the way you actually use them in day-to-day activities.

- The RLA subject test includes historical texts previously found only in the Social Studies subject test.
- The Mathematical Reasoning subject test contains questions based on graphics previously found only in the Science subject test.
- The Social Studies subject test includes reading and interpreting graphs and/or charts.
- The Science subject test contains questions that require you to use math to produce a numerical answer. Calculators are almost always provided for these questions.

STUDY PLAN

A study plan has two parts: time and materials. You need to know how much time you can spend studying. You also need to know what you'll be doing with that time and what materials you'll need.

Types of Studying

There are four types of studying:

- **BOOK WORK** Reading the lesson material in this book
- **PRACTICE** Doing practice questions or taking practice exams
- **REVIEW** Reexamining practice questions you missed or skipped and also reading the explanations
- **DRILLS** Using study aids (like flash cards) to test and improve memorization

---

Study Environments

Most types of studying require you to have a study friendly environment. This environment is quiet, well lit, and free from distractions (music, TV, mobile devices, and other people making noise). It has enough space for you to work and includes a firm, flat surface to lean on when writing. When doing book work, practice, or review, you'll want to be in a study friendly environment.

Drills are a different story, however. You can do drills in many environments where other kinds of study wouldn't work: on the bus or train, during a break at work, at the gym, or in similar settings. Most of the study aids used for drills (like flash cards or worksheets) are small and portable, making them easier to use when space is limited. Since most drills test memorization, like the definitions of vocabulary words or the factors of numbers, they require shorter periods of concentration. Unlike reading a paragraph or passage, which takes a long and uninterrupted span of time, a drill question is asked and answered quickly. Therefore, interruptions are easier to manage.

The Planning Process

When planning your study schedule, use the following suggestions:

1. Using a spreadsheet, a planning calendar, or good old pen and paper, create a template that you can use to show a weekly schedule. Use this template to lay out your general schedule for two or three weeks. Identify blocks of time that you could use for quiet, focused book work, practice, and review. These blocks should be at least 30 minutes long and no more than 2 hours in length. Then, review your schedule a second time, this time looking for opportunities for quick drills. These might be while commuting or during breaks in your work or school schedule.
2. Find your strengths and weaknesses. You should study certain topics early in the process and address other topics later. Skim through the review chapters in this book to determine which topics you remember distinctly and which ones you are less familiar with. Be prepared to devote more time and attention to those concepts that are less familiar to you.
3. Create some study aids. Study aids are things like flash cards, magazines, newspapers, journals, and similar items that you can carry with you. You'll use these for studying wherever you may be—at work, on the bus, and so on. If you'd like to use a premade set of flash cards, check out *Barron's GED® Test Flash Cards*. With 450 flash cards, it's easy for you to study information for the test in all four subject areas.

Get to Work!

After completing the steps described above, you will be aware of the time you have available to study and will be equipped with the material you need to work on. All that remains is to start working the plan and keep working the plan every day.

TEST-TAKING STRATEGY

Whenever you take any kind of exam, whether it is the GED® test or some other test, you must have a strategy. Obviously, you also need to be comfortable with the subject matter on the exam. However, having an effective test-taking strategy can help you make the most of the things you know. When you combine knowledge of a test's subject matter with knowledge of the test itself, you create a recipe for success.

Study the Test

You must always study for the particular test that you plan to take. However, you must also study the test itself. The more you know about a test's structure, organization, and rules, the better prepared you will be to take the test efficiently and effectively. Know the following details about the test:

CONTENT What subject matter will be tested?

FORMAT Is it a paper-and-pencil test or a computer-based test?

STRUCTURE How is the test organized? Is it divided into sections? Do these sections have a specific order?

QUESTION TYPES What kinds of questions are used on the test?

TIMING How much time do you have to take each section? How much time is available per question? Will different question types require you to spend different amounts of time on them?

SEQUENCING Must questions be answered in order or can you skip questions and return to them later?

SCORING How is the test scored? Does each question have the same point value, or do different question types carry different point values?

PASSING What is considered a passing score? How many points must you earn to pass the test? How many questions must you answer correctly to earn those points?

LEAVING BLANKS Is a question with no answer selected scored the same way as a question answered incorrectly?

QUESTION LEVELS Do questions differ in terms of complexity or difficulty? How can I recognize questions at different levels?

Not All Questions Are Created Equal

You must study and become familiar with the various kinds of questions you will face on the exam. Each question you see on the exam will have some characteristics that will help you to make choices. You can use these characteristics to choose whether to answer a question, when to answer a question, and how to answer a question.

QUESTION TYPE Some exams are limited to a small number of different question types. Other exams, like the updated GED® test, use a wide variety of question types. Each type will have its own structure or format and its own rules. Each is designed to test your knowledge and skills in a specific way. The best method of approaching a given question will depend on the question type.

SUBJECT MATTER Each question will focus on a specific subject matter (math, language arts, science, or social studies). On the GED® test, themes, or big ideas, often provide a common thread throughout the subject. The subject area of a given question will help you identify the theme you should focus on in your answer.

COMPLEXITY OR DIFFICULTY Most exams contain a mixture of questions, some that seem easier to the test taker and some that seem harder. This apparent difference is generally based on the number of steps required to answer the question, the number of choices to choose from, and the level of knowledge or skill being tested. The ability to recognize different levels of question complexity will help you make strategic choices during the test.

GROUPED QUESTIONS Some of the questions may be based on a shared piece of content. A group of reading questions may be based on a common passage. A group of math questions may be based on a common geometric diagram. Science or social studies questions may be based on a common chart or graph. Grouped questions require you to take a slightly different approach than individual questions.

POINT VALUE On some exams, each question is worth the same number of points so each question counts the same toward the overall exam score. On other exams, like the updated GED® test, different questions are worth different numbers of points. Unfortunately, you won't know the point value of any question on the updated GED® test, so do your best to rule out any obvious wrong answers and make an educated guess with the remaining ones.

Strategy for the Updated GED® Test

One feature of the exam that works very much in your favor is related to question sequence. Within one exam section, you may answer the questions in any order you choose. The exam software lets you flag questions for review and then return to them later. This will allow you to work through the section on your terms, earning points by using your strengths and avoiding questions where you are less confident.

To take best advantage of this aspect of the GED® test, plan to move through each section by putting questions into one of three categories.

1. **DO NOW** Some questions test areas where your confidence is high. You're very comfortable with the question type, the content, and the level of complexity. As you've practiced, you've learned that you are usually successful with these questions. By answering these questions immediately, you will keep your point total rising and will feel good about your progress in the section.

2. **DO LATER** For some questions, your confidence level will be somewhere in the middle. You're reasonably comfortable with the question but feel that it may take more time or effort to ensure you answer correctly. Flag these. Return to them once you've reviewed the whole section and answered all the Do Now questions. Go through these Do Later questions in order of preference, working slowly and carefully. Do this until you've answered them all or until you have only 3 minutes left in the section.

3. **TACKLE LAST** Every student has weaknesses, and every exam has questions related to those weak areas. Questions in areas where your confidence is low will likely take a lot of time and effort so save those for last. Try to eliminate wrong choices, then guess.

UNIT 1:
REASONING THROUGH
LANGUAGE ARTS

Language

1

▬▲▬▲▬▲▲▲▲▲▲▲▲▲▲▲▲▲▲▲▲▲▲▲▲▲▲

The GED® test evaluates your ability to edit and understand the use of standard written English in context. The purpose of this unit is to provide you with the skills needed to be successful on the test. These skills will enable you to answer document-based questions effectively. You will also be able to write effective short and extended responses that are generally free of grammatical, syntactical, and mechanical errors.

The following topics will be covered in this unit:

Lesson 1:   Parts of Speech

Lesson 2:   Parts of the Sentence

Lesson 3:   Independent and Subordinate Clauses

Lesson 4:   Types of Sentences

Lesson 5:   Agreement

Lesson 6:   Capitalization

Lesson 7:   Punctuation

Lesson 8:   Commonly Confused Words

Lesson 9:   Editing

LESSON 1: PARTS OF SPEECH

The English language consists of hundreds of thousands of words. However, these words can be broken up into just a few different categories. These categories are called parts of speech. Although the exam does not specifically ask test takers to identify a word's part of speech, understanding how different parts of speech work with each other will help you better understand grammatical rules.

Nouns

A noun is a person, place, thing, or idea. Nouns are usually things that are tangible. This means they appeal to the five senses so you can see, feel, hear, smell, and/or taste them. Examples of nouns that are tangible are *boy, city,* and *clothing*. A boy is a person. A city is a place. Clothing is a thing. Nouns, however, can also be intangible. Examples of these abstract ideas include:

happiness	sadness
running	walking
kindness	rudeness
love	hate

These are all familiar nouns. However, they cannot be touched or put into your hand.

Pronouns

A pronoun is a word that takes the place of a noun but functions in the same way. Some common pronouns include:

all	it	several
both	me	that
each	mine	them
him	most	us
her	none	we
I	she	you

Verbs

A verb is a word that shows action or a state of being. Examples of action words are *run, jump, work, sit, push, learn,* and *smile*. Each of these words is an action of some sort. However, not all verbs show action. The verb *to be* shows a state of being. Forms of the verb *to be* include:

am	was
are	will be
is	were
am being	have been

Adjectives

An adjective is a descriptive word that gives additional information about nouns and pronouns. Some of the characteristics that adjectives describe are size, shape, color, and quantity. Some examples of adjectives include:

Size	large, medium, small
Shape	round, square, triangular, rectangular, oval
Color	red, orange, yellow, green, blue
Quantity	one, two, three, four, five

Note that sometimes nouns can be used as adjectives and that sometimes adjectives can be used as nouns. Although we wouldn't use *large* as a noun, *oval* could be used as a noun.

Adverbs

An adverb is very similar to an adjective because it is a descriptive word. Rather than describing nouns, adverbs describe verbs, adjectives, or adverbs. Additionally, adverbs very often (but not always) end in -ly. Here are some examples:

slowly	fast	softly	loudly
happily	very	internally	externally

Prepositions

Prepositions are words that show the relationship to a noun. Prepositions tell us about the nature of something's time, placement, or direction. Some common prepositions include the following:

about	below	except	inside	over	up
against	between	for	into	through	with
around	by	from	off	toward	without
at	down	in	on	under	
before	during	in between	out	until	

Conjunctions

Conjunctions are the glue that holds sentences together. When we want to join together items or thoughts, we use conjunctions. We will discuss two types of conjunctions: coordinating and subordinating. Coordinating conjunctions connect similar ideas, contrasting ideas, and related ideas. The following are some common coordinating conjunctions:

or	nor	so	for	yet	but

The other type of conjunction is a subordinating conjunction, which we will discuss in Lesson 3 when we cover subordination.

Interjections

An interjection is an interrupting word. It usually shows emotion and is not a complete sentence. Examples of interjections include:

Hey!   Wow!   Ouch!   Hi!   Great!

LESSON 2: PARTS OF THE SENTENCE

Subjects

The subject of a sentence is who or what is doing the action. It can be singular or compound. A singular subject is when one person or thing completes the action. Consider the following sentence.

Jennifer went to the store.

In this sentence, Jennifer *is the subject because she performed the action of going to the store.*

A compound subject is when more than one person or thing does the action. Consider the following sentence.

Robert and Rick brought a cake to the party.

In this sentence, the subject is Robert and Rick *because they both brought the cake to the party.*

Every sentence must have a subject. However, the subject is not always stated directly. In the sentence above, the subject was stated explicitly. If I were telling the subject to bring a cake, the subject may be implied.

Bring a cake to the party.

In this sentence, the subject is assumed to be you, *or* the person to whom I'm speaking.

Predicates

The predicate of a sentence contains the verb, and, in some cases, additional information. The predicate indicates the action or state of being. Just like the subject, the predicate can be singular or compound. A singular compound contains one action. Consider the following sentence.

Jennifer **went** to the store.

In this sentence, went *is the verb and shows action. Everything that follows gives additional information.*

A compound predicate is when there is more than one action or state of being. Consider the following sentence.

The dog **ran and jumped** on the lawn.

In this sentence, there is more than one action (ran and jumped). *Everything that follows gives additional information.*

Direct Objects

The direct object is a noun and appears in some sentences with action verbs. The direct object is what or who receives the action. The direct object is never the subject.

Renaldo read the **passage** aloud.

In this sentence, passage *is the receiver of the action* read.

Indirect Objects

The indirect object is a noun and appears in some sentences with a direct object. The indirect object is who or what receives the direct object.

Brad threw **Molly** the Frisbee.

In this sentence, the Frisbee *is what is thrown and* Molly *receives it.*

Predicate Nouns

A predicate noun is sometimes found in a sentence that uses the verb *to be*. It tells what the subject is.

Billy was such a **joker**!

In this sentence, Billy *is the subject and* joker *tells us what Billy is.*

Predicate Adjectives

A predicate adjective is sometimes found in a sentence that uses the verb *to be*. It tells what the subject is like.

My mother was very **sweet** when I was sick.

In this sentence, My mother *is the subject, and* sweet *is what she was like.*

Prepositional Phrases

Prepositional phrases can appear in any type of sentence but are not essential. They provide the reader with additional information. All prepositional phrases begin with a preposition and end with a noun. However, prepositional phrases may include adjectives or adverbs.

Sheila went home **after work**.

In this sentence, the preposition is after, *and the noun is* work.

LESSON 3: INDEPENDENT AND SUBORDINATE CLAUSES

Independent Clauses

If someone walks into a room and says, "I went to the movies," you would be content with that information. It is a complete thought. Since it contains both a subject and a predicate, it is a *clause*. It is called an *independent clause* because it can stand on its own two feet. The following are independent clauses:

The teacher wrote the assignment on the whiteboard.

As a favor, I drove my neighbor to work.

Sonia's friends planned a surprise birthday party for her.

Subordinate Clauses

Although a complete sentence must have both a subject and a predicate, just because both are present does not mean the clause is a complete sentence. For example, if someone walks into a room and says, "When I went to the movies," you would be waiting for the rest of the information. The statement has a subject and a verb, but it is not a complete sentence because it begins with the word *when*. This is what we call a *subordinate clause*. Subordinate clauses, or dependent clauses as they are sometimes referred to, must be joined to an independent clause. All subordinate clauses begin with a subordinating conjunction.

Subordinating Conjunctions

A subordinating conjunction is similar to a regular conjunction in that it is a connecting word. However, a subordinating conjunction changes the clause that follows into a subordinate clause. These are examples of subordinating conjunctions:

after	how	unless
although	if	until
because	now that	when
even if	since	while
even though	though	

LESSON 4: TYPES OF SENTENCES

Now that we are familiar with the structure of sentences and the different types of clauses, we can take a look at different types of complete sentences. There are four types of sentences in English: simple, compound, complex, and compound/complex.

Simple Sentences

A simple sentence is one independent clause. It contains either a singular or a compound subject and either a singular or a compound predicate. Examples of simple sentences include:

James *worked* on his science project all night.

Kristen and Rob *took* the dog to the park.

Compound Sentences

A compound sentence consists of *two or more* independent clauses that are joined by a conjunction or a semicolon. Examples of compound sentences include:

Jasmine took her daughters to nursery school, **and** they played with the other children.

The play was enjoyable; it was just too long.

Complex Sentences

A complex sentence consists of one independent clause and one or more subordinate clauses. If the subordinate clause occurs at the beginning of the sentence, it is followed by a comma. If it occurs at the end of a sentence, it is not preceded by a comma. Examples of complex sentences include:

Even if things are not perfect, life is still pretty good!

Sue brought her lunch to school with her **so** *she could eat while she studied.*

Compound/Complex Sentences

A compound/complex sentence consists of two or more independent clauses and one or more subordinate clauses. Examples of compound/complex sentences include:

> Roberto forgot about his friend's birthday, but *when he remembered*, he sent her a gift.

> The trip was exciting, and we bought some souvenirs *when we came across a little boutique*.

Run-on Sentences

Although you should vary your sentence structure and enhance the quality of your writing by including more robust and dynamic sentences, make sure that the sentences do not become run-ons. A sentence becomes a run-on when multiple sentences are put together without the proper punctuation. For example:

> After sleeping late last Saturday, I went to the café down the block, I saw my friend while I was there, he was out for a bike ride and stopped to get a bottle of water.

This run-on should be broken up into several sentences. An appropriate revision would be:

> After sleeping late last Saturday, I went to the café down the block. I saw my friend while I was there. He was out for a bike ride and stopped to get a bottle of water.

In this revision, periods are used instead of the comma. The different thoughts in the run-on are now separated.

Sentence Fragments

A sentence fragment is a piece of a sentence and incomplete. When determining whether or not you have a sentence fragment, ask yourself, "What is the action, and who or what is performing the action?" Here's an example:

> This morning went to the airport to pick up his sister.

What is the action? The action is *went*. Who or what is performing the action? There is no performer of the action in this sentence, so we need to add a subject to make this a complete sentence. Appropriate revisions would be:

This morning, **Chris** went to the airport to pick up his sister.

This morning, **he** went to the airport to pick up his sister.

The first revision adds the proper noun, *Chris,* who is now the performer of the action, *went.* The second revision uses the pronoun *he* as the subject instead of using a proper noun.

LESSON 5: AGREEMENT

Verb Form Agreement

Verbs come in many forms. You must be consistent in your form when writing extended responses. It is also very important to be aware of the different forms when you're editing passages in the language section. This includes tense agreement, subject-verb agreement, and pronoun-antecedent agreement.

Tense Agreement

In English, verbs indicate when something happened, is happening, or will happen; this is called *verb tense.* Most of the time, tense form should be consistent within a sentence. The following sentence does not have tense agreement:

Jeremy went to the baseball game last week and is sitting in box seats.

In this sentence, the verb *went* is in past tense whereas *is sitting* is in the present. To correct this, one of the tenses must be changed. A proper revision would be:

Jeremy went to the baseball game last week and sat in box seats.

An example of an exception to this rule would be:

Andy is in Las Vegas and will see some shows.

This example purposefully has two different tenses. Andy is currently in Las Vegas. Sometime in the future, he will go to some shows.

Subject-Verb Agreement

A common writing mistake, and one that will be tested in the language section, is making errors in subject-verb agreement. In most cases, if the subject is plural, the verb must also be plural. If the subject is singular, so must be the verb. For example:

Dana attend meetings on Monday mornings with the other managers.

Dana is singular and *attend* is plural. Two possible revisions would be:

Dana **attends** meetings on Monday mornings with the other managers.
Dana and Sorin attend meetings on Monday mornings with the other managers.

Pronoun-Antecedent Agreement

As discussed in Lesson 1, pronouns take the place of nouns. The pronoun must agree with the noun that it replaces, which is called the antecedent. For example, if I were talking about a woman named Chelsea, I could use the pronouns *she* and *her* because they agree with the antecedent *Chelsea*. Pronouns and antecedents must also agree in quantity. If the sentence is discussing Bradley and James, *he* would be an inappropriate pronoun choice because it does not agree in quantity. The pronoun *they* agrees with the antecedent *Bradley and James* because more than one person is being discussed.

Unclear Pronoun Reference

When discussing more than one person or thing, make sure your writing clearly shows who or what the pronoun is referring to. The following is an example of an unclear pronoun reference:

Jan and Alexandra went to the movies, and she bought a tub of popcorn.

In the sentence, it is unclear who the pronoun *she* refers to. Did Jan buy the tub of popcorn or did Alexandra? In this example, it is necessary to use the person's name again instead of a pronoun. A proper revision would be:

Jan and Alexandra went to the movies, and Jan bought a tub of popcorn.

LESSON 6: CAPITALIZATION

There are many rules regarding the capitalization of letters within sentences. The three most important are beginning of sentences, proper nouns, and proper adjectives.

Beginning of Sentences

The first letter of the first word of every sentence must be capitalized. There are no exceptions to this rule. Keep in mind that you need to conform to standard English. Although you can make some mistakes and still receive full credit, capitalizing the first letter of the first word of each sentence is the most commonly encountered rule and perhaps the easiest mechanical rule to remember.

Proper Nouns

Proper nouns are the names of people, places, things, or ideas. They are always capitalized. Carlos, Statue of Liberty, and Olympics are all examples of proper nouns.

Proper Adjectives

Proper adjectives are similar to proper nouns in that they refer to the proper name of a person, place, thing, or idea. They are always capitalized. Irish soda bread is an example of a proper adjective.

LESSON 7: PUNCTUATION

One of the best ways to improve your punctuation skills is to become familiar with the general rules of punctuation.

Periods (.)

Periods, also known as full stops, are most often used at the end of a sentence. A period indicates that the sentence has ended. They are also used after an abbreviation, such as Dr., Mrs., Mr., Jr., Sr., Ph.D., or other common titles.

Question Marks (?)

Question marks are used at the end of sentences. They indicate that a question is being asked.

Exclamation Points (!)

Exclamation points are used to convey excitement, urgency, or shouting. They are also used to indicate interjections, such as "Stop!"

Commas (,)

Commas are commonly misused. Commas are intended to separate, not connect. This means they are used to separate items on a list, independent clauses, and certain phrases. Keep in mind that if you are using a comma to separate independent clauses, you must include a conjunction after the comma.

Semicolons (;)

People often use a comma when they really should use a semicolon. A semicolon separates and connects at the same time. For example, this shows a common mistake:

I went to the store, Katie went to the movies.

This is an improper use of a comma. Correct revisions would be:

I went to the store, and Katie went to the movies.
I went to the store; Katie went to the movies.

Both of these revisions separate the two different ideas but also connect the ideas since they are related.

Possessives and Contractions

Possessives and contractions often look similar because they both use apostrophes. However, they use apostrophes in different ways. In a possessive, the apostrophe is often, but not always, used to show ownership. In a contraction, it is used to show where letters are omitted.

EXAMPLES OF POSSESSIVES

John's dog   our home
Rita's car   their backyard
book's page   your friend
tree's branches   my party

COMMON CONTRACTIONS

are not	aren't		cannot	can't
is not	isn't		would have	would've
was not	wasn't		could have	could've
were not	weren't		should have	should've

LESSON 8: COMMONLY CONFUSED WORDS

Homonyms

Homonyms are words that sound the same but are spelled differently and have different meanings. All too often, an incorrect homonym is used in writing. Make sure that you know the difference between these commonly confused homonyms.

ACCEPT, EXCEPT

Accept means to receive something; *except* means something is not inc̣.

AFFECT, EFFECT

Affect means to influence something; *effect* is what happens as a result of an action.

BARE, BEAR

Bare is to be uncovered or naked; *bear* is an animal.

BOARD, BORED

Board is a piece of wood; *bored* is to have nothing to do.

BREAK, BRAKE

Break means to damage or ruin something; *brake* means to slow down or stop doing something.

EMIGRATE, IMMIGRATE

Emigrate means to come *from* somewhere; *immigrate* means to go *to* somewhere.

ENSURE, INSURE

Ensure is to make sure something happens; *insure* means to have a policy that will pay money should something be stolen or damaged.

FEET, FEAT

Feet are body parts; *feat* is an accomplishment.

ITS, IT'S

Its shows possession; *it's* is a contraction meaning "it is."

KNOW, NO

Know is to have knowledge of something; *no* is a negative response.

ONE, WON

One is a number; *won* is past tense for winning something.

PASSED, PAST

Passed is past tense for going by something or passing something along; *past* is what has already happened.

PRINCIPLE, PRINCIPAL

A *principle* is a rule; a *principal* is the leader of a school.

SURE, SHORE

Sure means "certainty"; *shore* means "coastline."

THAN, THEN

Than makes a comparison between two things; *then* indicates a certain time.

THERE, THEIR, THEY'RE

There indicates a location; *their* shows possession; *they're* is a contraction meaning "they are."

TO, TOO, TWO

To is a preposition indicating motion; *too* means "also" or "more than is wanted"; *two* is a number.

WHETHER, WEATHER

Whether indicates a choice; *weather* is temperature, humidity, precipitation, and so on.

WHOLE, HOLE

Whole is something that is complete; *hole* is an empty space.

YOUR, YOU'RE

Your shows possession; *you're* is a contraction meaning "you are."

LESSON 9: EDITING

In addition to using correct grammar, punctuation, and spelling, make sure you have structured your sentences correctly and have used words efficiently.

Wordiness and Awkward Structure

Wordiness and awkward structure refer to the flow of the sentences. Sometimes when we first write something, the sentence evolves as we are writing. As a result, sometimes we use too many words. This means we could say the same thing using fewer words. On the GED® test, you will be tested on your ability to recognize wordy and awkwardly structured sentences.

Non-Standard and Informal Language

The goal of the language questions on the exam is to test your knowledge of standard English. One way is by giving you answer choices that use non-standard English and informal language. In other words, some answer choices will sound more like they belong in a conversation you're having with a friend rather than in a more formal work of literature. As a rule of thumb, you should always elevate your language when you're writing. Likewise, you should be looking for choices with elevated language that are also grammatically and mechanically correct.

Review Test

▬▬▬▬▬▬▬▬▬▬▬▬▬▬▬▬▬▬▬▬▬▬▬▬▬▬

> **DIRECTIONS:** This review test contains passages with embedded Reasoning Through Language Arts questions where you have to select the best sentence or best completion of a sentence from the choices given.

QUESTIONS 1 THROUGH 8 ARE BASED ON THE FOLLOWING PASSAGE ABOUT LAND TREATMENT BY THE EPA:

ADJUSTING FOR DEPRECIATION OF LAND TREATMENT WHEN PLANNING WATERSHED PROJECTS

Introduction

1. | Select   ∨ |

(A) Watershed-based planning helps address water quality problems in a holistic manner by fully assessing the potential contributing causes and sources of pollution, than prioritizing restoration and protection strategies to address the problems (USEPA 2013).

(B) Watershed-based planning helping address water quality problems in a holistic manner by fully assessing the potential contributing causes and sources of pollution, then prioritizing restoration and protection strategies to address the problems (USEPA 2013).

(C) Watershed-based planning helps address water quality problems in a holistic manner by fully assessing the potential contributing causes and sources of pollution, then prioritizing restoration and protection strategies to address the problems (USEPA 2013).

(D) Watershed-based planning helps address water quality problems in a holistic manner by fully assessing the potential contributing causes and sources of pollution, then prioritizing restoration and protection strategies to address the problems (USEPA 2013)

The U.S. Environmental Protection Agency (EPA) requires that watershed projects funded directly under section 319 of the Clean Water Act implement a watershed-based plan (WBP) addressing the nine key elements identified in EPA's *Handbook for Developing Watershed Plans to Restore and Protect our Waters* (USEPA 2008). EPA further recommends that all other watershed plans intended to address water quality impairments also include the nine elements. The first element calls for the identification of causes and sources of impairment that must be controlled to

2. | Select   ∨ |
   | (A) achieving
   | (B) achievement
   | (C) achieved
   | (D) achieve

needed load reductions. Related elements include a description of the non-point source (NPS) management measures—or best management practices (BMPs)—needed to

3. | Select   ∨ |
   | (A) achieve required pollutant load reductions, a description of the critical areas in which the BMPs should be implemented, and an estimate of the load reductions expected from the BMPs.
   | (B) achieve required pollutant load reductions a description of the critical areas in which the BMPs should be implemented and an estimate of the load reductions expected from the BMPs.
   | (C) achieve required pollutant load reductions, a description of the critical areas in which the BMP's should be implemented, and an estimate of the load reductions expected from the BMP's.
   | (D) achieve required pollutant load reductions, a description of the critical areas in which the BMPs should be implemented. And an estimate of the load reductions expected from the BMPs.

Once the causes and sources of water resource impairment

4.
Select ⌄
(A) is
(B) being
(C) to be
(D) are

assessed, identifying the appropriate BMPs to address the identified problems, the best locations for additional BMPs, and the pollutant load reductions likely to be achieved with the BMPs depends on accurate information on the performance levels of both BMPs already in place and BMPs to be implemented as part of the watershed project. All

5.
Select ⌄
(A) to
(B) too
(C) two
(D) so

often, watershed managers and Agency staff have assumed that, once certified as installed or adopted according to specifications, a BMP continues to perform its pollutant reduction function at the same efficiency (percent pollutant reduction) throughout

6.
Select ⌄
(A) its
(B) it's
(C) it
(D) it is

design or contract life, sometimes longer. An important corollary to this assumption is that BMPs in place during project planning are performing as originally intended. Experience in NPS watershed projects across the nation, however, shows that, without diligent operation and maintenance, BMPs and their

7. Select ⌄
    (A) effects
    (B) affects
    (C) effected
    (D) affected

probably will depreciate over time, resulting in less efficient pollution reduction.

8. Select ⌄
    (A) Recognize of this fact is important at the project planning phase, for both existing and planned BMPs.
    (B) Recognition of these fact is important at the project planning phase, for both existing and planned BMPs.
    (C) Recognition of this fact is important at the project planning phase, four both existing and planned BMPs.
    (D) Recognition of this fact is important at the project planning phase, for both existing and planned BMPs.

Source: "Adjusting for Depreciation of Land Treatment When Planning Watershed Projects." *United States Environmental Protection Agency.* Last accessed September 9, 2016.
www.epa.gov/sites/production/files/2015-10/documents/tech_memo_1_oct15.pdf.

QUESTIONS 9 THROUGH 15 ARE BASED ON THE FOLLOWING PASSAGE
ABOUT URBAN HEAT ISLANDS BY THE EPA:

URBAN HEAT ISLANDS, CLIMATE CHANGE,
AND GLOBAL WARMING

Urban heat islands

9. | Select ∨ |

    (A) referring
    (B) refer
    (C) referee
    (D) to refer

to the elevated temperatures in developed areas compared to more rural sur-
roundings. Urban heat islands are caused by development and the changes in
radiative and thermal properties of urban infrastructure as well as the impacts
buildings can have on the local micro-climate—for example tall buildings can
slow the rate at which cities cool off at night. Heat islands are influenced by a

10. | Select ∨ |

    (A) city's
    (B) cities
    (C) citys
    (D) city is

geographic location and by local weather patterns, and their intensity changes
on a daily and seasonal basis.

    The warming that results from urban heat islands over small areas such as
cities is an example of local climate change. Local climate changes resulting
from urban heat islands fundamentally differ from global climate changes in
that their effects are limited to the local scale and decrease with distance from
their source.

11.
Select   ∨

(A) Global climate changes such as those caused by increases in the sun's intensity or greenhouse gas concentrations are not locally or regionally confined.

(B) global climate changes, such as those caused by increases in the sun's intensity or greenhouse gas concentrations, are not locally or regionally confined.

(C) Global climate changes, such as those caused by increases in the sun's intensity or greenhouse gas concentrations, is not locally or regionally confined.

(D) Global climate changes, such as those caused by increases in the sun's intensity or greenhouse gas concentrations, are not locally or regionally confined.

Climate change, broadly speaking, refers to any significant change in measures of climate

12.
Select   ∨

(A) (such as temperature; precipitation; or wind)

(B) (such as temperature. And precipitation. And wind.)

(C) (such as temperature, precipitation, or wind)

(D) (such as temperature, as well as precipitation, and maybe even wind)

lasting for an extended period (decades or longer). Climate change may result from:

- Natural factors, such as changes in the sun's intensity or slow changes in the Earth's orbit around the sun
- Natural processes within the climate system (e.g., changes in ocean circulation)
- Human activities that change the atmosphere's composition (e.g., burning fossil fuels) and the land surface (e.g., deforestation, reforestation, or urbanization).

The term climate change is often used

13.
Select ∨
(A) interchangeably
(B) interchangably
(C) interchangeabely
(D) intrachangably

with the term global warming, but according to the National Academy of Sciences, "the phrase 'climate change' is growing in preferred use to 'global warming' because it helps convey that there are [other] changes in addition to rising temperatures."

14.
Select ∨
(A) Global warming is an average increase in the temperature of the atmosphere near the Earths surface and in the lowest layer of the atmosphere, which can contribute to changes in global climate patterns.
(B) Global warming are an average increase in the temperature of the atmosphere near the Earth's surface and in the lowest layer of the atmosphere, which can contribute to changes in global climate patterns.
(C) Global warming is an average increase in the temperature of the atmosphere near the Earth's surface and in the lowest layer of the atmosphere, which can contribute to changes in global climate patterns.
(D) Global warming is an average increase in the temperature of the atmosphere near the Earth's surface and in the lowest layer of the atmosphere, which can contributed to changes in global climate patterns.

Global warming can occur from a variety of causes, both natural and human induced. In common usage, "global warming" often refers to the warming that can occur as a result of increased emissions of greenhouse gases from human activities. Global warming can be considered part of global climate change along with changes in precipitation, sea level, etc.

The impacts from urban heat islands and global climate change (or global warming) are often similar.

15.
Select ⌄
(A) For example;
(B) For example,
(C) For example
(D) For example...

some communities may experience longer growing seasons due to either or both phenomena.

Source: "Urban Heat Islands, Climate Change, and Global Warming." *United States Environmental Protection Agency.* Last accessed September 9, 2016. *www.epa.gov/sites/production/files/2014-06/documents/basicscompendium.pdf.*

Answers Explained

1. **(C)** Choice C is grammatically correct. Choice A incorrectly uses "than." There is no comparison being made. One event (assessing the potential causes and sources) happened, *then* another event happened (prioritizing restoration and protection strategies). Choice B uses "helping" instead of "helps." Choice D is missing punctuation at the end of the sentence.

2. **(D)** Only choice D uses the correct tense of "achieve" that makes sense in this context.

3. **(A)** Choice A is the only grammatically correct choice. Choice B does not uses commas in a series of three. Choice C incorrectly uses the possessive "BMP's." Choice D creates a fragment.

4. **(D)** Only choice D is grammatically correct and makes sense in the context of the sentence.

5. **(B)** Choice B uses the correct form of "too." Choices A and C use the wrong forms. Choice D does not make sense in the sentence.

6. **(A)** Choice A uses the correct form of "its." Choices B and D, which mean the same thing, use the wrong forms of "it's" and "it is." Choice C does not make sense in the sentence.

7. **(A)** Choice A correctly uses "effects" to identify the results of BMPs. Choice B, "affects," means that something impacts something else. Choices C and D incorrectly use the past tense forms of choices A and B.

8. **(D)** Choice D is grammatically correct. Choice A mistakenly uses "recognize" in place of "recognition." In choice B, the plural "these" does not agree with the singular "fact." Choice C uses the wrong form of "four."

9. **(B)** Choice B uses the correct tense and spelling of "refer." Choice A incorrectly adds "ing" to "refer." Choice C uses "referee" instead of "refer." Choice D incorrectly adds the word "to" before "refer."

10. **(A)** Choice A uses the correct, possessive form to indicate that the sentence is describing the geographic location of the city. Choice B incorrectly uses the plural "cities." Choice C is missing an apostrophe. Choice D does not make sense in the context of the sentence.

11. **(D)** Choice D is grammatically correct. Choice A is missing the commas that set apart "such as...concentrations." Choice B does not capitalize

the first letter of the first word in the sentence. In choice C, "is" does not agree with "changes."

12. **(C)** Choice C is grammatically correct. Choice A incorrectly uses semi-colons in place of commas. Choice B creates fragments. Choice D is awkward and wordy.

13. **(A)** Choice A is the only choice with the correct spelling of "interchangeably."

14. **(C)** Choice C is the only grammatically correct option. Choice A is missing the apostrophe in "Earth's." Choice B incorrectly uses "are" in reference to "global warming." Choice D mistakenly uses "contributed" instead of "contribute."

15. **(B)** Choice B is the only choice with correct punctuation after "For example."

Reading 2

The GED® test evaluates your ability to read, interpret, and respond to a variety of literary and informational texts. The length of the texts will range from 400 to 900 words and have 6 to 8 questions each. Several different question types will be used to evaluate your literacy skills in Reasoning Through Language Arts, Reading:

→ **MULTIPLE-CHOICE**

→ **FILL-IN-THE-BLANK**

→ **DRAG-AND-DROP**

→ **DROP-DOWN**

→ **SHORT-ANSWER**

→ **EXTENDED-RESPONSE**

The following skills will be covered in this unit:

Lesson 1: Identifying Main Ideas and Supporting Details

Lesson 2: Summarizing Details and Ideas

Lesson 3: Drawing Conclusions and Making Generalizations

Lesson 4: Making Inferences and Assumptions

Lesson 5: Analyzing Language

Lesson 6: Identifying Plot Elements

Lesson 7: Analyzing Relationships of Ideas

LESSON 1: IDENTIFYING MAIN IDEAS AND SUPPORTING DETAILS

Main Idea

When reading literary and informational texts, keep in mind that the author has written the passage for a reason and that each section of the passage has a purpose. In general, the passages you will encounter on the GED® test will have a particular idea that the author is trying to convey; this is called the main idea. The main idea is very often stated in the first sentence or two of a passage. However, this is not always the case. The main idea can also be stated in the middle of a passage, at the end of the passage, or even not at all, leaving the reader to determine the main idea.

Supporting Details

Authors can make claims and take positions on issues. However, if no evidence is provided to support those positions, their claims become worthless. In order to substantiate the main idea, authors use *supporting details*. A supporting detail is evidence that gives credibility to or proves the main idea.

Inferring the Main Idea

When the author does not specifically state the main idea of a paragraph or passage, the reader must put the stated and unstated pieces together and determine the main idea. This is called *inferring*. To infer the main idea, you must examine the supporting details and what the author implies. Since supporting details are the individual pieces of evidence that support a main idea, looking at what the supporting details have in common can enable you to determine the main idea. For example, an author may write about an individual who went to Costa Rica to go surfing, Montauk Point to go fishing, and Mt. Kilimanjaro to go mountain climbing. What do all these have in common? Each event took place in a very different location and involved some kind of outdoor sport. We can infer that the main idea is the person likes to travel and enjoys outdoor activities.

LESSON 2: SUMMARIZING DETAILS AND IDEAS

Summarizing

When summarizing, only the most important information should be included. Minor details can be left out. For example, if you were reading an excerpt from a biography about an author, the excerpt may focus on how she was a best-selling author. It may also mention that she was left-handed. Because it was the focus of the biography, her being a best-selling author is something you would include or look for in a summary. In contrast, being left-handed is likely nonessential and should have been left out of the summary.

The easiest way to summarize what has happened is to act like a detective and ask the following questions:

→ Who?
→ What?
→ When?
→ Where?
→ Why?
→ How?

Answering these questions will help you outline the most important information in the passage as well as help you become a better reader. The summary is defined as a short restatement of the most important ideas in the passage. If you're able to assemble these answers into a sentence or two, you have just effectively summarized a passage.

LESSON 3: DRAWING CONCLUSIONS AND MAKING GENERALIZATIONS

Drawing Conclusions

To draw a conclusion, you must consider the facts provided and then judge or decide what the information means. To keep with the theme of solving a crime, a detective looks for evidence. Once he or she has assembled a good deal of evidence, the detective may be able to come to a conclusion about what happened or who perpetrated the crime.

Making Generalizations

When a broad statement is made about a group, this is called a generalization. A generalization suggests that all group members share a certain common trait or characteristic.

LESSON 4: MAKING INFERENCES AND ASSUMPTIONS

Inferences

Making an inference involves analyzing the information you are given directly or indirectly and drawing conclusions based on that information. You must often make inferences when an author does not clearly state all of the information directly.

Assumptions

An author does not always need to define everything that he or she is writing about because it is assumed that the reader already knows something about the topic being discussed. For example, if a character in a story traveled to Chihuahua, the author would likely indicate that this is a city in Mexico because the reader may not have heard of that city. However, if a character went to a pet store and bought a Chihuahua, chances are the author would not have to indicate that a Chihuahua is a type of dog because most people would know this. The author assumes the reader knows this and therefore omits the definition.

LESSON 5: ANALYZING LANGUAGE

Style

When we talk about style in terms of literature, we're looking at all the elements of an individual's writing. Examples of style include:

FORMAL—This style is not personal, may be complicated, and is used for higher forms of writing such as scholarly journals.

INFORMAL—This style may be personal and is written more for everyday reading. An example of this is a local newspaper reporting on a parade or fair.

TECHNICAL—This style is usually used within a field of study for people who are familiar with that field such as doctors reading medical literature or information technology (IT) specialists reading something about a piece of technology.

SIMPLE—This style is straightforward and easy to follow.

COMPLEX—This style is more complicated than simple style and may be more difficult for someone unfamiliar with the content.

Tone

The tone of a work is very similar to tone of voice. Tone involves how something is said. If you saw a mother walking down the street with her son, and she said, "Come over here," her tone of voice would indicate if she was angry or just being cautious. In literature, the author's feelings about the subject—the tone—are conveyed through the style, literary elements, and statements about the topic being discussed.

Point of View and Purpose

The point of view and the purpose go hand in hand. An author's point of view is simply how he or she views the topic. This often comes through in the purpose. The purpose is the author's reason for writing the passage or section of the passage. The author's purpose for writing the piece can vary. The writing can:

INFORM—This type of writing is intended to provide the reader with information on a topic. This is characteristic of many newspaper articles.

ENTERTAIN—This type of writing is characteristic of fiction. The author wants the reader to gain pleasure from reading the work.

PERSUADE—This type of writing is intended to make the reader believe what the author is writing. This is characteristic of movie reviews, book reviews, and restaurant reviews.

Literal and Figurative Language

Authors may use both literal and figurative language in their writing. Literal language means that what is stated is actually true. In contrast, figurative language means that what is stated is not actually true. Instead, it is a way of expressing an idea. For example, if someone said, "I was so startled that I jumped three feet in the air," a literal interpretation would be that the person actually jumped three feet in the air. The figurative interpretation would be that the person was very surprised.

LESSON 6: IDENTIFYING PLOT ELEMENTS

Plot

The plot of a work of literature is the sum of events that occur to create the story. Depending on to whom you speak, a plot has either 5 or 7 of the distinct components listed below.

→ **EXPOSITION**
→ **CATALYST**
→ **RISING ACTION**
→ **CLIMAX**
→ **FALLING ACTION**
→ **RESOLUTION**
→ **CONCLUSION**

The *exposition* is the introductory part of the story, where the reader is given information about the setting and various characters. At some point, something occurs that complicates things in the story and sets the plot in motion; this is called the *catalyst*. As the plot progresses, the actions of the characters cause the excitement or tension to build; this is called the *rising action*. Tensions rise as the plot thickens and becomes more complicated. The peak of the plot and turning point of the story are called the *climax*. After the climax, the plot begins to slow down; this is called the *falling action*. Eventually, the conflict is resolved and the story is ended; these are called the *resolution* and *conclusion*.

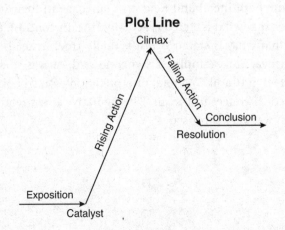

Plot Line

Theme

The theme of a work of literature is the main idea that the author has woven into the fabric of the work. Sometimes the theme is clearly presented. At other times, the reader must read more deeply into what the author is saying in order to find the theme. For example, an author may write about the struggles a person has had over the course of his lifetime. The author may include a chapter on how he struggled in school, another about how he struggled in love, another chapter about struggling at work, and another about struggling with money. The author describes at the end of each chapter how the person always overcame the struggle. Each chapter would have a different main idea, but the overall theme would be overcoming obstacles.

Setting

The setting encompasses all the information dealing with *when* and *where*. For example, the setting may indicate the time the story is taking place, such as the day, month, year, season, or time of day. It can also indicate the location, such as the country, state/province, city, or street. Additionally, it may include information about the environment, such as the temperature, condition of the location, sounds, and smells.

Characterization

When we talk about the attributes or characteristics of an individual, we may discuss things like demeanor, personality, and behavior. When asked to characterize someone, these are the elements about which we are being asked.

LESSON 7: ANALYZING RELATIONSHIPS OF IDEAS

Cause and Effect

Cause and effect relationships are common in the various sections of the GED® test. A cause is an action that makes something else happen, while an effect is what happens as a result of that action. These relationships can sometimes be confusing because whether an action is a cause or an effect depends on the context. For example, let's take the scenario that Sue bumped into Chuck, Chuck bumped into the table, and the lamp fell to the floor. Sue bumping into Chuck is what caused Chuck to bump into the table, which is the effect. However, Chuck bumping into the table is what caused the lamp to fall to the floor, which is the effect. Depending on the context, Chuck bumping into the table could be either a cause or an effect.

Comparing and Contrasting

When you are asked to compare items, you will be looking for ways in which they are similar. When asked to contrast items, you will be looking for ways in which they are different. For example, if comparing apples and oranges, you may indicate that they are both fruits and are both sweet. If contrasting apples and oranges, you may indicate that apples are usually red or green while oranges live up to their name and are usually orange.

Review Test

QUESTIONS 1 THROUGH 6 ARE BASED ON THE FOLLOWING PASSAGE:

KENNEDY'S INAUGURAL ADDRESS

1   So let us begin anew—remembering on both sides that civility is not a sign of weakness, and sincerity is always subject to proof. Let us never negotiate out of fear. But let us never fear to negotiate.

2   Let both sides explore what problems unite us instead of belaboring those problems which divide us.

3   Let both sides, for the first time, formulate serious and precise proposals for the inspection and control of arms—and bring the absolute power to destroy other nations under the absolute control of all nations.

4   Let both sides seek to invoke the wonders of science instead of its terrors. Together let us explore the stars, conquer the deserts, **eradicate** disease, tap the ocean depths and encourage the arts and commerce.

5   Let both sides unite to heed in all corners of the earth the command of Isaiah—to "undo the heavy burdens . . . (and) let the oppressed go free."

6   And if a beachhead of cooperation may push back the jungle of suspicion, let both sides join in creating a new endeavor, not a new balance of power, but a new world of law, where the strong are just and the weak secure and the peace preserved.

7   All this will not be finished in the first one hundred days. Nor will it be finished in the first one thousand days, nor in the life of this Administration, nor even perhaps in our lifetime on this planet. But let us begin.

8   In your hands, my fellow citizens, more than mine, will rest the final success or failure of our course. Since this country was founded, each generation of Americans has been summoned to give testimony to its national loyalty. The graves of young Americans who answered the call to service surround the globe.

9   Now the trumpet summons us again—not as a call to bear arms, though arms we need—not as a call to battle, though embattled we are—but a call to bear the burden of a long twilight struggle, year in and year out, "rejoicing in hope, patient in tribulation"—a struggle against the common enemies of man: tyranny, poverty, disease and war itself.

10   Can we forge against these enemies a grand and global alliance, North and South, East and West, that can assure a more fruitful life for all mankind? Will you join in that historic effort?

11   In the long history of the world, only a few generations have been granted the role of defending freedom in its hour of maximum danger. I do not shrink from this responsibility—I welcome it. I do not believe that any of us would exchange places with any other people or any other generation. The energy, the faith, the devotion which we bring to this endeavor will light our country and all who serve it—and the glow from that fire can truly light the world.

12   And so, my fellow Americans: ask not what your country can do for you—ask what you can do for your country.

Source: "President John F. Kennedy's Inaugural Address (1961)."
Our Documents. Last accessed August 10, 2016.
www.ourdocuments.gov/doc.php?doc=91&page=transcript.

1. What is the main idea of President Kennedy's speech?
    (A) We must all work together to support our country.
    (B) Few generations have faced such danger.
    (C) The country should have a fresh start.
    (D) All must go to battle.

2. What can be inferred by the statement, in the eleventh paragraph, that reads, "In the long history of the world, only a few generations have been granted the role of defending freedom in its hour of maximum danger"?
   (A) Democracy is the best type of government.
   (B) There have been few generations of people.
   (C) The history of the world is longer than most people think.
   (D) If people don't defend freedom, it may be lost.

3. In the fourth paragraph, President Kennedy said, "Together let us explore the stars, conquer the deserts, eradicate disease, tap the ocean depths and encourage the arts and commerce." All of the following would fit into those categories EXCEPT
   (A) funding of programs that assist endangered species.
   (B) establishing free trade agreements.
   (C) increasing military funding to support space exploration.
   (D) offering college scholarships to students in the arts.

4. Based on the context of the word, which of the following is the best definition of the word "eradicate" in the fourth paragraph?
   (A) lessen
   (B) control
   (C) develop remedies for
   (D) completely eliminate

5. President Kennedy's speech can best be described as _____.

6. The tone of President Kennedy's speech can best be described as
   (A) conciliatory.
   (B) disciplinary.
   (C) energizing.
   (D) apologetic.

QUESTIONS 7 THROUGH 12 ARE BASED ON THE FOLLOWING PASSAGE:

DON QUIXOTE

1   At this point they came in sight of thirty forty windmills that there are on the plain, and as soon as Don Quixote saw them he said to his squire, "Fortune is arranging matters for us better than we could have shaped our desires ourselves, for look there, friend Sancho Panza, where thirty or more monstrous giants present themselves, all of whom I mean to engage in battle and slay, and with whose spoils we shall begin to make our fortunes; for this is righteous warfare, and it is God's good service to sweep so evil a breed from off the face of the earth."

2   "What giants?" said Sancho Panza.

3   "Those thou seest there," answered his master, "with the long arms, and some have them nearly two leagues long."

4   "Look, your worship," said Sancho, "what we see there are not giants but windmills, and what seem to be their arms are the sails that turned by the wind make the millstone go."

5   "It is easy to see," replied Don Quixote, "that thou art not used to this business of adventures; those are giants; and if thou art afraid, away with thee out of this and betake thyself to prayer while I engage them in fierce and unequal combat."

6   So saying, he gave the spur to his steed Rocinante, **heedless** of the cries his squire Sancho sent after him, warning him that most certainly they were windmills and not giants he was going to attack. He, however, was so positive they were giants that he neither heard the cries of Sancho, nor perceived, near as he was, what they were, but made at them shouting, "Fly not, cowards and vile beings, for a single knight attacks you."

7   A slight breeze at this moment sprang up, and the great sails began to move, seeing which Don Quixote exclaimed, "Though ye flourish more arms than the giant Briareus, ye have to reckon with me."

8   So saying, and commending himself with all his heart to his lady Dulcinea, imploring her to support him in such a peril, with lance in rest and covered by his buckler, he charged at Rocinante's fullest gallop and fell upon the first mill that stood in front of him; but as he drove his lance-point into the sail the wind whirled it round with such force that it

shivered the lance to pieces, sweeping with it horse and rider, who went rolling over on the plain, in a sorry condition. Sancho hastened to his assistance as fast as his ass could go, and when he came up found him unable to move, with such a shock had Rocinante fallen with him.

9   "God bless me!" said Sancho, "did I not tell your worship to mind what you were about, for they were only windmills? And no one could have made any mistake about it but one who had something of the same kind in his head."

10   "Hush, friend Sancho," replied Don Quixote, "the fortunes of war more than any other are liable to frequent fluctuations; and moreover I think, and it is the truth, that that same sage Friston who carried off my study and books, has turned these giants into mills in order to rob me of the glory of vanquishing them, such is the enmity he bears me; but in the end his wicked arts will avail but little against my good sword."

11   "God order it as he may," said Sancho Panza, and helping him to rise got him up again on Rocinante, whose shoulder was half out; and then, discussing the late adventure, they followed the road to Puerto Lapice, for there, said Don Quixote, they could not fail to find adventures in abundance and variety, as it was a great thoroughfare. For all that, he was much grieved at the loss of his lance, and saying so to his squire, he added, "I remember having read how a Spanish knight, Diego Perez de Vargas by name, having broken his sword in battle, tore from an oak a ponderous bough or branch, and with it did such things that day, and pounded so many Moors, that he got the surname of Machuca, and he and his descendants from that day forth were called Vargas y Machuca. I mention this because from the first oak I see I mean to rend such another branch, large and stout like that, with which I am determined and resolved to do such deeds that thou mayest deem thyself very fortunate in being found worthy to come and see them, and be an eyewitness of things that will with difficulty be believed."

12   "Be that as God will," said Sancho, "I believe it all as your worship says it; but straighten yourself a little, for you seem all on one side, may be from the shaking of the fall."

13   "That is the truth," said Don Quixote, "and if I make no complaint of the pain it is because knights-errant are not permitted to complain of any wound, even though their bowels be coming out through it."

14   "If so," said Sancho, "I have nothing to say; but God knows I would rather your worship complained when anything ailed you. For my part, I confess I must complain however small the ache may be; unless this rule about not complaining extends to the squires of knights-errant also."

Source: de Cervantes, Miguel. Excerpt from *Don Quixote*. Reprint of the John Ormsby Translation Edition, Project Gutenberg, 2015. *www.gutenberg.org/cache/epub/996/pg996-images.html*.

7. Sancho can best be characterized as _____.

8. Initially, how did Don Quixote feel about the loss of his lance?
    (A) panicked
    (B) confused
    (C) relieved
    (D) upset

9. Write the following characteristics in the correct boxes to match them with the appropriate character.

    Imaginative   Realistic   Devoted   Bold

Sancho Panza	Don Quixote

10. Based on the passage, what does Don Quixote value?
    (A) negotiating
    (B) heroism
    (C) mediation
    (D) peace

11. Based on the context of the word, which of the following is the best definition of the word "heedless" in the sixth paragraph?
    (A) distorted
    (B) loud
    (C) inaudible
    (D) careless disregard

12. Which of the following can be concluded about Quixote?
    (A) He has delusions of grandeur.
    (B) He has always been a great knight.
    (C) He speaks Spanish.
    (D) He prefers business to adventure.

QUESTIONS 13 THROUGH 18 ARE BASED ON THE FOLLOWING PASSAGE:

LITTLE WOMEN

1   "Merry Christmas, little daughters! I'm glad you began at once, and hope you will keep on. But I want to say one word before we sit down. Not far away from here lies a poor woman with a little newborn baby. Six children are huddled into one bed to keep from freezing, for they have no fire. There is nothing to eat over there, and the oldest boy came to tell me they were suffering hunger and cold. My girls, will you give them your breakfast as a Christmas present?"

2   They were all unusually hungry, having waited nearly an hour, and for a minute no one spoke, only a minute, for Jo exclaimed impetuously, "I'm so glad you came before we began!"

3   "May I go and help carry the things to the poor little children?" asked Beth eagerly.

4   "*I* shall take the cream and the muffings," added Amy, heroically giving up the article she most liked.

5   Meg was already covering the buckwheats, and piling the bread into one big plate.

6   "I thought you'd do it," said Mrs. March, smiling as if satisfied. "You shall all go and help me, and when we come back we will have bread and milk for breakfast, and make it up at dinnertime."

7   They were soon ready, and the procession set out. Fortunately it was early, and they went through back streets, so few people saw them, and no one laughed at the queer party.

8   A poor, bare, miserable room it was, with broken windows, no fire, ragged bedclothes, a sick mother, wailing baby, and a group of pale, hungry children cuddled under one old quilt, trying to keep warm.

9   How the big eyes stared and the blue lips smiled as the girls went in.

10   "Ach, mein Gott! It is good angels come to us!" said the poor woman, crying for joy.

11   "Funny angels in hoods and mittens," said Jo, and set them to laughing.

12   In a few minutes it really did seem as if kind spirits had been at work there. Hannah, who had carried wood, made a fire, and stopped up the broken panes with old hats and her own cloak. Mrs. March gave the mother tea and gruel, and comforted her with promises of help, while she dressed the little baby as tenderly as if it had been her own. The girls meantime spread the table, set the children round the fire, and fed them like so many hungry birds, laughing, talking, and trying to understand the funny broken English.

13   "Das ist gut!" "Die Engel-kinder!" cried the poor things as they ate and warmed their purple hands at the comfortable blaze. The girls had never been called angel children before, and thought it very agreeable, especially Jo, who had been considered a 'Sancho' ever since she was born. That was a very happy breakfast, though they didn't get any of it. And when they went away, leaving comfort behind, I think there were not in all the city four merrier people than the hungry little girls who gave away their breakfasts and contented themselves with bread and milk on Christmas morning.

14   "That's loving our neighbor better than ourselves, and I like it," said Meg, as they set out their presents while their mother was upstairs collecting clothes for the poor Hummels.

Source: Alcott, Louisa May. Excerpt from *Little Women*. Reprint of the 1896 Boston Edition, Project Gutenberg, 2011. *www.gutenberg.org/files/37106/37106-h/37106-h.htm.*

13. Based on the passage, write all of the following words that do NOT define the word "impetuously" in context in the box below.

suddenly
sullenly
quietly
doubtfully

14. Jo's and Hannah's actions can be categorized as all of the following EXCEPT
   (A) thoughtful.
   (B) considerate.
   (C) divisive.
   (D) helpful.

15. Place the following events, in chronological order, in the following boxes.

Mrs. March collected clothes upstairs.
Mrs. March gave the mother tea.
Beth was eager to help the poor children.
Hannah made a fire.

16. The actions of Jo and Hannah most likely had a _____
    effect on the children of the poor woman.

17. What does the pause in the second paragraph suggest?
    (A) The children wanted to help the poor family.
    (B) The children had to weigh their hunger against helping the poor
        family.
    (C) The children were praying for the poor family.
    (D) The children were shy.

18. Which literary element was the author using when she said, "A poor,
    bare, miserable room it was, with broken windows, no fire, ragged
    bedclothes, a sick mother, wailing baby, and a group of pale, hungry
    children cuddled under one old quilt, trying to keep warm"?
    (A) metaphor
    (B) imagery
    (C) personification
    (D) hyperbole

Answers Explained

1. **(A)** President Kennedy indicates various ways in which citizens must work together. Choice B is incorrect. Although this is mentioned, it is a supporting detail, not the main idea. Choices C and D are incorrect.

2. **(D)** The quote clearly indicates that freedom is in danger and therefore could be lost.

3. **(A)** Funding for endangered species does not fit into the categories indicated.

4. **(D)** "Eradicate" means to "completely eliminate."

5. "**Motivational**," "**inspirational**," or any similar word would be the best answer.

6. **(C)** President Kennedy used language that is motivational and was intended to spur people into action.

7. "**Loyal**," "**committed**," "**steadfast**," or any similar word would be the best answer.

8. **(D)** The passage indicates that Don Quixote grieved, so it is logical that he was upset. Choices A, B, and C are incorrect. No evidence supports these answers.

9.

Sancho Panza	Don Quixote
Realistic	Imaginative
Devoted	Bold

10. **(B)** Don Quixote says in paragraph 1 that this is "righteous warfare," which indicates heroism.

11. **(D)** Quixote ignores Panza's warning.

12. **(A)** Based on his belief that he would face the "giants" alone, Don Quixote believes that he is greater than he actually is.

13. "Sullenly," "quietly," and "doubtfully" should all have been written in the box. "Suddenly" is the only word that should not have been written

in the box because the word "impetuously" was used to describe a sudden break in the moment of silence.

14. **(C)** The girls could be described as choice A, B, or D. However, "divisive" indicates that they have caused division, which they have not.

15. First, Beth was eager to help the poor children. Then Hannah made a fire. Next, Mrs. March gave the mother tea. Finally, Mrs. March collected clothes upstairs.

16. **"Positive," "good,"** or any similar word would be the best answer.

17. **(B)** If the children were certain, they would have answered right away. A pause indicates thought.

18. **(B)** The sentence enables one to picture the scene.

Extended Responses | 3

The extended-response section of the Reasoning Through Language Arts subject test gives test takers the chance to express their ideas to an assigned prompt. Test takers must develop their ideas logically and include details to support their assertions. In addition, they must use proper grammar and include varied, precise, and appropriate words.

In layman's terms, you need to elevate your language, make sure there are few errors, and express yourself clearly!

The following topics will be covered in this unit:

Lesson 1: Format

Lesson 2: Beginning

Lesson 3: Middle

Lesson 4: End

Lesson 5: Planning

Lesson 6: Constructing Your Response

The test evaluators use a fairly complex system of evaluating your writing. However, it can be broken down into three categories:

1. Quality and validity of your argument
2. Organization and level of language
3. Conformity to standard English

LESSON 1: FORMAT

A well-written extended response has three main components:

→ **BEGINNING**
→ **MIDDLE**
→ **END**

This may seem overly simplistic. However, the evaluators are simply looking for your writing to have a clear structure with a logical order.

LESSON 2: BEGINNING

The introductory paragraph is like a first impression. It sets the tone for the rest of the extended response. The purpose of the introductory paragraph is to let the reader know what you are going to discuss in the body paragraphs. As with the extended response as a whole, certain things should be included in an introductory paragraph:

→ **INTRODUCTORY SENTENCE**

→ **LIST OF SUPPORTING DETAILS/EXAMPLES**

→ **CONTROLLING IDEA/THESIS STATEMENT**

The Introductory Sentence

The introductory sentence is the very first sentence of the extended response. It should grab the reader's attention and give a sense of the topic. Several types of introductory sentences work well as a "hook":

→ **GENERAL STATEMENT ABOUT THE TOPIC**
(i.e., *Electric cars, while not widely popular, have proven to reduce emissions and promote a more green mode of transportation.*)

→ **QUOTE**
(i.e., *"My fellow Americans, ask not what your country can do for you; ask what you can do for your country."—John F. Kennedy*)

→ **QUESTION**
(i.e., *What would our daily lives look like if another world war took place?*)

→ **STATEMENT OF A FACT**
(i.e., *In America, 207 million people had smartphones in 2016.*)

Keep in mind that however you choose to begin your introductory paragraph, it must fit within the context of the extended response as a whole.

List of Supporting Details/Examples

The next sentence should be a list of the details that will be discussed in the body paragraphs to support the thesis statement. You should not elaborate on the details, as that is the purpose of the body of the extended response; simply list the details and examples.

For example, using the "quote" introductory sentence, the following italicized sentences list supporting details and examples:

"My fellow Americans, ask not what your country can do for you; ask what you can do for your country." *In his 1961 inaugural address, John F. Kennedy believed that we Americans could provide for our own needs. Today, however, tax rates have skyrocketed, making this a difficult task for business owners and the self-employed.*

Controlling Idea/Thesis Statement

The thesis statement is the controlling idea of your extended response. It should address the questions:

Why are you writing this?
What is your point?
What do you want to prove?

For example, building on the paragraph on the previous page, the following italicized sentence would be a sensible controlling idea/thesis statement:

"My fellow Americans, ask not what your country can do for you; ask what you can do for your country." In his 1961 inaugural address, John F. Kennedy believed that we Americans could provide for our own needs. Today, however, tax rates have skyrocketed, making this a difficult task for business owners and the self-employed. *If Congress lowered the taxes that directly affect small businesses and self-employed individuals, a small business boom could bring about jobs and increase localized spending throughout the country.*

When put together, these sentences form the beginning or introductory paragraph. Although the introductory sentence should always come first, the list of supporting details and examples may come either before or after the thesis statement.

LESSON 3: MIDDLE

The body paragraphs make up the majority of the extended response. Therefore, they must be complete and properly organized. Much like the introductory paragraph, certain types of sentences go at the beginning, middle, and end of each body paragraph. Each of these paragraphs should discuss one of the details listed in the introductory paragraph and contain the following:

→ **TRANSITIONAL SENTENCE**
→ **TOPIC SENTENCE**
→ **EXAMPLES AND SUPPORTING DETAILS**
→ **CONCLUDING SENTENCE**

Having all of these components in this order in each paragraph will help ensure that the paragraph is organized and complete.

Transitional Sentence

When moving from the introductory paragraph to a body paragraph or from one body paragraph to another, transition smoothly. Use transitional words and phrases.

Topic Sentence

The topic sentence should tell the reader the main idea of the paragraph. It is very similar to the thesis statement in that it should indicate the purpose of the paragraph.

Examples and Supporting Details

When taking a position on an issue, you must include an adequate amount of evidence to support that position. Examples of evidence that is sufficient to support your thesis statement include quotes and/or paraphrases from both sources. Without information directly from your sources, your argument will be weak, and you may be scored much lower. Choose carefully, though! Do not fill your entire essay with quotes and leave out your own careful analysis.

Concluding Sentence

The concluding sentence should tie up any loose ends. More importantly, it should tell the reader how the information in the paragraph relates to the thesis statement.

Depending on the number of body paragraphs and the complexity of the sentences, a good length for a body paragraph is typically 4 to 7 sentences. However, the length is less important than the quality of the information. A well-written, well-supported short paragraph is far better than a poorly written, inadequately supported long paragraph.

Example of a Body Paragraph

With lower taxes and more tax incentives, self-employed and small business owners would be able to hire more workers. These workers would have more income to spend in their local economy. With fewer unemployed people, the local, state, and federal governments will all have a smaller financial burden. In "Create a Small Business Boom," the author argues that local governments would be positively impacted the most from more small businesses and self-employed workers. The author writes that "[f]ewer burdens on the local government and increased revenue makes for a strong and healthy local economy."

LESSON 4: END

Just as a well-written introductory paragraph is important in making a good first impression, the conclusion is important in making a good final impression. In fact, the conclusion contains much of the same information as the introductory paragraph, just in different words. The conclusion should contain the following items:

→ **RESTATEMENT OF THE CONTROLLING IDEA/THESIS STATEMENT**
→ **SUMMARY OF THE MOST IMPORTANT DETAILS**
→ **CONCLUDING SENTENCE/CLINCHER**

Restatement of the Controlling Idea/Thesis Statement

Saying the same exact thing twice doesn't strengthen your argument; it just sounds repetitive. Therefore, be careful when restating the controlling idea or thesis statement. Make sure that how you phrase the idea in the introductory and concluding paragraphs is different.

Summary of the Most Important Details

Just like with the controlling idea, do not repeat the details from the body paragraphs word for word. Rather than listing the details again, paraphrase your most interesting or important points.

Concluding Sentence/Clincher

The concluding sentence will stay with the reader. Be sure it will make a strong impact.

Example of a Conclusion

John F. Kennedy's challenge continues to resonate with many Americans, even more than 50 years later. As Smith argued in his article, lower taxes would greatly affect all self-employed and small business owners across the country in many positive ways. With a reduced financial burden from our own government, more people will stand up and ask, "What can I do for my country?"

LESSON 5: PLANNING

While writing extended responses in this book, we recommend you use a diagramming technique to plan your essay. Diagramming helps you not only plan your essay, but also helps you visualize the material. This is especially important when you compare and contrast or put events in a logical order.

Below is a Venn diagram that is useful for planning extended responses that ask you to compare and contrast. The far left and far right areas are where you will list the ways in which each is unique. Where the circles overlap in the middle is where you will list the ways in which they are similar.

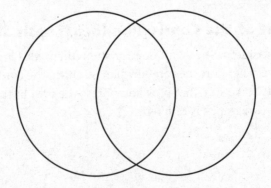

The following is a planning web. This is especially useful when you are listing characteristics of a single item or how multiple things relate to a single item.

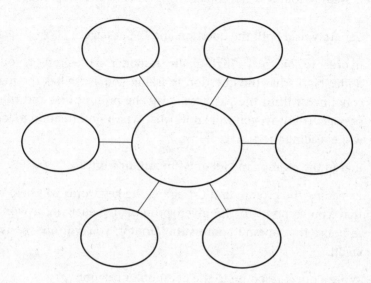

If nothing else, keep it simple and come up with a list!

1.	
2.	
3.	
4.	
5.	

LESSON 6: CONSTRUCTING YOUR RESPONSE

Here are 7 steps to follow when constructing an extended response.

STEP 1 Carefully read both the question and the passage.

In order to construct a high-quality response to the prompt, you must understand what the question is asking you as well as the material contained within the passages. Read the prompt first and then the passage. This way, you will know what type of information to look for while reading the passage.

STEP 2 Reread the prompt and identify important words.

Rereading the prompt and extracting the key words will help ensure that you respond to the given prompt. If you write a wonderful response that doesn't address the prompt, you will not receive any credit.

STEP 3 Write a direct response to the question or prompt.

Begin by making sure you have responded to the prompt. If you do so, it is more likely that your response will stay on track and that you will write about what is being asked of you.

STEP 4 Refer back to the passage, and find details that support your position.

A large portion of the score on the extended response will have to do with your argument. An argument is more effective when you include evidence to back it. Make sure you cite a sufficient amount of evidence from both sources. Remember, "evidence" includes direct quotes and paraphrases.

STEP 5 Arrange your ideas logically.

Now that you have assembled your supporting details, make sure that the essay is written in a logical order. You can order the ideas by time, size, significance, or some other logical methods.

STEP 6 Write a rough draft.

Write out a preliminary version of the response. Remember that since you are typing your extended response, it will be very easy to go back and change things or to cut out and move entire sections if need be.

STEP 7 Reread and revise your essay.

The goal is for the essay to be as good as possible. If you can avoid it, don't submit the essay until you've reread and revised it. Ask yourself the following questions:

- Have I responded to the prompt?
- Have I included enough evidence?
- Do my ideas follow a logical order?
- Are any words misspelled?
- Have I confused any homonyms?
- Have I used proper punctuation, including periods, commas, semi-colons, and apostrophes?
- Do I need to break up any run-on sentences?
- Can I combine any strings of short, choppy sentences?

After you have asked yourself these questions and made all appropriate changes, read your response one last time. If you are satisfied, submit it.

SCORING FOR THE EXTENDED RESPONSE

The score that you will receive for your extended response in Section 2 of the Reasoning Through Language Arts subject test will be graded, according to three traits, by multiple evaluators. Those traits are **Creation of Arguments and Use of Evidence**, **Development of Ideas and Organizational Structure**, and **Clarity and Command of Standard English Conventions**. Each trait is worth up to 2 points; the highest score you can receive on your essay is 6 points total. Below is a checklist that can be used to evaluate any extended response that you write. If you check off all of the following requirements, you most likely would receive a 5 or 6 on your extended response.

- ☐ My purpose/thesis answers the prompt.
- ☐ My purpose/thesis is based on the reading passage.
- ☐ My essay gives specific evidence (direct/indirect quotes) from the reading passages.
- ☐ My evidence is sufficient and supports my thesis/argument.
- ☐ My ideas are logical and well-developed and elaborate the main points of my essay.

☐ My essay has an introduction, at least 2–3 body paragraphs, and a conclusion.

☐ I used clear transitions between paragraphs and main points.

☐ I used a formal tone, appropriate to the intended audience.

☐ I used specific vocabulary and/or terms (I avoided vague words like "things" or "stuff").

☐ I used varied sentence structures.

☐ I used proper grammar (with few to no mistakes)—capitalization, punctuation, pronoun usage, subject-verb agreement.

☐ I avoided wordiness and awkward sentences.

☐ I avoided run-ons and sentence fragments.

NOTE: An essay with minor mistakes can still receive a perfect score. Evaluators take into consideration that you are writing a draft under timed circumstances.

Review Test

■▼▼■▼▼▼▼▼▼▼▼▼▼▼▼▼▼▼▼▼▼▼▼▼▼■■

DIRECTIONS: Read and use the passages that follow to construct an extended response to this prompt.

Over the years, the United States has had varying policies on Native Americans as is suggested in the two passages below. In your extended response, compare and contrast the attitudes toward Native Americans and indicate whether the Treaty of Fort Laramie was beneficial or detrimental to Native Americans.

Cite specific information and examples to support your position. Be sure to develop your response fully.

(Note that, for this prompt, a sample extended response has been provided for you.)

THE POLICIES OF PRESIDENT ANDREW JACKSON

1   With the onset of westward expansion and increased contact with Indian tribes, President Jackson set the tone for his position on Indian affairs in his message to Congress on December 6, 1830. Jackson's message justified the removal policy already established by the Indian Removal Act of May 28, 1830.

2   The Indian Removal Act was passed to open up for settlement those lands still held by Indians in states east of the Mississippi River, primarily Georgia, Tennessee, Alabama, Mississippi, North Carolina, and others. Jackson declared that removal would "incalculably strengthen the southwestern frontier." Clearing Alabama and Mississippi of their Indian populations, he said, would "enable those states to advance rapidly in population, wealth, and power."

3   White inhabitants of Georgia were particularly anxious to have the Cherokees removed from the state because gold had been discovered on

tribal lands. Violence was commonplace in Georgia, and in all likelihood, a portion of the tribe would have been decimated if they had not been removed.

4   Removal of the Indian tribes continued beyond Jackson's tenure as President. The most infamous of the removals took place in 1838, two years after the end of Jackson's final term, when the Cherokee Indians were forcibly removed by the military. Their journey west became known as the "Trail of Tears," because of the thousands of deaths along the way.

Source: "President Andrew Jackson's Message To Congress 'On Indian Removal' (1830)." *Our Documents.* Last accessed August 10, 2016. *www.ourdocuments.gov/doc.php?flash=true&doc=25.*

FORT LARAMIE

1   ARTICLES OF A TREATY MADE AND CONCLUDED BY AND BETWEEN

2   Lieutenant General William T. Sherman, General William S. Harney, General Alfred H. Terry, General O. O. Augur, J. B. Henderson, Nathaniel G. Taylor, John G. Sanborn, and Samuel F. Tappan, duly appointed commissioners on the part of the United States, and the different bands of the Sioux Nation of Indians, by their chiefs and headmen, whose names are hereto subscribed, they being duly authorized to act in the premises.

3   ARTICLE I. From this day forward all war between the parties to this agreement shall for ever cease. The government of the United States desires peace, and its honor is hereby pledged to keep it. The Indians desire peace, and they now pledge their honor to maintain it.

4   If bad men among the whites, or among other people subject to the authority of the United States, shall commit any wrong upon the person or property of the Indians, the United States will, upon proof made to the agent, and forwarded to the Commissioner of Indian Affairs at Washington city, proceed at once to cause the offender to be arrested and punished according to the laws of the United States, and also reimburse the injured person for the loss sustained.

5   If bad men among the Indians shall commit a wrong or depredation upon the person or property of nay one, white, black, or Indian, subject to the authority of the United States, and at peace therewith, the Indians

herein named solemnly agree that they will, upon proof made to their agent, and notice by him, deliver up the wrongdoer to the United States, to be tried and punished according to its laws, and, in case they willfully refuse so to do, the person injured shall be reimbursed for his loss from the annuities, or other moneys due or to become due to them under this or other treaties made with the United States; and the President, on advising with the Commissioner of Indian Affairs, shall prescribe such rules and regulations for ascertaining damages under the provisions of this article as in his judgment may be proper, but no one sustaining loss while violating the provisions of this treaty, or the laws of the United States, shall be reimbursed therefor.

Source: "Treaty of Fort Laramie (1868)."*Our Documents*. Last accessed August 10, 2016. *www.ourdocuments.gov/doc.php?flash=true&doc=42&page=transcript.*

CONSTRUCTING A RESPONSE

When reviewing your extended response, make sure you have asked yourself the following questions:

- Have I responded to the prompt?
- Do I have enough evidence?
- Do my ideas follow a logical order?
- Are there any misspellings?
- Have I confused any homonyms?
- Have I used proper punctuation, including periods, commas, semicolons, apostrophes, and so forth?
- Do I need to break up any run-on sentences?
- Can I combine any strings of short, choppy sentences?

The prompt asks you to compare and contrast the attitudes toward Native Americans and indicate whether the Treaty of Fort Laramie was beneficial or detrimental to Native Americans. Make sure that you have chosen a side; either the treaty was beneficial or it was not. Make sure you have clearly articulated your position in the introductory part of the response. Following your introduction, compare and contrast the attitudes and cite specific evidence from both of the passages that you feel supports your position. Be sure to explain why. Finally, restate your position in the conclusion.

SAMPLE RESPONSE

The following is a sample, high-scoring response.

In a race to expand the American frontier, President Andrew Jackson forced Native Americans out of their own lands and territories, leading to strained relations with the first inhabitants of this great land. Over time, however, the American government came to recognize the importance of improving relations with Native Americans, resulting in a formal peace treaty. The Treaty of Fort Laramie proved to be beneficial for both U.S. citizens and Native Americans by offering a fair and peaceable solution to decades of war and injustice brought about by President Jackson's prejudiced policies.

While both President Jackson and the Treaty of Fort Laramie were concerned about increased contact with Indian tribes, they had completely different agendas. President Jackson was intent upon westward expansion, no matter the cost. He saw Native Americans as a hindrance to American progress. His message to Congress, entitled "On Indian Removal," was intended to "strengthen the American southwestern frontier." By making room for American settlers, those states would be able to "advance rapidly in population, wealth, and power," according to Jackson.

No benefits, however, were given to any Native Americans who were stripped of their land. They were simply moved west. If they didn't comply, they were forcibly removed by the military. Jackson also argued that if they weren't removed, the tribes would have been "decimated" in areas like Georgia.

Decades later, after thousands of Native Americans died during these forced relocations and both sides battled each other for land and territory, special U.S. commissioners were tasked to find a solution. With its sole intent to bring peace between Americans and Native Americans, the Treaty of Fort Laramie was signed in 1868. This agreement was beneficial to Native Americans because it stopped the unfair treatment that they had experienced for so long. Under the terms of this treaty, U.S. citizens were finally held accountable for any crimes against the Native Americans, and vice versa.

After decades of war and injustice, the Treaty of Fort Laramie finally brought about lasting peace between U.S. citizens and Native Americans. This treaty guaranteed the protection of Native Americans from 1868 onward. Whereas President Jackson saw Native Americans as a threat to America, this treaty finally recognized Native Americans as important individuals in this country whose rights and liberties should be protected now and always.

DIRECTIONS: Read and use the passages that follow to construct an extended response to this prompt.

There have been many great people who have changed the course of history. How did the lives of Charles Darwin and Theodore Roosevelt compare to one another, and what childhood events may have influenced them?

Cite specific information and examples to support your position. Be sure to develop your response fully.

CHARLES DARWIN

1   I was born at Shrewsbury on February 12th, 1809, and my earliest recollection goes back only to when I was a few months over four years old, when we went to near Abergele for sea-bathing, and I recollect some events and places there with some little distinctness.

2   My mother died in July 1817, when I was a little over eight years old, and it is odd that I can remember hardly anything about her except her deathbed, her black velvet gown, and her curiously constructed worktable. In the spring of this same year I was sent to a day school in Shrewsbury, where I stayed a year. I have been told that I was much

slower in learning than my younger sister Catherine, and I believe that I was in many ways a naughty boy.

3   By the time I went to this day school (Kept by Rev. G. Case, minister of the Unitarian Chapel in the High Street. Mrs. Darwin was a Unitarian and attended Mr. Case's chapel, and my father as a little boy went there with his elder sisters. But both he and his brother were christened and intended to belong to the Church of England; and after his early boyhood he seems usually to have gone to church and not to Mr. Case's. It appears ("St. James' Gazette," Dec. 15, 1883) that a mural tablet has been erected to his memory in the chapel, which is now known as the 'Free Christian Church.') my taste for natural history, and more especially for collecting, was well developed. I tried to make out the names of plants (Rev. W.A. Leighton, who was a schoolfellow of my father's at Mr. Case's school, remembers his bringing a flower to school and saying that his mother had taught him how by looking at the inside of the blossom the name of the plant could be discovered. Mr. Leighton goes on, "This greatly roused my attention and curiosity, and I enquired of him repeatedly how this could be done?"—but his lesson was naturally enough not transmissible.—F.D.), and collected all sorts of things, shells, seals, franks, coins, and minerals. The passion for collecting which leads a man to be a systematic naturalist, a virtuoso, or a miser, was very strong in me, and was clearly innate, as none of my sisters or brother ever had this taste.

Source: Darwin, Charles. Excerpt from *The Autobiography of Charles Darwin.* Reprint of the 1887 Edition, Project Gutenberg, 2013. *www.gutenberg.org/files/2010/2010-h/2010-h.htm.*

THEODORE ROOSEVELT

1   My grandfather on my father's side was of almost purely Dutch blood. When he was young he still spoke some Dutch, and Dutch was last used in the services of the Dutch Reformed Church in New York while he was a small boy.

2   About 1644 his ancestor Klaes Martensen van Roosevelt came to New Amsterdam as a "settler"—the euphemistic name for an immigrant who came over in the steerage of a sailing ship in the seventeenth century

instead of the steerage of a steamer in the nineteenth century. From that time for the next seven generations from father to son every one of us was born on Manhattan Island.

3   My father's paternal ancestors were of Holland stock; except that there was one named Waldron, a wheelwright, who was one of the Pilgrims who remained in Holland when the others came over to found Massachusetts, and who then accompanied the Dutch adventurers to New Amsterdam. My father's mother was a Pennsylvanian. Her forebears had come to Pennsylvania with William Penn, some in the same ship with him; they were of the usual type of the immigration of that particular place and time. They included Welsh and English Quakers, an Irishman,—with a Celtic name, and apparently not a Quaker,—and peace-loving Germans, who were among the founders of Germantown, having been driven from their Rhineland homes when the armies of Louis the Fourteenth ravaged the Palatinate; and, in addition, representatives of a by-no-means altogether peaceful people, the Scotch Irish, who came to Pennsylvania a little later, early in the eighteenth century. My grandmother was a woman of singular sweetness and strength, the keystone of the arch in her relations with her husband and sons. Although she was not herself Dutch, it was she who taught me the only Dutch I ever knew, a baby song of which the first line ran, "Trippe troppa tronjes." I always remembered this, and when I was in East Africa it proved a bond of union between me and the Boer settlers, not a few of whom knew it, although at first they always had difficulty in understanding my pronunciation—at which I do not wonder. It was interesting to meet these men whose ancestors had gone to the Cape about the time that mine went to America two centuries and a half previously, and to find that the descendants of the two streams of emigrants still crooned to their children some at least of the same nursery songs.

Source: Roosevelt, Theodore. Excerpt from *Theodore Roosevelt: An Autobiography by Theodore Roosevelt.* Reprint of the 1920 Edition, Project Gutenberg, 2012. *www.gutenberg.org/files/3335/3335-h/3335-h.htm.*

CONSTRUCTING A RESPONSE

When reviewing your extended response, make sure you have asked yourself the following questions:

- Have I responded to the prompt?
- Do I have enough evidence?
- Do my ideas follow a logical order?
- Are there any misspellings?
- Have I confused any homonyms?
- Have I used proper punctuation, including periods, commas, semicolons, apostrophes, and so forth?
- Do I need to break up any run-on sentences?
- Can I combine any strings of short, choppy sentences?

The prompt asks how the lives of Charles Darwin and Theodore Roosevelt compare to one another and what may have influenced them as children. Make sure that you draw comparisons—how they are the same, not different. Make sure you have clearly articulated your position in the introductory part of your response. Following your introduction, cite specific evidence from their childhoods that you feel supports your position and be sure to explain why. Finally, restate your position in the conclusion.

UNIT 2:
MATHEMATICAL
REASONING

Mathematical Reasoning Overview | 4

The Mathematical Reasoning subject test, which we will call the "Math subject test," measures your math skills in two ways. The first deals with math in an academic way, focusing on the terms, concepts, and methods that math students learn in school. Problems may involve more formal presentations of math: equations, functions, geometric diagrams, and so on. These are called math world questions because they test math in a formal way.

The Math subject test also measures your math skills in more familiar, real-world settings. These questions are often in the form of word problems involving familiar objects or situations. Your job is to translate the story into mathematical terms and then perform some math operations to find the answer. These are called real-world questions because they test math using real settings.

You'll need to be comfortable in both worlds. However, you must keep your priorities straight. To do well on this subject test, you will need to be very comfortable dealing with math in the real world.

Subject Matter

The Mathematical Reasoning test covers two areas of content:

1. Quantitative Problem Solving (45%)
2. Algebraic Problem Solving (55%)

Quantitative subjects include:

- Numbers and operations
- Ratios, proportions, and rates
- Word problems
- Geometry
- Statistics

Algebraic subjects include:

- Expressions
- Equations
- The coordinate plane
- Functions

Question Types

On the computer-based Math subject test, the following types of questions will appear:

→ **MULTIPLE-CHOICE**

→ **FILL-IN-THE-BLANK**

→ **DROP-DOWN**

→ **HOT SPOT**

→ **DRAG-AND-DROP**

Note that certain question types, such as drop-down, will be modified in this book so you can practice them using pen and paper.

Subject Integration

Some math skills will also be tested on the Science and Social Studies subject tests. Math questions on these tests will focus on skills used in statistics, like interpreting graphs and charts, calculating averages and other measures of center, and analyzing data.

Practice Fundamentals

One way to build study time into your daily routine is to use portable study tools (like flash cards) to help you memorize important information. You can create cards to help you study:

- Multiplication tables
- Factors and multiples
- Number conversions (fraction to decimal to percent)
- Divisibility rules
- Formulas for area and perimeter
- Any other fact-based math you want to memorize

All math questions will require you to use these fundamentals. As you memorize more of these math facts, you will find that all math questions become easier.

PRACTICE CALCULATION BOTH WAYS

You can make calculations using two different methods: manually or with a calculator. Practice using both methods.

Manual Calculation

Your mental math skills are important. The best way to sharpen them is to do math in your head or on paper. Look for opportunities to make some quick calculations by hand. Double-check sales receipts and recalculate the sales tax, recalculate your utility bills, add up the transactions on bank statements, or create and track a weekly budget and record your expenses. Work on paper, even if you are comfortable doing mental math, so that you can review your calculations later.

Using a Calculator

The exam will provide you with an online scientific calculator for part of the exam. You should be familiar with the kinds of functions that will be available. Buy or borrow a scientific calculator and learn how to use it. The GED Testing Service® provides an online demonstration of the calculator that they will provide, so you can compare it to whichever calculator you learn on.

PRACTICE DATA ANALYSIS

Certain math skills related to statistics are tested on the Science and Social Studies subject tests. The integrated subjects include measures of center (mean, median, mode), weighted averages, range, identifying outliers, and similar subjects related to analyzing numerical data. Make these skills a priority since they will help you earn points in three different parts of the test.

Learn to Estimate

Once your fundamentals and calculation skills are sharp, you'll be able to use them to estimate. Estimation is a very powerful tool when working on math questions. Rounding numbers in a problem before doing the calculation can make the problem noticeably easier. Number conversions like "21% is about 1/5" or "one-eighth is about 12%" can be very useful in estimating parts of wholes.

Numbers and Operations

5

Success on the Math subject test relies heavily on the fundamental skills covered in this section. Having a solid foundation in the basics, including how to perform all the basic operations (adding, subtracting, multiplying, and dividing), is critical for succeeding on the exam. If these skills are not strong, you can't do more advanced math. Since most students are already fairly familiar with these basic skills, we present them at a summary level along with some practice in case you need to remove the rust.

LESSON 1: DIGITS AND NUMBERS

DIGITS The symbols we use to construct numbers: 0, 1, 2, 3, 4, 5, 6, 7, 8, and 9.

NUMBERS Combinations of digits used to represent amounts or values.

INTEGERS Whole numbers, including all positive and negative whole numbers and zero (zero is neutral).

LESSON 2: THE NUMBER LINE

The *number line* is a horizontal line with zero in the middle that extends forever in either direction. Along the line, small *tick marks* indicate the location of numbers that are greater or less than zero.

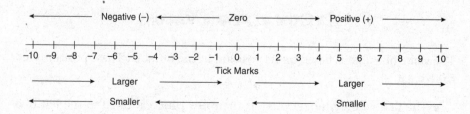

- Numbers to the right of zero are called **positive** *numbers*. They increase in value (get larger) as they move away from zero. Positive numbers are greater than zero.
- Numbers to the left of zero are called **negative** *numbers*. They decrease in value (get smaller) as they move away from zero. Negative numbers are less than zero.
- Zero is called **neutral**, because it is neither positive nor negative.

Positive numbers are distinguished from negative numbers using symbols called **signs**. A plus (+) is used to indicate positive numbers, and a minus (–) is used to indicate negative numbers. Any number without a sign is assumed to be positive.

LESSON 3: ABSOLUTE VALUE

Absolute value is the unit distance on the number line between a number and 0. For all positive and negative numbers, absolute value is always positive. Absolute value is symbolized like this with two vertical lines: $|\ \ |$. The absolute value of 0, $|0|$, is 0.

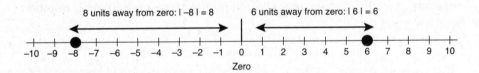

8 units away from zero: $|-8| = 8$ 6 units away from zero: $|6| = 6$

Zero

- The absolute value of 6 or $|6|$ is 6.
- The absolute value of –8 or $|-8|$ is 8.
- The absolute value of 0 or $|0|$ is 0.

LESSON 4: PLACE VALUES

The value of a digit is based on its position in the number. These positions are called places.

- The first whole number place is the **ones place**, located to the left of a starting point called the **decimal point**.
- Whole number places increase in value from right to left by multiples of 10.

- Commas are used to divide periods (groups of three places).

Place	____ ,			____ ,				.
Place name:	Millions	Hundred thousands	Ten thousands	Thousands	Hundreds	Tens	Ones	Decimal Point
Number:	1,000,000	100,000	10,000	1,000	100	10	1	
Prior number × 10:	100,000 × 10	10,000 × 10	1,000 × 10	100 × 10	10 × 10	1 × 10	1	
Exponent:	× 10^6	× 10^5	× 10^4	× 10^3	× 10^2	× 10^1		

The **exponent** row in the table above is used in **scientific notation**.

LESSON 5: ROUNDING

Round numbers are numbers that end in one or more zeros. They are useful when estimating.

- Numbers are rounded to a specific place. 1,475 rounded to the hundreds place is 1,500.
- The digit in the place to be rounded is called the rounding digit.
- If the digit to the right of the rounding digit is 5 or greater, the rounding digit is rounded up by adding 1.
- If the digit to the right is 4 or smaller, the rounding digit remains unchanged. This is called rounding down.
- All digits to the right of the selected place are replaced with zeros.

Number	7,263	3,509
Nearest 10:	Round **down** to 7,260	Round **up** to 3,510
Nearest 100:	Round **up** to 7,300	Round **down** to 3,500
Nearest 1,000:	Round **down** to 7,000	Round **up** to 4,000

LESSON 6: OPERATIONS

ADDING AND SUBTRACTING

When adding, the numbers being added are the addends and the result is the sum.

When subtracting, the first number is the minuend, the second number is the subtrahend, and the result is the difference.

$$
\begin{array}{rl}
\text{addends} \searrow & 4 \\
& \underline{+5} \\
\text{sum} \longrightarrow & 9
\end{array}
$$

$$
\begin{array}{rl}
\text{minuend} \longrightarrow & 6 \\
& \underline{-2} \longleftarrow \text{subtrahend} \\
\text{difference} \longrightarrow & 4
\end{array}
$$

MULTIPLYING

When multiplying, the first number is the multiplicand, the second number is the multiplier, and the result is the product.

The multiplicand and multiplier are factors of the product, and the product is a multiple of both factors.

$$
\begin{array}{rl}
\text{multiplicand} \longrightarrow & 4 \longleftarrow \text{factors} \\
& \underline{\times 2} \longleftarrow \text{multiplier} \\
\text{product} \longrightarrow & 8 \longleftarrow \text{multiple}
\end{array}
$$

Multiplication can be expressed using the word "times," the times sign (×), a dot, or parentheses.

Multiplication Symbol	Times ×	Dot •	Parentheses ( )
	4 × 2	4 • 2	4(2) or (4)(2)

Distributive Property in Multiplication

Several math properties apply to operations like addition and multiplication. However, the most important one on the Math subject test is the *distributive* property in multiplication. This property applies to expressions like the following:

$$3(4 + 5)$$

Order of operations tells us to add inside the parentheses first and then multiply:

$$3(4 + 5) = 3(9) = 27$$

The distributive property says that we will get the same result if we multiply the number outside the parentheses (3) by each of the numbers inside them (4 and 5) and then perform the operation between the inside numbers (+):

$$3(4 + 5) = 3(4) + 3(5) = 12 + 15 = 27$$

In cases that involve only numbers, like the one above, you should follow the order of operations and add inside the parentheses first. The distributive property becomes very important later on in algebra when not everything is a number.

DIVIDING

When dividing, the number being divided is the *dividend*, the other number is the *divisor*, and the result is the *quotient*. The amount left over, if any, is the *remainder*. If there is no remainder, the divisor is a *factor* of the dividend and the dividend is a *multiple* of the divisor.

$$5 \leftarrow \text{quotient}$$
$$\text{divisor} \longrightarrow 3\overline{)15} \leftarrow \text{dividend}$$

Division can be expressed using the division symbol, slash, fraction bar, or long division symbol.

Division Symbol	Division ÷	Slash /	Fraction Bar —	Long Division $\overline{)}$
	15 ÷ 3	15/3	$\frac{15}{3}$	$3\overline{)15}$

LESSON 7: SIGNED NUMBER OPERATIONS

ADDING

- When adding two positive numbers, the sum is positive: $6 + 3 = 9$
- When adding two negative numbers, the sum is negative: $-8 + -3 = -11$
- When adding a positive number and a negative number, first find the difference between them. If the positive number is farther from 0 than the negative number, the result is positive: $5 + -3 = 2$. If the negative number is farther from 0 than the positive number, the result is negative: $5 + -9 = -4$

SUBTRACTING

When subtracting two positive numbers:

- If the first number is larger, the difference is positive: $7 - 4 = 3$
- If the second number is larger, the difference is negative: $4 - 7 = -3$

When subtracting a negative second number:

- First change the subtraction operation to addition.
- Then change the sign of the second number to positive:

$$6 - (-2) = 6 + 2 = 8 \text{ and } -5 - (-3) = -5 + 3 = -2$$

When subtracting a positive second number from a negative first number:

- First change the subtraction operation to addition.
- Then change the sign of the second number to negative:

$$-3 - 6 = -3 + -6 = -9$$

MULTIPLYING AND DIVIDING

If the signs are the same, the result is positive:

- $4 \cdot 6 = 24$
- $-3 \cdot -8 = 24$
- $18 \div 3 = 6$
- $-27 \div -3 = 9$

If the signs are not the same, the result is negative:

- $4 \cdot -6 = -24$
- $-3 \cdot 8 = -24$
- $18 \div -3 = -6$
- $-27 \div 3 = -9$

LESSON 8: FACTORS AND MULTIPLES

Consider the following example: $4 \times 6 = 24$

- 4 and 6 are *factors* of 24. Factors are numbers that divide evenly into a given number.
- 24 is a *multiple* of both 4 and 6. Multiples are the results when a given number is multiplied by other numbers.
- We sometimes also say that 4 and 6 go into 24, and that 24 is divisible by 4 and 6.

The distributive property of multiplication can be applied in reverse by using factors. Suppose we begin with $28 + 42$:

- Both 28 and 42 are multiples of 7. $28 \div 7 = 4$ and $42 \div 7 = 6$.
- Therefore, we can re-express the original expression: $7(4 + 6)$.
- This is called the factored form of the expression, because 7 is a factor of both numbers. Dividing out a common factor is called factoring.

PRIME NUMBERS

A number that has no factors other than itself and 1 is a **prime** number. All other numbers are **composite** numbers. The first 10 prime numbers are:

$$2, 3, 5, 7, 11, 13, 17, 19, 23, 29$$

Note that 1 is neither a prime nor a composite number.

PRIME FACTORIZATION

You can factor a composite number into a product of prime numbers. This is called prime factorization. It involves repeatedly dividing composite factors by prime factors until only prime factors are left. The process and result can be presented in a factor tree.

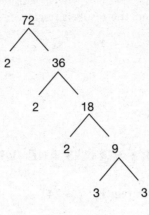

The prime factorization of 72 is expressed as $2 \times 2 \times 2 \times 3 \times 3$ or $2^3 \times 3^2$.

DIVISIBILITY RULES

Use the rules below when trying to identify factors.

A Number Is Divisible By	When
2	The last digit is 2, 4, 6, 8, or 0. (This means the number is even. Numbers not divisible by 2 are odd.) 32 and 18 are divisible by 2. 37 and 29 are not divisible by 2.
3	The sum of its digits is divisible by 3. 327 is divisible by 3 (3 + 2 + 7 = 12, and 12 is divisible by 3). 241 is not divisible by 3 (2 + 4 + 1 = 7).
4	The last two digits, when taken as a number, are divisible by 4. 1,024 is divisible by 4 because 24 is divisible by 4.
5	The last digit is 0 or 5. 30 and 55 are divisible by 5. 72 and 53 are not divisible by 5.
6	The number is even and the sum of digits is divisible by 3 (rules for 2 and 3 together). 84 is divisible by 6 because it is even and because 8 + 4 = 12 and 12 is divisible by 3.

8	The last three digits, when taken as a number, are divisible by 8. 1,824 is divisible by 8 because 824 is divisible by 8.
9	The sum of digits is divisible by 9. 2,331 is divisible by 9 ($2 + 3 + 3 + 1 = 9$). 3,124 is not divisible by 9 ($3 + 1 + 2 + 4 = 10$).
10	The last digit is 0. 380 and 1,250 are divisible by 10. 987 and 3,458 are not divisible by 10.

LESSON 9: EXPONENTS

Using exponents allows test takers to multiply the same number repeatedly. It is often referred to as raising a number to a power.

$$\text{base} \longrightarrow 4^3 \longleftarrow \text{exponent}$$

The number is expressed as a combination of a *base*, which is the number to be multiplied, and an *exponent*, or a *power*, which is the number of times to multiply.

SQUARING AND CUBING

In the following example, 5 is the base and 2 is the exponent. Raising a base to the second power is often called squaring. Therefore, 5 to the 2nd power can be referred to as "5 squared."

$$5^2 = 5 \bullet 5 = 25$$

Raising a base to the third power is often called cubing. Therefore, 2 to the 3rd power can be referred to as "2 cubed."

$$2^3 = 2 \bullet 2 \bullet 2 = 8$$

RULES FOR OPERATIONS ON EXPONENTS

Certain operations can be performed on exponents with the same base.

- **Multiplication**—Add the exponents: $3^3 \times 3^5 = 3^8$
- **Division**—Subtract the exponents: $3^5 \div 3^3 = 3^2$

- **Raising a Power to a Power**—Multiply the exponents: $(3^3)^{.5} = 3^{15}$
- **Raising a Product to a Power**—Apply the exponent to each term and express as a product: $(3 \times 5)^2 = 3^2 \times 5^2$
- **Raising a Fraction to a Power**—Apply the exponent to the numerator and denominator and express as a fraction: $\left(\dfrac{3}{5}\right)^2 = \dfrac{3^2}{5^2}$
- **Negative Exponent**—Express as a fraction with numerator 1 and the positive exponent in the denominator: $10^{-4} = \dfrac{1}{10^4}$
- **Fractional Exponent**—When the numerator is 1, apply the denominator to the base as a root: $9^{\frac{1}{2}}$ is $\sqrt{9}$. $8^{\frac{1}{3}}$ is $\sqrt[3]{8}$. When the numerator is not 1, apply the numerator to the base as a power, and then apply the denominator to the result as a root: $8^{\frac{2}{3}}$ is $\sqrt[3]{8^2}$

Remember that you cannot perform any of these operations if the numbers have different bases. For example, $2^3 \times 3^5$ is in its simplest exponential form.

LESSON 10: ROOTS

A *root* is a special kind of factor of a multiple called the *radicand*. When the root is multiplied by itself a specified number of times, the product is the radicand.

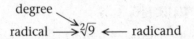

degree

radical $\longrightarrow \sqrt[2]{9} \longleftarrow$ radicand

The symbol for a root ($\sqrt{}$) is called the radical. The expression sometimes includes a degree, which indicates the number of times the root should be multiplied by itself to produce the radicand.

SQUARE ROOTS AND CUBE ROOTS

The *square root* of positive integer x is the positive number that, when squared, yields a product of x. For example, $\sqrt{49} = 7$ because $7 \bullet 7 = 49$. (The degree is not shown for square roots.)

The *cube root* of positive integer x is the positive number that, when cubed, yields a product of x. For example, $\sqrt[3]{125} = 5$ because $5 \bullet 5 \bullet 5 = 125$.

Perfect Squares and Estimating Square Roots

A perfect square is a number that has an integer (whole number) as a square root. Most numbers are not perfect squares, and their square roots include many decimal places.

The process for manually calculating the square root of a number that is not a perfect square is complicated. The good news is that you'll never need it. The test provides you with a calculator that has a square root function. You'll often be able to estimate a square root using your knowledge of the perfect squares. The first 20 perfect squares are shown in the following table:

Square	Root
1	1
4	2
9	3
16	4
25	5
36	6
49	7
64	8
81	9
100	10
121	11
144	12
169	13
196	14
225	15
256	16
289	17
324	18
361	19
400	20

For example, to estimate the value of $\sqrt{15}$, look for perfect squares that are close to 15. The largest perfect square that is smaller than 15 is 9, and the square root of 9 is 3. The smallest perfect square that is larger than 15 is 16 and the square root of 16 is 4. Since 15 is between 9 and 16, and is much closer to 16, we can estimate that $\sqrt{15}$ is between 3 and 4 and is much closer to 4.

Factoring and Distributing

You can also factor and distribute under the radical:

$$\sqrt{450} = \sqrt{225 \bullet 2} = \sqrt{225} \bullet \sqrt{2} = 15\sqrt{2}$$

This can be useful in estimating as well. Since $\sqrt{2} \approx 1.4$, we know that the root above is close to 21 because 15×1.4 equals 21.

Distributing can also be helpful when working with radicals:

$$\sqrt{12} \bullet \sqrt{3} = \sqrt{12 \bullet 3} = \sqrt{36} = 6$$

LESSON 11: ORDER OF OPERATIONS

The *order of operations*, sometimes called *PEMDAS*, is listed below:

1. **PARENTHESES** Any operations found inside parentheses should be done first, regardless of the type of operation. This also applies to other grouping symbols, like braces and brackets. A radical is also treated as a grouping symbol.

2. **EXPONENTS** Any powers should be done next.

3. **MULTIPLICATION AND DIVISION** All multiplication and division should be done from left to right before doing any addition or subtraction.

4. **ADDITION AND SUBTRACTION** All addition and subtraction should be done last, from left to right.

Apply the order of operations to the following numerical expression:

$$3(5 - 2) - 21 \div 3 + 2(7 - 5)^2$$

1. **Work inside the parentheses**: $5 - 2 = 3$ and $7 - 5 = 2$

$$3(3) - 21 \div 3 + 2(2)^2$$

2. **Calculate the exponents**: $2^2 = 4$

$$3(3) - 21 \div 3 + 2(4)$$

3. **Do the multiplication** and **division** from left to right:

$$3 \bullet 3 = 9, \ 21 \div 3 = 7, \text{ and } 2 \bullet 4 = 8$$

$$9 - 7 + 8$$

4. **Do the addition** and **subtraction** from left to right:

$9 - 7 = 2$ and $2 + 8 = 10$. The answer is 10.

LESSON 12: FRACTIONS

A fraction expresses a part of a whole: $\frac{3}{5}$ represents "3 of 5 equal parts." The number representing the part is called the *numerator,* and is on the top. The number representing the whole is called the *denominator* and is on the bottom.

EQUIVALENT FRACTIONS AND REDUCING

Two fractions are equivalent if applying a common multiplier to the numerator and denominator of one fraction produces the other fraction. For example, $\frac{3}{5}$ is equivalent to $\frac{6}{10}$ by a factor of 2:

$$\frac{3}{5} = \frac{3 \cdot 2}{5 \cdot 2} = \frac{6}{10}$$

Reducing a fraction to **lowest terms** means finding the equivalent form that uses the smallest numbers. The fraction $\frac{16}{20}$ can be reduced by a factor of 4 because 4 is a factor of both 16 and 20. The numerator 4 goes into 16 four times, and 4 goes into 20 five times:

$$\frac{16}{20} = \frac{16 \div 4}{20 \div 4} = \frac{4}{5}$$

The fraction $\frac{4}{5}$ is an equivalent form of $\frac{16}{20}$.

COMPARING FRACTIONS

If two fractions have equal numerators, the fraction with the smaller denominator is bigger:

$$\frac{3}{5} > \frac{3}{7}$$

If two fractions have equal denominators, the fraction with the larger numerator is bigger:

$$\frac{3}{5} > \frac{2}{5}$$

If two fractions are completely different, you can compare them by cross multiplying. Alternatively, you can rename the fractions so they have a common denominator. Then compare the fractions.

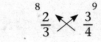

The larger product indicates the larger fraction. Since 9 > 8, that means $\frac{2}{3} < \frac{3}{4}$ or $\frac{3}{4} > \frac{2}{3}$.

ADDING AND SUBTRACTING FRACTIONS

Use the *multiplication method*:

- Cross multiply.
- Apply the original operation to the products. If you are supposed to add the fractions, add the products. If you are supposed to subtract the fractions, subtract the products.
- Write the sum or difference as the numerator of a new fraction.
- Multiply the original denominators.
- Write the product as the denominator of your new fraction.
- Reduce if needed.

$$\frac{2}{3} \times \frac{1}{6} = \frac{15}{18} = \frac{5}{6}$$

$$\frac{2}{3} \times \frac{1}{6} = \frac{9}{18} = \frac{1}{2}$$

Alternatively, you can rename the fractions so they have a common denominator. Then add (or subtract) only the numerators. Use the common denominator in your answer.

MULTIPLYING FRACTIONS

Multiply numerator by numerator and denominator by denominator straight across:

$$\frac{2}{3} \times \frac{3}{4} = \frac{2 \times 3}{3 \times 4} = \frac{6}{12} = \frac{1}{2}$$

If common factors exist between numerators and denominators, you may cancel them before multiplying.

DIVIDING FRACTIONS

Dividing fractions can be tricky. Just remember the following saying. "When dividing don't ask why, just reverse and multiply." In other words, invert the second fraction in a division problem and then multiply:

$$\frac{1}{4} \div \frac{2}{3} = \frac{1}{4} \times \frac{3}{2} = \frac{1 \times 3}{4 \times 2} = \frac{3}{8}$$

MIXED NUMBERS AND IMPROPER FRACTIONS

Mixed numbers combine a whole number with a fraction. For example, $3\frac{3}{4}$ is a mixed number.

Improper fractions have a numerator that is greater than or equal to the denominator. An example is $\frac{5}{3}$.

Mixed numbers can be converted to improper fractions:

- Multiply the denominator of the fraction by the whole number.
- Add the numerator of the fraction to the product.
- Write the sum as the numerator of a new fraction over the original denominator.

$$3\frac{3}{4} = \frac{12+3}{4} = \frac{15}{4}$$

Improper fractions can be converted to mixed numbers:

- Reduce to lowest terms if needed.
- Divide the numerator by the denominator to get the quotient with remainder.
- Write the quotient as a whole number. Use the remainder as the numerator of a new fraction over the original denominator.

$$\frac{46}{14} = \frac{23}{7} \qquad 23 \div 7 = 3r2 \qquad 3\frac{2}{7}$$

LESSON 13: DECIMALS

Decimals use number places called decimal places to express parts of wholes based on decimal fractions.

Place Name	Decimal Point	Tenths	Hundredths	Thousandths	Ten Thousandths
Fraction		$\dfrac{1}{10}$	$\dfrac{1}{100}$	$\dfrac{1}{1,000}$	$\dfrac{1}{10,000}$
Decimal		0.1	0.01	0.001	0.0001
Exponent		$\times 10^{-1}$	$\times 10^{-2}$	$\times 10^{-3}$	$\times 10^{-4}$

The exponent row in the table above is used in scientific notation.

When saying decimals aloud, people often use the name of the decimal fraction: For example, 0.3 is three tenths, 0.06 is six-hundredths, 0.007 is seven-thousandths. Reciting the digits from left to right is another common method: 0.3 is point three or 0.007 is point zero zero seven.

DECIMAL OPERATIONS

To add and subtract decimals, line up the decimal points, fill in zeros on the end as needed, and add and subtract as usual:

$$
\begin{array}{r}
0.523 \\
+\,0.264 \\
\hline
0.787
\end{array}
\qquad\qquad
\begin{array}{r}
0.487 \\
-\,0.110 \\
\hline
0.377
\end{array}
$$

To multiply decimals, first multiply as usual. Add up the decimal places in all the factors, and place the decimal point at that spot in the product. For instance, if the first factor has 1 decimal place and the second has 2, the product will have 1 + 2 = 3 decimal places.

$$\begin{array}{r} 2.3 \\ \times\, 0.3 \\ \hline 0.69 \end{array} \qquad \begin{array}{r} 0.25 \\ \times\, 0.3 \\ \hline 0.075 \end{array}$$

$$\begin{array}{r} 0.23 \\ \times\, 0.3 \\ \hline 0.069 \end{array} \qquad \begin{array}{r} 0.025 \\ \times\, 0.3 \\ \hline 0.0075 \end{array}$$

To divide decimals, multiply the divisor by 10 until it becomes an integer. You can do this by moving the decimal point to the right one place for every multiple of 10. Do the same to the dividend and then divide as usual. Make sure to move the decimal point in the dividend the same number of places to the right. You may have to add zeros to the dividend to do this.

$$2.3\overline{)460.}$$

$$\begin{array}{r} 200 \\ 23\overline{)4600.} \\ \underline{46} \\ 000 \end{array}$$

LESSON 14: SCIENTIFIC NOTATION

Scientific notation is a standardized way of representing numbers using multiplication by powers of 10. Since both whole numbers and decimal numbers are based on multiples of 10, multiplying by powers of 10 relocates (or shifts) the decimal point without affecting the digits in the number.

- The degree (power) of the exponent in scientific notation indicates the number of places to shift the decimal point. The sign of the exponent indicates the direction of the shift.
- Positive exponents shift the decimal point to the right, and the numbers get larger. 10^2 shifts the decimal point 2 places to the right and multiplies the decimal number by 100.
- Negative exponents shift the decimal point to the left, and the numbers get smaller. 10^{-3} shifts the decimal point 3 places to the left and divides the decimal number by 1,000 (multiplies it by $\frac{1}{1,000}$).

To convert a number to scientific notation, place the decimal point so that the first nonzero digit is in the ones place:

- 12,345,678,900,000,000,000,000 becomes 1.2345678900000000000000
- 0.0000000000000000987654321 becomes 9.87654321

After the decimal point has been relocated, powers of 10 are used to show where it originally was.

- We moved the decimal point 22 places to the left to produce 1.2345678900000000000000. We would write the original number as $1.23456789 \times 10^{22}$. (Note that the zeros on the right end were removed.)
- This tells someone to move the decimal 22 places to the right to reproduce the original number, 12,345,678,900,000,000,000,000. (Note that the person would have to restore the zeros that were removed.)
- We moved the decimal point 16 places to the right to produce 9.87654321. We would write the original number as $9.87654321 \times 10^{-16}$. (Note that the zeros on the left end were removed.)
- This tells someone to move the decimal 16 places to the left to reproduce the original number, 0.0000000000000000987654321. (Note that the person would have to restore the zeros that were removed.)
- The value of the number does not change when it is converted to scientific notation. Only the number of digits that are used to express the number is changed.

LESSON 15: PERCENTAGES

A percentage expresses a partial quantity (part) out of a total (whole) of 100. The word percent means "out of 100" and is expressed using the percent sign: %. 72% (seventy–two percent) is 72 out of 100.

One way to calculate a percentage is to multiply by the decimal equivalent of the percentage. To get the decimal equivalent of a percentage, move the decimal point two places to the left and delete the percent sign. For example, to take 35% of 60:

- Convert 35% to 0.35
- Multiply $60 \times 0.35 = 21$

LESSON 16: CONVERTING FRACTIONS, DECIMALS, AND PERCENTS

FRACTION TO DECIMAL

To convert a fraction to a decimal, divide the numerator by the denominator:

$$\frac{4}{5} = 5\overline{)4.0}^{\,0.8} = 0.8$$

Although most conversions produce *terminating decimals* that eventually stop producing a remainder, some produce *repeating decimals* that continue to produce a remainder indefinitely. The fraction $\frac{1}{3}$ produces a repeating decimal:

$$\frac{1}{3} = 3\overline{)1.000000000000000\ldots}^{\,0.333333333333333\ldots} = 0.333\ldots = .33\overline{3} = 0.33$$

- Repeating digits can be symbolized with a bar (—) above a digit that repeats indefinitely.
- Repeating digits can also be rounded ($\approx$ means "almost equal to").

PERCENT TO DECIMAL

To convert a percent to a decimal, divide the percent by 100. Instead, you can move the decimal point 2 places to the left, adding zeros if needed:

- 20% becomes 0.20 (or 0.2)
- 4% becomes 0.04
- 37.5% becomes 0.375

DECIMAL TO PERCENT

To convert a decimal to a percent, multiply the decimal by 100. Instead, you can move the decimal point 2 places to the right, adding zeros if needed:

- 0.25 becomes 25%
- 0.3 becomes 30%
- 0.07 becomes 7%
- 0.125 becomes 12.5%

Ratios, Unit Rates, and Proportions

6

A *ratio* describes the relationship between one part and another part. A ratio can be expressed in a number of ways:

- **WORDS** the ratio of 3 to 5

- **RATIONAL (FRACTION) FORM** $\frac{3}{5}$

- **COLON** 3:5

All of these mean that there are 3 of one kind of thing for every 5 of another kind of thing. A class may have 3 male students for every 5 female students, and this is a ratio of 3 to 5.

Ratios can be equivalent to each other. They can be expanded and reduced like fractions. A ratio of 12:9 $\left(\frac{12}{9}\right)$ is equivalent to a ratio of 4:3 $\left(\frac{4}{3}\right)$ because 3 is a common factor of both parts of the first ratio ($12 \div 3 = 4$ and $9 \div 3 = 3$).

Ratios are an extremely important concept on the Math subject test because other concepts (like fractions, proportions, and rational equations) build on ratios.

THE RATIO BOX

Most ratio questions on the test will ask you to use the ratio of parts in a whole to find the actual numbers. For example:

The ratio of boys to girls in a math club is 2 to 3. If there are 70 students in the club, how many girls are in the club?

Questions such as this can be answered using a very effective tool called the ratio box.

STEP 1 **SET UP A RATIO BOX**

The best way to set up a ratio box is like this:

	Ratio	Multiply By	Actual Number
Boys	2		
Girls	3		
Total			70

As shown here, a ratio box has four columns. The first holds the labels for each part along with a label for the total. The second column is the "Ratio" column. It holds the numbers in the ratio (in this case, 2 and 3). The third column is the "Multiply By" column. It will hold a multiplier that you figure out using the other columns. The fourth column is the "Actual Number" column. It holds the actual numbers for the parts and the whole (in this case, the 70 actual students).

Along with the row for the column labels, the ratio box has rows for each part of the ratio and an additional row for the total. You will always add this "Total" row when setting up a ratio box.

STEP 2 **ADD UP THE PARTS**

The next step in using the ratio box is to add up the numbers representing the parts. Then put the result in the "Total" row of the "Ratio" column.

	Ratio	Multiply By	Actual Number
Boys	2		
Girls	3		
Total	5		70

In this example, the numbers for the parts are 2 and 3. Since 2 + 3 = 5, you would write 5 in the "Total" row of the "Ratio" column.

STEP 3 **FIND THE MULTIPLIER**

The next step is to find the multiplier that is used to go from the ratio numbers to the actual numbers. This multiplier remains constant. In fact, it is the key to working out the answer to the question. Find a row that has a number in both the "Ratio" column and the "Actual Number" column.

In this example, the row that contains a value in both columns is the "Total" row. To determine the multiplier, divide the actual number value by the ratio value. Since $70 \div 5 = 14$, the multiplier is 14.

	Ratio	Multiply By	Actual Number
Boys	2	14	
Girls	3	14	
Total	5	14	70

The multiplier is constant, so it will be the same for each part of the ratio. The multiplier goes into each cell in the "Multiply By" column as shown above.

STEP 4 **USE THE MULTIPLIER**

The next step is to multiply the ratio numbers by the multiplier for any value not already present in the "Actual Number" column. This gives you the rest of the actual numbers.

	Ratio	Multiply By	Actual Number
Boys	2	14	28
Girls	3	14	42
Total	5	14	70

Since $2 \bullet 14 = 28$, 28 goes into the "Boys" row. Since $3 \bullet 14 = 42$, 42 goes into the "Girls" row.

You can check that these numbers are correct by adding them together. The problem says that 70 students are in the club. Since $28 + 42 = 70$, these numbers are correct because they agree with the information in the problem.

STEP 5 **ANSWER THE QUESTION**

The original question was:

The ratio of boys to girls in a math club is 2 to 3. If there are 70 students in the club, how many girls are in the club?

The completed ratio box looks like this:

	Ratio	Multiply By	Actual Number
Boys	2	14	28
Girls	3	14	42
Total	5	14	70

The ratio box shows that there are 28 boys and 42 girls in the club. The total number of girls is 42.

LESSON 2: UNIT RATES

A *rate* is a ratio that involves words or phrases like *"per"* (60 miles per hour, $14 per hour) or *"for every"* (1 free coffee for every 3 purchased). Whenever a question asks for an answer involving a unit (like a mile, a minute, an hour, and so on), divide the total amount by the total number of units to calculate the amount per unit. For example, $14 per hour would be 14 dollars ÷ 60 minutes or 23.3 cents per minute.

LESSON 3: PROPORTIONS

A *proportion* sets two ratios equal to one another:

$$\frac{1}{4} = \frac{4}{16}$$

Two ratios are proportional when one of them can be converted to the other using the same multiplier for both the numerator and the denominator:

$$\frac{1}{4} \cdot \frac{4}{4} = \frac{4}{16}$$

In a proportion, the cross products of the two ratios are equal:

$$16 = 16$$
$$\frac{1}{4} \diagup\!\!\!\!\diagup \frac{4}{16}$$

The rule of equal cross products can be used to find a missing term in a proportion if given the other three terms:

- Set up the proportion using a consistent structure.
- Cross multiply two of the known terms.
- Divide the product by the third known term.

Consider the following example:

The class has a ratio of three males to five females, and there are fifteen female students. How many male students are in the class?

First, the two ratios must present the parts in the same order:

- Ratio part: 3 males, 5 females
- Actual part: 15 female students, unknown number of male students

$$\frac{3 \text{ males}}{5 \text{ females}} = \frac{x \text{ male students}}{15 \text{ female students}}$$

- In the proportion shown above, males are on the top in both ratios and females are on the bottom. (Note that we use the letter x to represent the number we don't know.)

Now cross multiply. Then divide by the third known term:

$$\frac{3}{5} = \frac{x}{15}$$

- $3 \times 15 = 45$ and $45 \div 5 = 9$. There are nine male students in the class.

To verify this answer, check the cross products:

$$\frac{3}{5} = \frac{9}{15} \rightarrow 3(15) = 5(9) \rightarrow 45 = 45$$

PROPORTION METHOD FOR PERCENTAGES

Proportions give us a very powerful way to calculate percentages manually. Most percentages can be expressed this way:

A part is equal to a percent of a whole, such as "80 is equal to 25% of 320."

In any percentage question, one of these three elements will be missing:

- Missing part: What number is equal to 25% of 320?
- Missing percent: 80 is equal to what percent of 320?
- Missing whole: 80 is equal to 25% of what number?
- The part is always next to the word "is."
- The whole is always next to the word "of."

Percentage questions can be set up as proportions using the following format:

$$\frac{part\ (is)}{whole\ (of)} = \frac{percent\ (\%)}{100}$$

Missing part: What number is equal to 25% of 320?

$$\frac{x\ (is)}{320\ (of)} = \frac{25}{100} \rightarrow 100x = 8,000 \rightarrow 8,000 \div 100 = 80$$

Missing percent: 80 is equal to what percent of 320?

$$\frac{80\ (is)}{320\ (of)} = \frac{x}{100} \rightarrow \frac{8}{32} = \frac{x}{100} \rightarrow 800 = 32x \rightarrow 800 \div 32 = 25\%$$

Note that we reduced the ratio on the left by a factor of 10 before we cross multiplied. This is a good way to make the calculation easier.

Missing whole: 80 is equal to 25% of what number?

$$\frac{80\ (is)}{x\ (of)} = \frac{25}{100} \rightarrow \frac{80}{x} = \frac{1}{4} \rightarrow x = 320$$

Note that this time, we reduced the ratio on the right.

PERCENT CHANGE

Some questions will ask you to work with an increase or a decrease of a number or a percentage. The increase or decrease goes "from" one (original) value "to" another (new) value. An increase makes the new value higher, and a decrease makes it lower.

To answer these questions, you'll need to work with the following proportion:

$$\frac{difference}{original} = \frac{\%}{100}$$

The difference is the amount of change from the original value to the new value:

- For increases, the new value will be larger: *difference = new – original.* An increase from 6 to 11 is a difference of 11 – 6 = 5.
- For decreases, the new value will be smaller: *difference = original – new.* A decrease from 19 to 12 is a difference of 19 – 12 = 7.

The percent (%) change is the difference represented as a percentage of the original. When given a value for percent change, pay attention to whether the change is an increase or a decrease.

For a *percentage increase*, the new value will be larger than the original. Let's look at a common situation to explain this topic—tipping a server after a meal.

(1) Assume that a meal costs $60 before the tip. This $60 is the original price.

(2) Your server did an excellent job, so you decide to tip 20%. Determine what amount equals 20%.

$$\frac{\text{difference (tip)}}{\text{original}} = \frac{x}{100}$$

$$\frac{\text{difference (tip)}}{\$60} = \frac{20}{100} = \frac{1}{5} \rightarrow \text{difference (tip)} = \frac{(\$60)(20)}{100} = \$12$$

Therefore, a 20% tip equals $12.

(3) You actually pay $72 for the meal ($60 + $12 = $72). This $72 is the new price.

You can look at this situation in two ways: either the original price as a percent of the new price or the new price as a percent of the original price.

- Original as a percent of new:

$$\frac{\text{original price}}{\text{new price}} = \frac{x}{100}$$

$$\frac{\$60}{\$72} = \frac{5}{6} = \frac{x}{100} \rightarrow \frac{(100)(5)}{6} = x = 83.33 \ldots \approx 83\%$$

The original price is about 83% of the new price.

- New as percent of original:

$$\frac{\text{new price}}{\text{original price}} = \frac{100}{x}$$

$$\frac{\$72}{\$60} = \frac{6}{5} = \frac{x}{100} \rightarrow \frac{(100)(6)}{5} = x = 120 = 120\%$$

The new price is 120% of the original price.

Note that although the numbers are all the same—original amount is $60, new amount is $72, and difference is $12—the way you look at the numbers affects the percentage increase.

For a *percentage decrease*, the new value will be smaller than the original. Let's look at a common situation to explain this topic—buying a shirt on sale.

(1) Assume that the shirt originally costs $40. The $40 is the original price.
(2) The sale discounts the original price by 10%. Determine what amount equals 10%.

$$\frac{\text{difference (discount)}}{\text{original}} = \frac{x}{100}$$

$$\frac{\text{difference (discount)}}{\$40} = \frac{10}{100} = \frac{1}{10} \rightarrow \text{difference (discount)} = \frac{(\$40)(10)}{100} = 4$$

Therefore, a 10% discount equals $4.

(3) You actually pay $36 for the shirt ($40 – $4 = $36). This $36 is the new price.

You can look at this situation in two ways: either the original price as a percent of the new price or the new price as a percent of the original price.

- Original as a percent of new:

$$\frac{\text{original price}}{\text{new price}} = \frac{x}{100}$$

$$\frac{\$40}{\$36} = \frac{10}{9} = \frac{x}{100} \rightarrow \frac{(100)(10)}{9} = x = 111.11 \ldots \approx 111\%$$

The original price is about 111% of the new price.

■ New as percent of original:

$$\frac{\text{new price}}{\text{original price}} = \frac{x}{100}$$

$$\frac{\$36}{\$40} = \frac{9}{10} = \frac{x}{100} \rightarrow \frac{(100)(9)}{10} = x = 90 = 90\%$$

The new price is 90% of the original price.

Note that although the numbers are all the same—original amount is $40, new amount is $36, and difference is $4—the way you look at the numbers affects the percentage decrease.

In any percent change question, one of these three elements will be missing:

■ Missing difference: What number is equal to a 20% change from 250?
■ Missing percentage: 50 is equal to what percent change from 250?
■ Missing new or original: 80 is equal to a 20% change from what number?

Proportions can be used to answer any of these question types:

MISSING DIFFERENCE Assume the new number is 15% greater than the original, which is 600. What number is equal to 15% of 600?

$$\frac{x}{600} = \frac{15}{100} \rightarrow 9,000 = 100x \rightarrow 9,000 \div 100 = 90$$

The number equal to 15% of 600 is 90. Even though it wasn't asked, you should know that the new number is 600 + 90 = 690.

MISSING PERCENTAGE Assume the original is 180, and it is reduced by 45. 45 is equal to what percent of 180?

$$\frac{45}{180} = \frac{x}{100} \rightarrow \frac{1}{4} = \frac{x}{100} \rightarrow 100 = 4x \rightarrow 100 \div 4 = 25$$

The number 45 is 25% of 180.

MISSING NEW Assume the original was 300 and was reduced by 25%. (Remember that this makes the new number 75% of the original, because 100% − 25% = 75%.) What number is 75% of 300?

$$\frac{x}{300} = \frac{75}{100} \rightarrow \frac{x}{300} = \frac{3}{4} \rightarrow 4x = 900 \rightarrow 900 \div 4 = 225$$

The number 225 is 75% of 300.

MISSING ORIGINAL Assume the new is 195 after an increase of 30%. (Remember that this makes the new 130% of the original, because 100% + 30% = 130%.) 195 is 130% of what number?

$$\frac{195}{x} = \frac{130}{100} \rightarrow \frac{195}{x} = \frac{13}{10} \rightarrow 13x = 1,950 \rightarrow 1,950 \div 13 = 150$$

The number 195 is 130% of 150.

RATE CALCULATIONS

Proportions can be used to perform calculations involving rates, like speed in miles per hour. At 60 miles per hour, how far will you travel in 4 hours?

To answer this question: First set up a proportion with the per unit (hours in this case) on the top of the left ratio:

$$\frac{1 \text{ hour}}{60 \text{ miles}} = \frac{4 \text{ hours}}{x \text{ miles}}$$

Solve the proportion:

$$\frac{1}{60} = \frac{4}{x} \rightarrow x = 240$$

At 60 miles per hour, you will travel 240 miles in 4 hours.

SCALE CONVERSIONS

Proportions can also be used to convert scales, such as the relationship between distances on a map and real distances. Suppose a map has a scale where 1 inch = 5 miles. If a distance on the map is 6 inches, how many miles is the real distance?

$$\frac{1 \text{ inch}}{5 \text{ miles}} = \frac{6 \text{ inches}}{x} \rightarrow x = 30 \text{ miles}$$

The real distance is 30 miles.

Measurement and Geometry

7

LESSON 1: MEASUREMENT

Measurement is a method of describing and comparing things using numerical units. Some of the types of things that are typically measured include:

- Dimensions (lengths, widths, heights, depths)
- Weight or mass
- Time
- Temperature
- Angles (degrees)
- Shapes (perimeter, area, volume)
- Amounts of money
- Data or memory size (gigabytes, megabytes)

All measurements consist of a number and a unit.

- The *number* answers the question "how many." In the measurement 6 grams, the number is 6.
- The *unit* answers the question "of what." In the measurement 40 seconds, the unit is seconds.

SYSTEMS OF MEASUREMENT

A measurement system is a group of standard units used to measure various quantities that represent characteristics of objects. The types of quantities that make up a measurement system include:

- Length
- Weight or mass
- Capacity (volume)
- Temperature

Units in a measurement system can be grouped together into larger units (12 inches in a foot) or broken down into smaller units (3 feet in a yard). Changing units makes it easier to measure things that are very large or very small.

Metric Units

Metric units are sometimes called international units, and they are standard units of measure in the scientific community as well as in many countries around the world. Since metric measurements will be used in all of the material you see on the Science subject test, you must become familiar with them if you aren't already.

The fundamental units in the metric system are the following:

- Length—The meter (m). Length is typically measured with rulers and measuring tapes.
- Mass—The gram (g). Mass is typically measured with scales.
- Capacity—The liter (L). Capacity is typically measured by filling containers with liquids or other substances.
- Temperature—Degrees Celsius (C) or Kelvins (K). Celsius is also called centigrade. Temperature is typically measured using a thermometer.

On the Math subject test, you will mostly have to work with the fundamental units and the kilo-, centi-, and milli- prefixes.

- When grouping smaller units into larger units, each larger unit consists of 10 of the next smaller unit. For example, there are 10 millimeters (mm) in 1 centimeter (cm).
- When breaking larger units into smaller units, each larger unit consists of 10 of the next smaller unit. For example, 1 decimeter (dm) is 10 centimeters (cm).

The table below lists these unit relationships.

Metric Prefixes and Their Values

Prefix	Prefix Abbreviation	Exponent	Number
tera	T	10^{12}	1,000,000,000,000
giga	G	10^9	1,000,000,000
mega	M	10^6	1,000,000
kilo	k	10^3	1,000
hecto	h	10^2	100
			1
deci	d	10^{-1}	0.1
centi	c	10^{-2}	0.01
milli	m	10^{-3}	0.001
micro	μ	10^{-6}	0.000001
nano	n	10^{-9}	0.000000001

The use of multiples of 10 makes the metric system very compatible with scientific notation since both are based on multiples of 10. For example, 1.2×10^3 centiliters (cL) is equal to 12 liters (L):

$$1 \text{ cL} = 0.01 \text{ L} \rightarrow 1.2 \text{ cL} = 0.012 \text{ L} \rightarrow 0.012 \text{ L} \times 10^3 = 12 \text{ L}$$

Customary Units

Customary units are sometimes called imperial units, and they are the standard units of measurement in the United States.

The fundamental units in this system are the following:

- Length—The foot (ft or ')
- Weight—The pound (lb)
- Capacity—The cup (c)
- Temperature—Degrees Fahrenheit (°F)

Conversions Between Customary Units

Length				
1 foot (ft)	=	12 inches (in)		
1 yard (yd)	=	3 feet	=	36 inches
1 mile (mi)	=	1,760 yards	=	5,280 feet
Weight				
1 pound (lb)	=	16 ounces (oz)		
1 ton (T)	=	2,000 pounds		
Capacity				
1 cup (c)	=	8 fluid ounces (fl oz)		
1 pint (pt)	=	2 cups	=	16 fl oz
1 quart (qt)	=	2 pints	=	32 fl oz
1 gallon (gal)	=	4 quarts	=	128 fl oz

Conversions Between Units of Time

1 minute (min)	=	60 seconds (sec)
1 hour (hr)	=	60 minutes
1 day	=	24 hours
1 week (wk)	=	7 days
1 month (mo)	=	approximately 4 weeks; between 28 and 31 days
1 year (yr)	=	365 days
1 leap year	=	366 days

Temperature

On the exam, temperatures will be expressed in either degrees Celsius (°C) or degrees Fahrenheit (°F). Both systems use a fundamental unit called a degree (°).

Think of temperature scales as number lines. Temperatures can be positive or negative. One difference between the two systems is the zero point, which is based on the freezing point of a liquid:

- Zero degrees Celsius (0°C)—Freezing point of water
- Zero degrees Fahrenheit (0°F)—Freezing point of a water-like liquid called brine

The other significant difference is in the interval between units on the scale (1 degree F is a little less than 2 degrees C). The intervals are different because:

- Celsius has 100 degrees between the freezing and boiling points of water.
- Fahrenheit has 180 degrees between these two points.

Temperatures in Celsius and Fahrenheit

Event	°C	°F
Water boils	100	212
Water freezes	0	32

CONVERTING BETWEEN SYSTEMS

You can convert between the metric and customary systems.

	Metric	**Customary**
Length	1 meter	3.28 feet 1.09 yards
Weight	1 gram 1 kilogram	0.035 ounces 2.20 pounds
Capacity	1 liter	1.06 quarts 0.26 gallons
Temperature	1 degree C	1.8 degrees F

Note that some of the conversion rates above have been rounded to two decimal places.

Converting between systems is done using proportions. For example, a 20-degree Celsius change is equivalent to a change of how many degrees Fahrenheit?

$$\frac{1.8°F}{1°C} = \frac{x°F}{20°C} \rightarrow x = 36 \rightarrow 36°F$$

Note that this example compares number of degrees and not temperatures. If you are asked to convert temperatures, you will be provided with the formula:

$$°F = (1.8)(°C) + 32°$$

The temperature 20°C is equivalent to 68°F: $(1.8)(20) + 32 = 36 + 32 = 68$. This formula is required because of the different zero points on the two scales.

LESSON 2: DIMENSIONS, LINES, AND ANGLES

DIMENSIONS   A dimension is a property of shapes. Length, width, and height are all dimensions.

POINTS AND LINES

POINT   A point is a location in space. Points are zero dimensional, which means they have no length, width, or height. Points are usually labeled with a single capital letter like A.

ENDPOINT An endpoint is a point that defines one end of a *ray* or line *segment*.

LINE A line is a collection of points. Lines are one dimensional, which means they have length but no width or height.

- A line is commonly represented with two points, but these are not the endpoints. Lines extend infinitely in both directions, as shown by the dotted lines above. Lines contain an infinite number of points.
- Lines are labeled with reference to the points that define them. The line above is called $\overleftrightarrow{BC}$ (line *BC*).

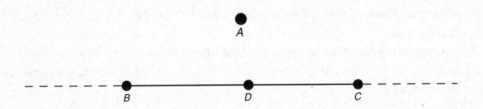

COLLINEAR Points on a common line are collinear. In the figure above, points *B*, *C*, and *D* are collinear.

NONCOLLINEAR Three or more points that cannot be connected by a single line are noncollinear. In the previous figure, points *A*, *B*, and *C* are noncollinear. Even though two points fall on the line, the third doesn't.

RAY A ray is a portion of a line that extends infinitely in one direction from a given endpoint. The ray in the figure below is called $\overrightarrow{EF}$ (ray *EF*).

LINE SEGMENT A line segment is a portion of a line with two endpoints. The segment below is called $\overline{GH}$ (segment *GH*).

MIDPOINT The midpoint is a point on a line segment that is at an equal distance from both endpoints. It is the middle or halfway point. In the segment below, point *J* is the midpoint of $\overline{GH}$.

PLANES AND SPACE

PLANE A plane is a two-dimensional surface made up of points. A plane has length and width but no height.

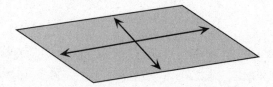

SPACE Space is three dimensional. It has length, width, and height. It contains all points, lines, and planes.

ANGLES

INTERSECTION An intersection is a point common to two lines, segments, or rays. It represents a place where they meet or cross.

ANGLE An angle is formed when two rays intersect at a common endpoint called a *vertex*. Angles are marked with a curved line called an *arc*.

VERTEX A vertex is the point where two rays meet to form an angle.

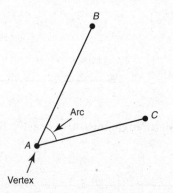

ACUTE ANGLE An acute angle measures less than 90°.

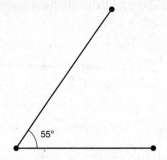

RIGHT ANGLE A right angle measures exactly 90°. It is marked with a small square symbol.

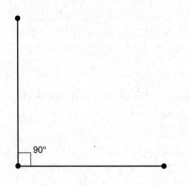

OBTUSE ANGLE An obtuse angle measures more than 90° but less than 180°.

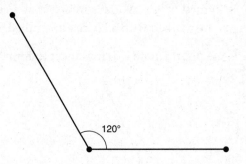

STRAIGHT ANGLE A straight angle measures exactly 180°.

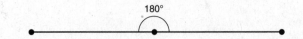

ADJACENT ANGLES   Two angles are adjacent when they share a common side and vertex.

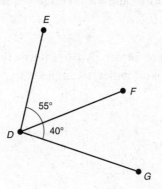

COMPLEMENTARY ANGLES   Two angles are complementary when their measures add to 90°.

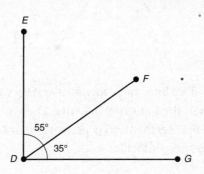

SUPPLEMENTARY ANGLES   Two angles are supplementary when their measures add to 180°.

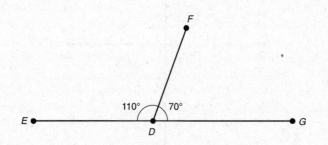

CONGRUENT When two or more lines or two or more angles have the same measure, they are congruent. Congruency is represented with the ≅ symbol. The sentence "the measure of angle *A* is congruent to the measure of angle *B*" is written as m∠*A* ≅ m∠*B*.

VERTICAL ANGLES They are formed by two intersecting lines or line segments. Vertical angles are pairs of nonadjacent angles with a common vertex. Vertical angles are congruent.

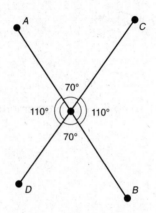

PERPENDICULAR LINES Two lines are perpendicular if they intersect to form right angles (90°) as shown in the following drawing. The symbol for perpendicular is ⊥, so $\overline{AB} \perp \overline{CD}$ means "segment *AB* is perpendicular to segment *CD*." Note that planes can also be perpendicular.

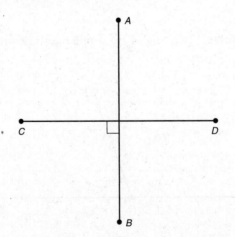

PARALLEL LINES Two lines are parallel if they never cross (or intersect). Planes can also be parallel. The symbol for parallel is ||, so $\overline{AB} \parallel \overline{CD}$ means segment *AB* is parallel to segment *CD* in the following drawing.

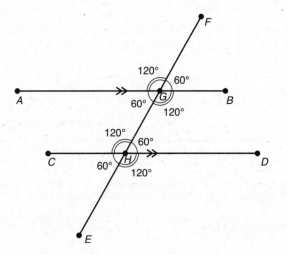

TRANSVERSAL A transversal is a line that intersects or crosses two or more parallel lines. $\overline{EF}$ is a transversal in the drawing below.

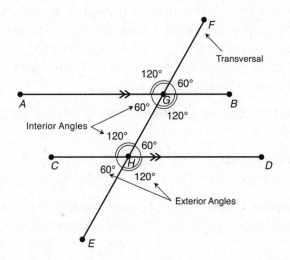

INTERIOR ANGLES Interior angles are formed inside (or between) two parallel lines crossed by a transversal. In the drawing above, ∠*AGH*, ∠*BGH*, ∠*CHG*, and ∠*DHG* are interior angles.

EXTERIOR ANGLES   Exterior angles are formed outside two parallel lines crossed by a transversal. In the previous drawing, ∠*FGA*, ∠*FGB*, ∠*CHE*, and ∠*DHE* are exterior angles.

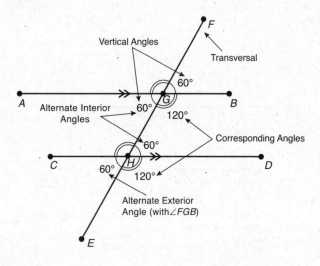

CORRESPONDING ANGLES   When two parallel lines are crossed by a transversal as shown in the above diagram, two sets of vertical angle pairs are created. One set of four angles occurs at each point of intersection (one for the top line and one for the bottom line). When an angle in the top set and an angle in the bottom set occupy the same position (upper right, lower left, and so on) in the set, they are called corresponding angles. Corresponding angles are congruent. ∠*BGH* and ∠*DHE* are both in the lower right position in their respective sets of angles, so they are corresponding angles.

ALTERNATE ANGLES   Congruent angles on opposite sides of the transversal are alternate angles.

ALTERNATE INTERIOR ANGLES   Alternate angles inside the parallel lines are alternate interior angles. ∠*AGH* and ∠*DHG* are alternate interior angles.

ALTERNATE EXTERIOR ANGLES   Alternate angles outside the parallel lines are alternate exterior angles. ∠*CHE* and ∠*FGB* are alternate exterior angles.

LESSON 3: GRAPHING POINTS AND LINES

Coordinate geometry deals with points and lines in the *coordinate plane*. This plane is sometimes called the **x, y** plane because it is defined by two perpendicular number lines called the *x*-axis and *y*-axis:

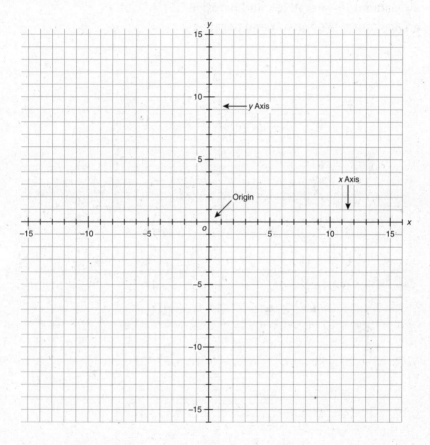

The two number lines (axes) intersect at their zero points, creating the *origin*.

POINTS AND QUADRANTS

The coordinate plane provides a standard method of describing the locations of points using the *x*- and *y*-axes to provide *coordinates* (numerical addresses) for the points. The coordinates of the origin are (0, 0).

ORDERED PAIR   An ordered pair is a pair of numbers in the format (*x*, *y*) representing the coordinates, or location, of a point in the coordinate plane.

QUADRANT   A quadrant is a one-quarter portion of the coordinate plane and contains all points with a specific combination of coordinate signs. Quadrants are numbered with Roman numerals and go in counterclockwise order:

- Quadrant I—positive *x* and positive *y*
- Quadrant II—negative *x* and positive *y*
- Quadrant III—negative *x* and negative *y*
- Quadrant IV—positive *x* and negative *y*

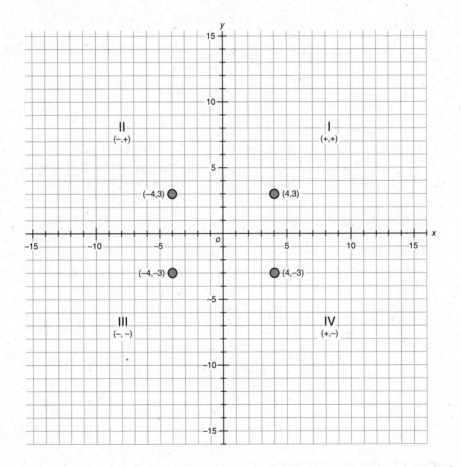

To plot a point using its coordinates:

- Start at the origin (0, 0) and move along the *x*-axis according to the *x*-coordinate (right for positive, left for negative).
- From your location on the *x*-axis, move up or down according to the *y*-coordinate (up for positive, down for negative).

To determine the coordinates of a point on a graph:

- Start at the origin and move to the point's location.
- Move along the *x*-axis first, then up or down.
- Note the number of units you move horizontally and vertically.
- The horizontal movement is the *x*-coordinate.
- The vertical movement is the *y*-coordinate.

GRAPHING LINES

- Two points on the coordinate plane define a line.
- A line extends beyond its endpoints in both directions to connect an infinite number of points.

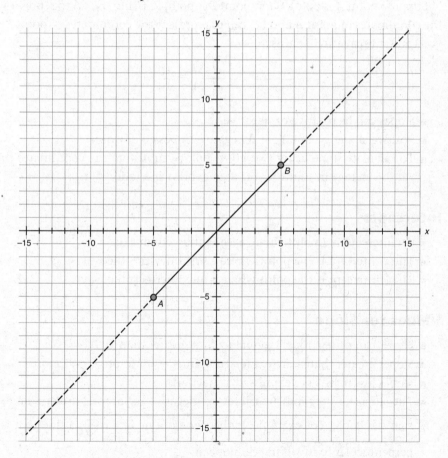

- Line *AB* in the graph is defined by points *A* and *B*. However, the line actually contains every point between points *A* and *B* as well as every point beyond them in either direction.

Slope

Slope defines the slant of a line in the coordinate plane. It is a ratio between the vertical change and the horizontal change required to move from one point on the line to another. This is sometimes called "rise over run" $\left(\frac{\text{rise}}{\text{run}}\right)$ or "change in y over change in x" $\left(\frac{\Delta y}{\Delta x}\right)$. You can calculate the slope of a line if you know the coordinates of two points on the line. For example, if point A (–5, –5) and point B (5, 5) are both on the same line, you can use their coordinates to calculate the slope. Start by choosing one of them to be point 1 and the other to be point 2. Then, subtract the x and y coordinates. Express the results as a ratio.

Suppose point A is point 1 and point B is point 2. Using (x_1, y_1) to represent the coordinates of point A and (x_2, y_2) to represent the coordinates of point B, you can set up a ratio like this:

$$\frac{y_2 - y_1}{x_2 - x_1} = \frac{5 - (-5)}{5 - (-5)} = \frac{10}{10} = 1$$

- Slopes can be positive or negative.
- Positive slopes go uphill, and negative slopes go downhill.
- To calculate slope using two given points, substitute the coordinates to get the change in y and x, and then express as a ratio.

Intercepts

- An intercept is a point where a line intersects an axis.
- The x-intercept is the point where a line intersects the x-axis.
- The y-intercept is the point where a line intersects the y-axis.

Values for Slope

- Slopes can be less than 1, equal to 1, or greater than 1.
- Slopes greater than 1 are expressed as integers or improper fractions.
- Slopes less than 1 are expressed as fractions.
- The slopes of perpendicular lines are negative reciprocals (inverted and sign switched). For example, if the slope of one line is $\frac{2}{5}$, a line that is perpendicular to it will have a slope of $-\frac{5}{2}$.
- The slopes of parallel lines are identical.

Lines Parallel to the Axes

Lines parallel to the axes are special cases because either the change in y or the change in x (the slope) will be zero.

PARALLEL TO THE x-AXIS   The change in $y = 0$. This is a horizontal line with 0 slope.

PARALLEL TO THE y-AXIS   The change in $x = 0$. This is a vertical line whose slope is undefined because of the 0 in the denominator of the slope formula.

LESSON 4: TWO-DIMENSIONAL FIGURES

TWO-DIMENSIONAL FIGURE   A two-dimensional figure is a "flat shape" (occurring in a plane) made up of line segments.

POLYGONS

POLYGON   A two-dimensional figure formed when three or more line segments are joined at their endpoints (or *vertices*) is a polygon. The segments are called *sides*, and the number of sides in a polygon is equal to the number of angles in the polygon.

- "Poly" means "many," and "gon" means angle. Therefore, polygons have many (three or more) angles.
- Common polygons include triangles, rectangles, squares, and other shapes with corners. Circles are not polygons because circles have no corners.
- Some polygons have pairs of sides that are parallel.
- Some polygons have pairs of sides that are perpendicular.
- Some polygons have two or more sides that are congruent.

EQUIANGULAR   An equiangular polygon is one where all angles are congruent. Congruent angles are marked with the same number of arcs.

EQUILATERAL   "Equi" means equal, and "lateral" means side. An equilateral polygon is one where all sides are congruent.

- Congruent sides are often marked with one or more lines, similar to the way that angles are marked with arcs. Sides having the same number of marks are congruent.
- A shape can be equilateral without being equiangular.

OPPOSITE (SIDE OR ANGLE) The segments that form angles in a polygon sometimes intersect with the endpoints of another side of the polygon. When this happens, the angle and intersecting side are said to be opposite one another.

- There is a consistent relationship between the measures of angles in a polygon and the sides that are formed by those angles (the sides opposite the angles). This relationship allows you to compare the relative sizes of sides and angles in a polygon.
- If two angles are congruent, the sides opposite them must also be congruent. This works in reverse as well.
- The largest angle in a polygon must be opposite the longest side.
- The smallest angle must be opposite the shortest side.

REGULAR POLYGON A regular polygon is both equilateral and equiangular. Squares are the most common regular polygons.

For any regular polygon, the total measure of all interior angles is $180(n - 2)$, where n is the number of sides. Since regular polygons are equiangular, you can divide this total by the number of sides to get the measure of a single angle.

PERIMETER The sum of all the sides of the polygon, or the distance around the outside of the polygon, is the perimeter.

AREA OF A POLYGON The area of a polygon is the amount of space inside the polygon. Area is usually measured in square units, as when a floor is measured in square feet. The different types of polygons have different formulas for calculating area. However, all of these formulas involve operations with a *base* and an *altitude* (or height).

BASE (POLYGON) A side serving as the bottom edge of a polygon and used to calculate area is the base of a polygon. Polygons can be rotated. Any side can serve as a base, not just the one that appears to be the bottom in a picture.

ALTITUDE (POLYGON) An altitude is a line, extending from the top of the polygon to the base, that is perpendicular to the base.

- In shapes with perpendicular sides (rectangles, squares, right triangles), both the base and the altitude are sides of the polygon.
- In shapes lacking any perpendicular sides (non-right triangles, parallelograms) only the base will be a side. The altitude must always be perpendicular to the base.

QUADRILATERALS

QUADRILATERAL   A quadrilateral is any four-sided polygon, including *parallelograms*, *rectangles*, and *squares*. There are several types of quadrilaterals, and their interior angles always add to 360°.

SQUARE   A square is a quadrilateral with four congruent sides. The intersecting sides are perpendicular, and the opposite sides are parallel. The length of a side of a square is represented by *s*.

PERIMETER (SQUARE)   Perimeter is the sum of all sides of a polygon. In a square, all sides are congruent: $P = s + s + s + s$. As a shortcut, you can also multiply *s* times 4: $P = 4s$.

AREA (SQUARE)   In a square, all four sides are congruent. Even though the process of calculating the area of a square involves multiplying a base times an altitude, the formula for area of a square is usually given as side squared: $A = s^2$

RECTANGLE   A rectangle is a quadrilateral with two pairs of congruent sides. Intersecting sides are perpendicular. Opposite sides are parallel and congruent.

PERIMETER (RECTANGLE)   In a rectangle, the base (*b*) is sometimes called the length (*l*) and the height (*h*) is sometimes called the width (*w*). Perimeter is the sum of all sides of a polygon. In a rectangle, there are two pairs of congruent sides (two lengths and two widths): $P = l + w + l + w$. As a shortcut, you can also add *l* times 2 plus *w* times 2: or $P = 2l + 2w$.

AREA (RECTANGLE)   The area of a rectangle can be found with the formulas $A = lw$ or $A = bh$.

PARALLELOGRAM   A parallelogram is a quadrilateral with two pairs of congruent sides. Intersecting sides are not necessarily perpendicular, so the height (*h*) is an altitude perpendicular to the base (*b*). The side of the parallelogram that is not the base is called the side (*s*). Opposite sides of a parallelogram are parallel and congruent, and opposite angles are also congruent.

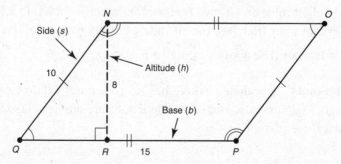

PERIMETER (PARALLELOGRAM) Perimeter is the sum of all sides of a polygon. In a parallelogram, calculating perimeter works the same as in a rectangle, but uses different symbols: $P = 2s + 2b$. The perimeter of parallelogram $QNOP$ on page 137 is $(2 \times 15) + (2 \times 10) = 30 + 20 = 50$.

AREA (PARALLELOGRAM) In a parallelogram, the altitude (height) is not necessarily a side because intersecting sides are not necessarily perpendicular. Once you have located or determined the height, the formula is the same as that for a rectangle: $A = bh$. The area of parallelogram $QNOP$ is $15 \times 8 = 120$.

TRIANGLES

TRIANGLE A triangle is a three-sided polygon. Its interior angles must add to 180°. The longest side is always opposite the largest angle. The shortest side is always opposite the smallest angle. Triangles are named using the three vertices, similar to the way angles are named. The figure below is called triangle ABC or $\triangle ABC$.

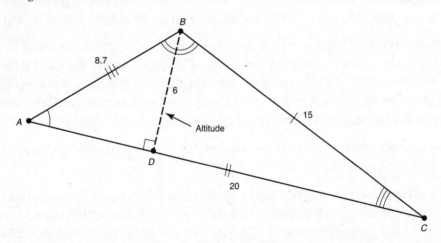

AREA (TRIANGLE) The formula for the area of a triangle is $A = \frac{1}{2}bh$, where the height (h) is an altitude (perpendicular to the base). In all types of triangles except right triangles, the altitude will not be a side of the triangle. The area of triangle ABC above is $\frac{1}{2} \cdot 20 \cdot 6 = 60$.

SCALENE TRIANGLE A scalene triangle has no congruent sides or congruent angles. Each angle measure and each side length are different. Triangle ABC above is a scalene triangle.

ISOSCELES TRIANGLE An isosceles triangle has two congruent sides and two congruent angles. Triangle *BCA* below is an isosceles triangle. Note that the height of an isosceles triangle is not a side. The area of triangle *BCA* below is $\frac{1}{2} \cdot 10 \cdot 12 = 60$.

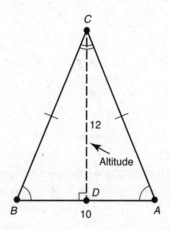

EQUILATERAL TRIANGLE An equilateral triangle has three congruent sides and three congruent angles. Each angle in an equilateral triangle measures 60°. Triangle *DEF* below is an equilateral triangle. Note that the height of an equilateral triangle is not a side.

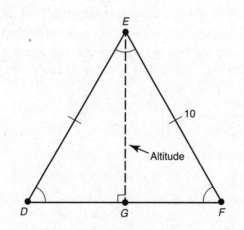

ACUTE TRIANGLE An acute triangle has three angles each measuring less than 90° (three acute angles). Triangle *PQR* below is acute.

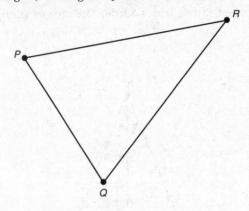

OBTUSE TRIANGLE An obtuse triangle has one angle measuring less than 180°. In an obtuse triangle, like *STU* below, the other two angles must be acute.

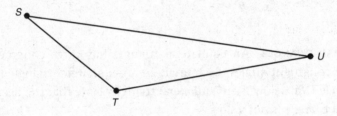

RIGHT TRIANGLE A right triangle has one right angle (90°). In a right triangle, the side opposite the right angle is called the *hypotenuse*. The other two sides are called the *legs*, and the two angles opposite the legs are complementary (must add to 90°). Triangle *DEF* below is a right triangle.

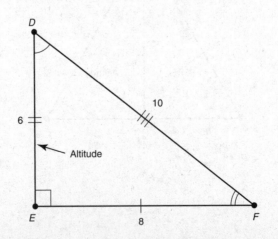

PYTHAGOREAN THEOREM The Pythagorean theorem only applies to right triangles. This rule says that the sum of the squared lengths of the legs of a right triangle will be equal to the squared length of the hypotenuse. This theorem is usually expressed as $a^2 + b^2 = c^2$, where a and b are the legs of the triangle and c is the hypotenuse.

CIRCLES

CIRCLE A circle is a line through a set of points that are all at an equal distance (or equidistant) from a common point called the center. Circles measure 360°. A circle does not have corners, so it is not considered a polygon. It doesn't have a base or a height. It has dimensions with different names.

CHORD A chord is any line segment passing through the circle whose endpoints are both on the circle. A diameter is a specific type of chord. In the figure below, $\overline{ST}$ is a chord.

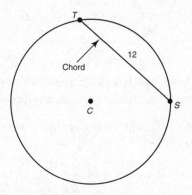

ARC A portion of the circumference defined by two points on the circle is an arc. Arcs are measured in degrees or radians. In the following diagram, the portion containing points L, M, and N is an arc.

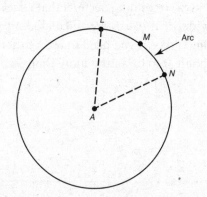

RADIUS   The radius is the distance from the center to any point on the circle. The plural of "radius" is "radii" (ray-dee-eye). All radii in the same circle are equal.

DIAMETER   A diameter is a line segment passing through the center of the circle whose endpoints are both on the circle. The diameter is equal to twice the radius.

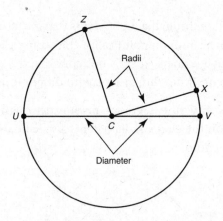

TANGENT   A line that intersects the circle at exactly one point. A tangent line is perpendicular to a radius or diameter that contains the intersection point.

CENTRAL ANGLE   An angle with its vertex at the center of the circle, formed by two radii that intersect.

UNIT CIRCLE   A unit circle is a circle with a radius of 1, a circumference of 2π, and an area of π. This circle is used frequently in trigonometry.

PI (π)   The ratio of a circle's perimeter (called *circumference*) to its diameter is the same in every circle. The value is called pi (π). Its value is equal to $\frac{22}{7}$, or approximately 3.14. Pi is a continuing decimal that never establishes a pattern no matter how many decimal places are calculated. In most cases, you will treat pi as a variable, like x or y. If you need to use π to get a numerical answer, you can probably estimate it to be a little more than 3.

CIRCUMFERENCE (CIRCLE)   The perimeter of a circle is called its circumference. It represents the distance around the outside of the circle. Since the diameter is twice the radius, you can use either one to find circumference: $C = \pi d$ or $C = 2\pi r$. The circumference of circle C that follows is $\pi(2)(8) = 16\pi$.

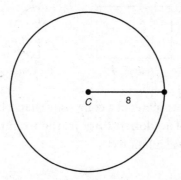

AREA (CIRCLE)   The amount of space inside a circle is the area. The formula for the area of a circle is $A = \pi r^2$. The area of circle C above is $\pi(8)(8) = 64\pi$.

SEMICIRCLE   A semicircle is half of a circle and is bounded on one side by the diameter. The formula for the circumference of a semicircle is one-half that of a circle: $C = \frac{1}{2}\pi d$ or $C\pi r$. The formula for the area is one-half that of a circle: $A = \frac{1}{2}\pi r^2$.

COMPOSITE SHAPES

- Composite shapes are nontraditional shapes created by combining traditional shapes.
- Questions will often ask you to find the area or perimeter of composite shapes.
- Break the shapes into traditional shapes using imaginary lines. Then calculate the values for the traditional shapes. Combine your results at the end.

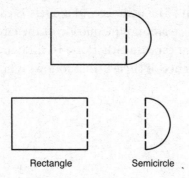

Rectangle   Semicircle

When calculating the perimeter of a composite shape, be careful not to include any imaginary lines. The dotted lines in the example above must not be included in perimeter calculations.

LESSON 5: THREE-DIMENSIONAL FIGURES

THREE-DIMENSIONAL FIGURES   Three-dimensional figures are shapes formed by the intersection of two-dimensional shapes—like squares, rectangles, circles, and triangles—in different planes.

- The two-dimensional shapes are called *faces*, and the lines that make up the two-dimensional faces are called the *edges*.
- The two important dimensions for solids are *surface area* and *volume*.

FACE   The sides of a three-dimensional figure are called the faces. The bottom face is sometimes called the *base*.

EDGE   The line where two faces of a three-dimensional figure touch is the edge.

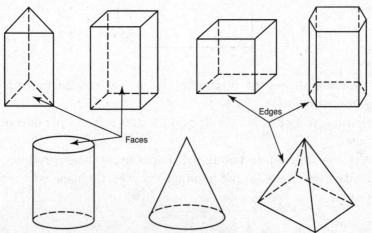

Faces   Edges

VOLUME   Volume is the total amount of space inside the figure. Volume in three-dimensional figures is similar in concept to area in two-dimensional shapes because it measures the space inside of a shape.

- Volume is often represented in *cubic units* like cubic feet (ft^3) or cubic yards (yd^3). This is because three dimensions are being multiplied, so the units are cubed.
- Volume can also be measured in liters or cups.
- Questions that ask about filling things with liquid (water and so on) are volume questions.

SURFACE AREA   Surface area is the sum of the areas of all faces of the figure. Surface area in three-dimensional figures is similar in concept to perimeter in two-dimensional shapes because it measures the outside of the shape.

PRISMS

PRISM   A prism is a solid figure with two opposite, congruent, and parallel faces (triangles, squares, pentagons, and so on). The top face is directly above the bottom face so that a line connecting their centers is perpendicular to both bases. Lines connect the corresponding vertices in the two bases.

- The volume of any prism on the Math subject test is computed using the area of the base (bottom face) multiplied by the height of the prism.
- The surface area of any prism is the sum of the areas of all faces of the prism. First calculate the sum of the areas of the two bases. Then calculate the sum of the areas of the other faces. Finally, add those two sums together.
- One useful shortcut is to use the perimeter of the base (*p*) times the height of the prism to get the total area of the nonbase faces. Then add this value to 2 times the area of a base (*B*).

RECTANGULAR PRISM (BOX)   A rectangular prism is made up of six rectangles and is commonly described as a box. Adjacent faces are perpendicular. The three dimensions of a rectangular prism are called length, width, and height.

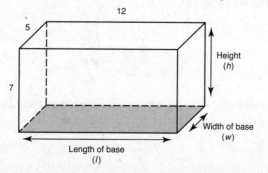

VOLUME (OF A BOX)   The volume of a box or a rectangular prism equals length times width times height: $V = lwh$. Note that this is the area of the base (bottom face) times the height. The volume of the box on page 145 is $12 \times 5 \times 7 = 420$.

SURFACE AREA (OF A BOX)   The formula for the surface area of a box or rectangular prism is $SA = ph + 2B$, where p is the perimeter of a base and B is the area of that base. Calculating the surface area of a box requires three steps. First calculate the area of a base (B) using $A = lw$. Then calculate the perimeter of a base (p). Finally, use the surface area formula. In the box on page 145, $p = (2 \times 5) + (2 \times 12) = 10 + 24 = 34$, $h = 7$, and $B = 12 \times 5 = 60$. The surface area of the box is $(34 \times 7) + (2 \times 60) = 238 + 120 = 358$.

CUBE   A cube is a rectangular prism made up of six squares (six congruent, square faces).

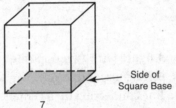

Side of
Square Base

7

VOLUME (OF A CUBE)   Since all faces and edges of a cube are congruent, the length, width, and height are all equal. Volume is often expressed as side cubed: $V = s^3$. The volume of the cube above is $7 \times 7 \times 7 = 343$.

SURFACE AREA (OF A CUBE)   Since all six faces of a cube are congruent squares, the surface area is six times the area of one face: $SA = 6s^2$. The surface area of the cube above is $6 \times 7 \times 7 = 294$.

CYLINDER   A cylinder is a prism with circular bases. It is commonly referred to as a tube.

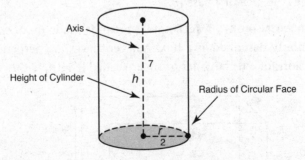

Axis

Height of Cylinder

h

7

Radius of Circular Face

$\dfrac{r}{2}$

VOLUME (OF A CYLINDER)   The volume is equal to the area of the circular base times the height of the cylinder: $V = \pi r^2 h$. The volume of the cylinder above is $\pi(2)(2)(7) = 28\pi$.

SURFACE AREA (OF A CYLINDER) The surface area is the sum of three areas: the top base, the bottom base, and the curved surface around the outside of the tube: $SA = 2\pi r^2 + 2\pi rh$:

- The formula for surface area of a cylinder is similar to that for a rectangular prism. The length represents the circumference of the circular base. The width represents the height of the cylinder.
- The area of each circle is πr^2, the circumference is $2\pi r$, and the height is h.
- The surface area of the cylinder on page 146 is

$$2\pi(2)(2) + 2\pi(2)(7) = 8\pi + 28\pi = 36\pi$$

PYRAMIDS

PYRAMID On the Math subject test, the word pyramid refers to a square pyramid. A square pyramid is a solid with a square base and triangular faces that all meet at a common point at the top called the *apex*.

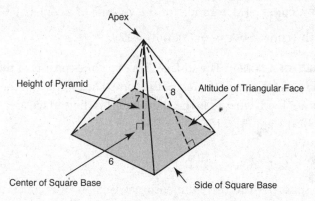

APEX The common vertex at the top of a pyramid is the apex.

VOLUME (OF A PYRAMID) The formula for the volume of a pyramid is $V = \frac{1}{3}Bh$. This formula uses the area of one base (B). Since the base is a square, B is equal to the square of one side of the base. The volume of the pyramid above is $\frac{1}{3}(6)(6)(7) = 84$.

SURFACE AREA (OF A PYRAMID) The surface area of a pyramid consists of the area of the square base plus the areas of the four triangular faces. The formula for the surface area of a pyramid is $\frac{1}{2}ps + B$, where p is the perimeter of a base, B is the area of that base, and s is the slant length or altitude of a triangular face.

- Calculating the surface area of a pyramid requires three steps. First calculate the area of the base (B) using $A = s^2$. Then calculate the perimeter of the base (p). Finally, use the surface area formula.

■ In the pyramid on page 147, $p = 4 \times 6 = 24$, $s = 8$, and $B = 6 \times 6 = 36$. The surface area of the pyramid is $\frac{1}{2}(24)(8) + 36 = 96 + 36 = 132$.

CONES

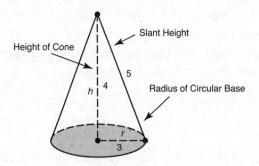

CONE A cone is similar to a pyramid except that a cone has a circular base.

VOLUME (OF A CONE) The formula for the volume of a cone is $V = \frac{1}{3}\pi r^2 h$. The volume of the cone above is $\frac{1}{3}\pi(3)(3)(4) = 12\pi$.

SURFACE AREA (OF A CONE) The surface area of a cone consists of the area of the circular base plus the area of the rest of the cone. The formula for the surface area of a cone is $\pi rs + \pi r^2$, where s is the slant length. The surface area of the cone above is $\pi(3)(5) + \pi(3)(3) = 15\pi + 9\pi = 24\pi$.

SPHERES

SPHERE A sphere is the three-dimensional version of a circle. It represents all points in space that are an equal distance from the center. The primary dimension in a sphere is the radius.

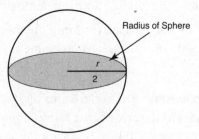

VOLUME (OF A SPHERE) The formula for the volume of a sphere is $V = \frac{4}{3}\pi r^3$. The volume of the sphere above is $\frac{4}{3}\pi(2)(2)(2) = \frac{32}{3}\pi = 10\frac{2}{3}\pi$.

SURFACE AREA (OF A SPHERE) The formula for the surface area of a sphere is $SA = 4\pi r^2$. The surface area of the sphere above is $4\pi(2)(2) = 16\pi$.

Data Analysis

8

Data presentation deals with ways that information can be represented visually. Statistics (measures of center, probability, and counting methods) deal with different ways of deriving new information from numbers.

DATA   Data are quantitative (numbers) or qualitative (words) information.

DATA PRESENTATION   Information presented using text, graphics, or both is data presentation.

LESSON 1: INTERPRETING DATA PRESENTATIONS

GRAPHS

A graph shows how a relationship between two things (variables) changes as the values of those things change, like change over time. For example, a graph might be used to plot the changes in temperature over the months of a year.

A graph is the intersection of two number lines. Each line is called an *axis* (the plural is "axes," pronounced "ak-seez"). One axis is horizontal (moving side to side) and is called the x-axis. The other line is vertical (moving up and down) and is called the y-axis.

Each axis is numbered at regular intervals (every 2 units, every 5 units, every 10 units, and so on). The numbers are aligned with lines or *tick marks*. These numbers show you the *scale* represented by each axis.

Information on a graph is presented with points, which are markers showing where a location on the x-axis intersects with a location on the y-axis. These numbers are called *coordinates*. They are usually written in an *ordered pair* in the form (x, y). An example of an ordered pair is $(6, 6)$.

Line Graph

A line graph is probably the most familiar kind of graph for most of us. Individual data points are plotted and then connected to form a line called a *series*. A line graph commonly contains more than one series of data points.

When this happens, the graph will contain a *key* or *legend* that explains what each line represents. To interpret line graphs, pay attention to trends and to the relative movement of lines (closer together vs. farther apart).

In the example below, the graph shows the month-by-month average temperatures for a sample city. For each month, the graph shows record high, average high, average low, and record low temperatures. Each of these temperature types is considered a data series, and is represented with a line that contains a different symbol. The legend at the right edge of the graph identifies the symbol used for each series.

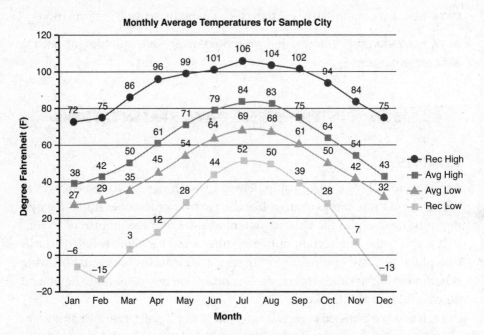

A line graph is very useful for describing change, particularly change over time. As we go from left to right, month by month, we see the temperatures rise until the middle of the x-axis (July) and then they tend to fall back toward their original values.

A line graph is generally used when the variation in each data series is smooth, which means that the points are easily connected with a single line. For each data series in the example above, there is only one temperature of each type for a given month. In other words, we don't have two or three record high temperatures for April.

Scatter Plot

A *scatter plot* is similar to a line graph in that it uses plotted points to represent data points. However, a scatter plot is used where the variation in data is not as smooth as in a line graph. The plot gets its name because the points in the series appear to be scattered around the plot area of the graph.

In the example below, the scatter plot presents the relationship between two variables associated with the eruptions of a geyser (a body of underground water that periodically forces water and steam out of a hole in the ground). The wait time in minutes before an eruption occurs is compared with the duration of the eruption in seconds.

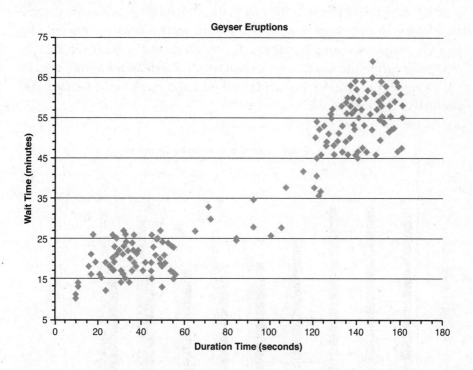

As we can see from the example, the data describing these eruptions is less smooth and orderly than the temperature data in the previous line graph. In some places here, more than one duration is plotted for a given wait time (see 26 minutes). In other places, more than one wait time is plotted for a given duration (see 24 seconds).

Scatter plots are used when the data are distributed in large concentrations of points close together called *clusters*. Those points that are plotted away from the clusters are called *outliers*.

CHARTS

Charts are used to represent relationships between quantities or amounts. In some cases, these amounts are portions of some large total or whole.

Bar Charts

Bar charts are similar to graphs in that they present data using an *x*-axis and a *y*-axis. Where they differ is in the way that each data point is presented. On a bar chart, each data point is shown as a shaded bar that extends from one axis to each data point's other coordinate. Bar charts may have either vertical bars that extend from the *x*-axis or horizontal bars that extend from the *y*-axis. In the example that follows, the bars extend from the *x*-axis to the *y*-coordinate for each data point.

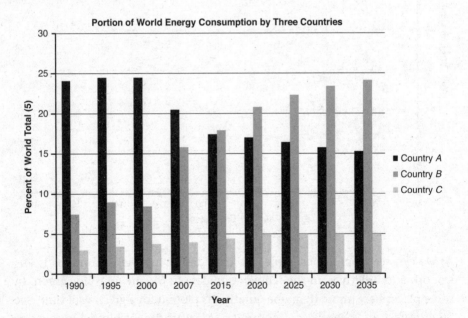

Bar charts will often have more than one data series (bar) for each coordinate. In the example shown above, each year has a bar for each of the three countries being presented. The use of bars makes it easy to compare relative amounts between bars.

Pie Charts

Also known as circle graphs, pie charts do not use the *x*- and *y*-axes found in other data presentations. Instead, they represent a total quantity (whole) as a shaded circle. This circle is often divided into portions that represent a part or subset of the total.

**Average Monthly Precipitation (in mm) for
Four Months in 2010: Northeast Region U.S.**

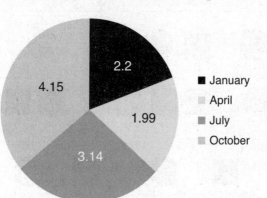

Pie charts let you easily see the relative composition of a total. The larger sections of the circle represent categories that take up larger portions of the total or whole. In the example above, average monthly precipitation (in millimeters) was measured in January, April, July, and October 2010.

By examining the pie chart, we can see that the second half of the year (July and October) received more precipitation than the first half. We can see that October received the greatest amount of precipitation of the four months measured.

TABLES

A table is a matrix or grid that organizes information into rows and columns. Tables make it easy to view and compare information when the data set is simple, when the range of data (from largest to smallest value) is very wide, or when data points contain large numbers of significant digits (large numbers or numbers with many decimal places).

DIAGRAMS

Diagrams are graphic illustrations of data that are usually nonnumerical. Diagrams are used to present processes and other kinds of information that cannot be easily graphed or charted. The example below shows pedigree information for a genetically inherited trait.

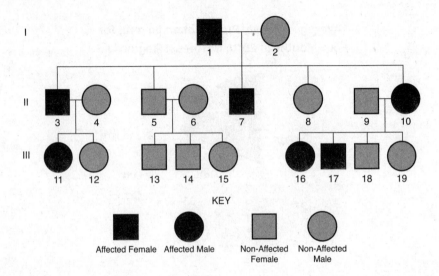

Diagrams are used to represent the most complex kinds of information. However, they are usually easily understood since they are essentially pictures with labels. In this example, shading and shapes that are easy to recognize are used to represent inheritance and gender. We can see the trait being passed from parent to child, from both males and females.

Diagrams are often used to present food webs, chains, and pyramids as well as chemical, biological, or mechanical processes.

UNDERSTANDING DATA REPRESENTATIONS

Examine

The first step in the process is to look at and read everything you see: titles, axis labels, axis numbers or words, keys or legends, notes, and so on. Read EVERYTHING. Many wrong answers come from missing an important piece of information in a graphic.

Analyze

The second step is to think about and organize the information you just examined.

- What do the two axes represent?
- What are the numerical scales for each axis? What units do the axes use?
- What does the data series (line or lines, plotted points, bars) represent?
- As it moves from left to right, what is happening to the data series?
- Is the data series increasing, decreasing, or doing both in different places?
- If more than one data series is present, how are they related to each other?
- Are lines getting closer together or farther apart?
- Are bars getting taller or shorter?
- Are there any outliers (dots on the edges away from the other dots) in the scatter plot?

Explain

The third step is the most important one in the process. Before moving to the questions, take time to summarize the results of your analysis in your own words. For example, you may think to yourself, "This line graph shows the average temperature and hours of daylight in New York City for each month in the year. The levels all start out low in January, then they steadily increase to a maximum in early August, and then they steadily decrease to a low in December."

Thinking about this explanation is important because the questions that follow will often focus on the elements you have in your explanation. After all, your explanation is like the main idea of the graph or chart. On the exam, the Science subject test will include short-answer questions that require you to write brief answers. Very often, these questions will ask you to provide a summary of a graph or chart. Your explanation makes you ready to do that.

LESSON 2: STATISTICS

SET   A set is a group of numbers sometimes called members, terms, or elements.

MEAN   The mean is the average of a set of numbers. It is calculated by adding the elements and dividing by the number of elements.

MEDIAN The median is the middle of the set of numbers. As many numbers in the set are larger than the median as are smaller than the median.

- In a set with an odd number of elements, the median is the middle element when the set is arranged in ascending order (smallest to largest).
- In a set with an even number of elements, the median is the average of the middle two elements when the set is arranged in ascending order.

MODE The mode is the most frequently occurring element in the set.

RANGE The range is the difference between the smallest element and the largest element in the set. It is sometimes called the spread of the data.

WEIGHTED AVERAGE A weighted average is an average where different elements in the set have different amounts of importance (or weight) in the calculation.

An example of a weighted average would be calculating a student's final grade:

- Suppose the student has a homework average grade of 85, an average of 95 on tests, and a participation grade of 60. A simple average of those three scores would be 80.
- Now suppose homework counts for 25%, tests count for 65%, and participation counts for 10% in the overall grade. To calculate the weighted average, multiply each element by its weight (85 × 0.25, 95 × 0.65, 60 × 0.1) and add the products together.
- The weighted average is 89. The weighted average is higher than the simple average because the test scores make up more than half of the final grade and the participation scores represent a very small portion of the grade.

LESSON 3: PROBABILITY

Probability describes the likelihood that something will occur.

- Something that will definitely happen has a probability of 1.
- Something that will definitely not happen has a probability of 0.
- The probability of anything else is expressed as a value between 0 and 1. It can be expressed as a fraction $\left(\frac{3}{8}\right)$, a decimal (0.375), or a percentage (37.5%).
- Assume you have some sort of test that you will repeat many times, like flipping a coin with heads and tails or rolling a six-sided die numbered

1 to 6. Each time you repeat the test, you will produce a result called an *outcome*.

■ Now assume you want to predict the number of times something will happen (called an *event*), like the number of times you will roll an even number (2, 4, 6).

■ Outcomes in which the event occurs (rolling a 4) are called positive. Outcomes in which the event does not occur (rolling a 1) are called negative.

■ Probability assumes that all possible results (rolling 1, 2, 3, 4, 5, or 6) are equally likely to occur. It compares the number of ways an event could occur (positive results) and the total number of all possible results (all results).

$$\text{Probability} = \frac{\text{Positive results}}{\text{All possible results}}$$

■ There are 6 possible results when rolling the six-sided die, and 3 of those (2, 4, and 6) would be positive results. $P = \frac{3}{6} = \frac{1}{2} = 0.5 = 50\%$.

INDEPENDENT EVENTS   Events whose outcomes do not depend on one another are independent events. On the Math subject test, all events are independent. For example, if you roll a six-sided die twice, the first result will not affect the second. The results do not depend on each other.

COMPOUND EVENTS   Two or more independent events that happen together are compound events. The probability of a compound event is the product of the probabilities of each independent event. For example, rolling two six-sided dice is a compound event. You would multiply the probability of rolling a specific number, say 4, on the first roll by the probability of rolling that same number on the second roll to find your answer.

LESSON 4: COUNTING METHODS

COUNTING METHODS   There are two different ways of counting the different possible arrangements of a set of elements.

■ In some cases, the order of elements does not matter. Therefore, 123 and 321 would be considered the same.

■ In other cases, order does matter, so 123 and 321 would be considered two distinct arrangements.

FACTORIAL The factorial is the number of different ways that a set of objects or elements can be placed in order. To calculate the factorial, the number of elements is multiplied by each successively smaller number, down to 1.

- The exclamation point (!) is used to symbolize factorial. 5 factorial is written as 5!
- For example, "5!" = $5 \times 4 \times 3 \times 2 \times 1 = 120$. This means that a set of 5 things can be placed in 120 different orders.

PERMUTATION Permutation is the number of ways that a group of objects selected from a larger group of objects can be placed in a particular order.

- The formula for a permutation is $\frac{n!}{(n-k)!}$, where n is the number of elements or objects and k is the number of places or spots we have to fill with selected elements.
- For example, suppose you need to select a 1st-, 2nd-, and 3rd-place winner in a contest with 6 contestants (A, B, C, D, E, and F).
- There are 6 elements (contestants), so n is 6. There are 3 places to fill (1st, 2nd, and 3rd), so k is 3. Apply the formula: $6! = 720$, $n - k = 3$, and $3! = 6$. This becomes $720 \div 6 = 120$.

COMBINATION Combination is the number of different ways that a group of k elements can be formed from a larger group of n elements when order does not matter. The formula is $\frac{n!}{(n-k)!k!}$

- For example, suppose you need to choose 3 contest winners from a group of 8 contestants.
- Apply the formula: $8! = 8 \times 7 \times 6 \times 5 \times 4 \times 3 \times 2 \times 1 = 40{,}320$, $n - k = 5$, $5! = 120$, and $3! = 6$.
- This becomes $40{,}320 \div (120 \times 6)$, or $40{,}320 \div 720 = 56$.

Calculating a combination can be simplified using the *cancellation method*. Since many of the same terms appear in both the numerator and denominator, it is possible to cancel out many of the terms and compute the rest manually:

$$\frac{(8)(7)(6)(\cancel{5})(\cancel{4})(\cancel{3})(\cancel{2})(\cancel{1})}{(\cancel{5})(\cancel{4})(\cancel{3})(\cancel{2})(\cancel{1}) \bullet (3)(2)(1)} = \frac{(8)(7)(\cancel{6})}{(\cancel{3})(\cancel{2})(1)} = \frac{(8)(7)}{(1)} = 8(7) = 56$$

Algebra

LESSON 1: EXPRESSIONS

Algebra deals with unknown quantities. These are called variables, and are represented with letters such as x, y, z, q, r, and s.

VARIABLE An unknown value is a variable. It is represented by a letter such as x, y, or z.

COEFFICIENT A number placed next to a variable to indicate multiplication is a coefficient.

- For example, $2x$ has a coefficient of 2. This means that the unknown value (x) is being multiplied by 2.
- Coefficients can be negative: $-3x$, $-5y$, etc.
- Coefficients can be fractions: $\frac{3x}{5}$ (or $\frac{3}{5}x$), $\frac{7x}{2}$ (or $\frac{7}{2}x$)
- A coefficient of 1 is not usually shown: $1x = x$

CONSTANT A value that does not change is a constant.

TERM A term is a value expressed with at least one variable, sometimes with a coefficient, and/or sometimes with an exponent. For example, $2x$ is a term and so is x^2. $2x^2y$ is one term. Each of the parts of the term (2, x^2, and y) are multiplied together so they are *factors* of the term.

SIMILAR TERMS Terms that contain the same variable or variables: $2x$ and $3x$ are similar, but $2x$ and $3y$ are not. Similar terms must include the same exponent (**degree**) for each variable. $2x^2$ and $3x^2$ are similar, but $2x^2$ and $3x$ are not. Similar terms are often called "like" terms, and terms that are not similar are often called "unlike" terms.

BASIC OPERATIONS (IN ALGEBRA)   All of the standard rules for basic operations apply to variables:

- **Adding:** $x + x = 2x$, $3x + 5x = 8x$
- **Subtracting:** $3x - 2x = x$, $2x - 3x = -x$
- **Multiplying:** $x \bullet y = xy$, $2y \bullet 4z = 8yz$, $x \bullet x = x^2$
- **Dividing (canceling):** $\dfrac{4x}{2x} = \dfrac{2}{1} = 2$; $\dfrac{9xy}{3xz} = \dfrac{3y}{z}$; $\dfrac{4x^3}{4x^2} = \dfrac{x}{1} = x$

OPERATORS   Operators are symbols for arithmetic operations ($+$, $-$, $\bullet$, $/$, x^2, $\sqrt{\ }$). They are used to form expressions.

EXPRESSION   An expression is a group of terms connected by operators, like $2x + 5$.

- The expression above has two terms ($2x$ and 5), one of which has two factors (2 and x).
- Expressions like the one above are often called linear expressions.
- An expression can also be a single term (monomial) with one or more factors, like $3z$.

MONOMIAL   An expression with only one term is a monomial, such as 5, x, $2y$, and z^3.

BINOMIAL   An expression with two terms, connected by addition or subtraction, is a binomial, such as $2x + 3$, $5x - 4$, and $x^2 + x$.

POLYNOMIAL   An expression with more than one term is a polynomial:

$$2x^2 - 3x + 4$$

- Polynomials include binomials and trinomials. Trinomials have 3 terms, as shown in the expression above.
- Exponents in polynomial terms must be non-negative integers.
- Polynomial terms are arranged in descending order of powers, so x^2 comes before x, which comes before any constant term. If the expression included an x^3 term, it would come before the x^2 term.
- Trinomials are usually referred to as polynomials.
- Binomials are sometimes referred to as binomials and sometimes as polynomials.

RATIONAL EXPRESSION   An expression that represents a ratio $\left(\dfrac{a}{b}\right)$ between two polynomials where b is not equal to zero is a rational expression: $\dfrac{x^2 + 4}{x + 2}$

RADICAL EXPRESSION An expression that includes a radical is a radical expression: $\sqrt{x+4}$

EVALUATING AND SIMPLIFYING EXPRESSIONS

EVALUATING AN EXPRESSION An expression can be evaluated by substituting numbers for the variables in the expression.

- When $x = 2$, the linear expression $2x + 3$ evaluates to 7.

$$2x + 3 = 2(2) + 3 = 4 + 3 = 7$$

- When $x = 2$, the polynomial expression $2x^2 - 3x + 4$ evaluates to 6.

$$2x^2 - 3x + 4 = 2(2^2) - 3(2) + 4 = 2(4) - 6 + 4 = 8 - 6 + 4 = 2 + 4 = 6$$

- When $x = 2$, the rational expression $\dfrac{x^2 + 5}{x + 2}$ evaluates to $\dfrac{9}{4}$.

$$\frac{x^2 + 5}{x + 2} = \frac{4 + 5}{2 + 2} = \frac{9}{4}$$

SIMPLIFYING Expressions containing multiple terms that are similar (like terms) can be made simpler by combining the similar terms. For example, the expression

$$2x^2 + 3 - x + 3x^2 + 2x - 1$$

contains several sets of like terms and can be simplified to $5x^2 + x + 2$.

DISTRIBUTING AND FACTORING EXPRESSIONS

DISTRIBUTING The distributive property says that the expression $a(b + c)$ is the same as the expression $ab + ac$. To illustrate this, let's review an example that uses numbers:

$$11(7 + 4)$$

In this case, the order of operations tells us to add inside the parentheses $(7 + 4)$ to get 11, and then multiply $11(11)$ to get 121. This is the appropriate way to work on an expression like the one above, which contains only numerical values (i.e., no variables).

The distributive property, however, gives us another way to arrive at the same result. This approach involves multiplying the first term (11) by each of the terms inside the parentheses and then adding the resulting products:

$$11(7 + 4) = 11(7) + 11(4) = 77 + 44 = 121$$

This approach can be applied to an algebraic expression that contains nonnumerical values:

$$a(b + c)$$

In this case, the distributive property tells us to multiply a by each of the terms inside the parentheses (b and c):

$$a(b + c) = a(b) + a(c) = ab + ac$$

The main thing to remember with this kind of distribution is that "distributing" a term means to multiply it by each term in another expression. The word "distribute" means "to give something out," and, in the example above, the term a is being "given out" (or multiplied by) the terms in the expression $b + c$. This is sometimes called *expanding* and results in the *distributed form* of the expression. Consider the following examples:

$$3(2x - 3) = 3(2x) - 3(3) = 6x - 9$$
$$3x(x + 5) = 3x(x) + 3x(5) = 3x^2 + 15x$$

In each example, a term is being "given out" to each of the terms in an expression. This core concept can be applied the same way to more complicated situations:

$$3(x^2 + x + 4) = 3(x^2) + 3(x) + 3(4) = 3x^2 + 3x + 12$$
$$3x(x^2 + 2x - 5) = 3x(x^2) + 3x(2x) - 3x(5) = 3x^3 + 6x^2 - 15x$$

This concept of distribution is a very important part of working with polynomials. No matter how complicated the terms and expressions become, the main concept is the same: **to distribute a term into an expression, multiply it by all the terms in the expression**.

FACTORING It is useful to think of factoring as distributing in reverse. When factoring, the goal is to take the expanded or distributed form of an expression and "work backwards" to the *factored form*. To do this, we need to find a term that is a factor of (divides evenly into) each term in the expression we are factoring. Consider this example:

$$8x^2 + 4x + 12$$

To factor this expression, we need to identify a number that will divide evenly into $8x^2$, $4x$, and 12. Since not all terms in the expression contain a variable, we need a number that is a factor of 12 and of the coefficients of the other terms (8 and 4). Both 2 and 4 are possibilities, but it is usually preferred to work with the largest factor we can find, so we should "factor" (or divide) a 4 out of the expression:

- The factor is 4.
- $8 \div 4 = 2$, so $8x^2 \div 4 = 2x^2$
- $4 \div 4 = 1$, so $4x \div 4 = x$
- $12 \div 4 = 3$

The resulting terms can be expressed in a new form:

$$4(2x^2 + x + 3)$$

In effect, when we factor a polynomial this way, we are "reverse distributing" the factor that is being "taken out": **to factor an expression, divide each term in the expression by the greatest common factor**.

ADDING AND SUBTRACTING POLYNOMIALS

Sometimes expressions can involve adding or subtracting polynomials.

To add, remove the parentheses and simplify:

$$(2x^2 + 3 - x) + (3x^2 + 2x - 1) = (2x^2 + 3x^2) + (2x - x) + (3 - 1) = 5x^2 + x + 2$$

To subtract, change the minus sign to a plus sign and change each sign in the polynomial being subtracted (this is called *distributing the negative*):

$$(3x^2 + 2x - 1) - (2x^2 + 3 - x) = (3x^2 + 2x - 1) + (-2x^2 - 3 + x) =$$
$$(3x^2 - 2x^2) + (2x + x) + (-1 - 3) = x^2 + 3x - 4$$

MULTIPLYING EXPRESSIONS

The concept of distributing can be used to multiply expressions together. In these cases, each term in one expression is distributed into (multiplied by) each term in another expression. One fundamental case where this occurs is when one binomial (two term) expression is multiplied by another binomial expression:

$$(x + 3)(x + 4)$$

The method of distributing in cases like this one is called **FOIL**:

- FOIL stands for First, Outer, Inner, Last. It lists the order in which you should multiply the terms.
- First: This refers to the first term in each binomial: $x \bullet x = x^2$
- Outer: This refers to the terms on the outside, or the first term in the first binomial and the second term in the second binomial: $x \bullet 4 = 4x$

- Inner: This refers to the terms on the inside, or the second term in the first binomial and the first term in the second binomial: $3 \bullet x = 3x$
- Last: This refers to the second term in each binomial: $3 \bullet 4 = 12$
- Arrange the terms in descending order of exponent values (**degree of the term**):

$$x^2 + 4x + 3x + 12$$

Simplify:

$$x^2 + 7x + 12$$

The rules of signed numbers apply when using FOIL. For example:

$$(x + 5)(x - 4)$$

- First: $x \bullet x = x^2$
- Outer: $x \bullet -4 = -4x$
- Inner: $5 \bullet x = 5x$
- Last: $5 \bullet -4 = -20$

Arrange and simplify:

$$x^2 - 4x + 5x - 20 = x^2 + x - 20$$

FOIL IN REVERSE (FACTORING)

FOIL can be used in reverse to factor a polynomial into the product of two binomials.

- Certain kinds of polynomials take the form $ax^2 + bx + c$.
- The symbols a and b are placeholders for coefficients; b is the coefficient of x.
- The symbol c represents a constant (a number).
- Even though they are letters when in the format $ax^2 + bx + c$, the values for a, b, and c will be numbers in a polynomial expressed using this format.

To factor a polynomial, look for pairs of numbers that are factors of c and add to b. Use the following example:

$$x^2 + 5x + 6$$

- Factor pairs of 6 (c) include (1, 6) and (2, 3). Negative factors are also possible.
- Since $1 + 6$ does not add to 5 (b), this pair is not valid.

- Since 2 + 3 do add to 5, this pair of factors is valid. They each become a second term in one of the two binomials that will make up the factored form of the polynomial:

$$(x + 2)(x + 3)$$

- To verify that you have factored correctly, FOIL the expression you produced:

$$(x + 2)(x + 3) = x^2 + 3x + 2x + 6 = x^2 + 5x + 6$$

This process can be applied to polynomials with coefficients that are negative and/or greater than 1.

WORKING WITH RATIONAL EXPRESSIONS

A rational expression is an expression involving a ratio between two polynomials. It is presented in a form similar to a fraction, with one polynomial as the numerator and another as the denominator:

$$\frac{x^2 + 4}{x + 2}$$

Simplifying rational expressions or performing operations on rational expressions can involve factoring and distributing polynomials.

Simplifying

Rational expressions can often be simplified by canceling terms that appear in both the top and the bottom of the ratio. For example:

$$\frac{x^2 - 4}{x + 2}$$

- By using one of the common factored forms, $(x + y)(x - y) = x^2 + y^2$, we can factor the expression above.
- $x^2 - 4 = (x + 2)(x - 2)$, so the expression becomes:

$$\frac{(x + 2)(x - 2)}{(x + 2)}$$

- Since $(x + 2)$ is in both the top and the bottom of the ratio, it can be canceled out:

$$x - 2$$

In many cases, the simplified form will still be a rational expression:

$$\frac{x^2 + x - 12}{x^2 - 9} = \frac{(x+4)(x-3)}{(x+3)(x-3)} = \frac{x+4}{x+3}$$

Multiplying and Dividing

Factoring, canceling, and distributing can help simplify the process of multiplying and dividing rational expressions.

To multiply a rational expression, factor it first:

$$\frac{x+4}{y^2 - 16} \cdot \frac{y+4}{x^2 + 5x + 4} = \frac{(x+4)}{(y+4)(y-4)} \cdot \frac{(y+4)}{(x+4)(x+1)} = \frac{1}{(y-4)(x+1)}$$

Division of rational expressions can be complicated. Remember to flip the bottom expression and multiply:

$$\frac{\dfrac{x^2 - 25}{x+7}}{\dfrac{x+5}{x^2 - 49}} = \frac{(x^2 - 25)}{(x+7)} \cdot \frac{(x^2 - 49)}{(x+5)}$$

$$= \frac{(x+5)(x-5)}{(x+7)} \cdot \frac{(x+7)(x-7)}{(x+5)}$$

$$= \frac{(x-5)}{1} \cdot \frac{(x-7)}{1}$$

$$= x^2 - 12x + 35$$

Adding and Subtracting

Adding and subtracting rational expressions can be complicated. You must use the rules for operations with fractions, including common denominators.

- When adding or subtracting numerical fractions, we sometimes convert both fractions to a common denominator:

$$\frac{1}{2} + \frac{1}{3} = \frac{3}{6} + \frac{2}{6} = \frac{5}{6}$$

- This same rule applies to rational expressions where the denominators are polynomials. This means that factoring and distributing will often be required:

$$\frac{4x}{x+2} + \frac{x}{x+3}$$

- Get a common denominator by multiplying the top and bottom of each ratio by the denominator of the other:

$$\frac{4x}{(x+2)} \cdot \frac{(x+3)}{(x+3)} = \frac{4x(x+3)}{(x+2)(x+3)} = \frac{4x^2+12x}{x^2+5x+6}$$

$$\frac{x}{(x+3)} \cdot \frac{(x+2)}{(x+2)} = \frac{x(x+2)}{(x+3)(x+2)} = \frac{x^2+2x}{x^2+5x+6}$$

- Add the two numerators, and express the new fraction over the common denominator:

$$\frac{4x^2+12x}{x^2+5x+6} + \frac{x^2+2x}{x^2+5x+6} = \frac{5x^2+14x}{x^2+5x+6}$$

- Factor and simplify if needed:

$$\frac{5x^2+14x}{x^2+5x+6} = \frac{x(5x+14)}{x^2+5x+6}$$

- Depending on the result, you may find additional ways to factor and cancel.

LESSON 2: EQUATIONS

EQUATION   An equation is an algebraic expression set equal to a constant or it is an expression set equal to another expression. This is called equating the two sides of the equal sign, which is how equations get their name. The following are equations:

$$2x + 15 = 6x - 5$$
$$x^2 + 6x + 5 = 0$$

FUNCTION   An equation containing two variables where each value for an independent (input) variable x produces only one value for a dependent (output) variable $f(x)$. The equation $f(x) = 2x + 5$ is a function.

FORMULA   An equation, usually containing two or more variables used to calculate a desired value or property. Formulas are used to calculate area and volume, as well as to find the zeros of quadratic equations.

COMBINING SIMILAR TERMS

Similar terms in an equation can be combined. Start with the equation:

$$2x + 3 + 3x - 4 = 19$$

After combining similar terms, the equation becomes:

$$5x - 1 = 19$$

Similar terms can also be combined across the equal sign. Start with the equation:

$$7x - 2 = 3x + 6$$

- There are multiple sets of similar terms in the equation above: $(7x, 3x)$ and $(-2, 6)$. However, the similar terms are on opposite sides of the equal sign.
- These terms can be combined by moving them across the equal sign using inverse operations.

INVERSE OPERATIONS

Inverse operations are used to move terms across the equal sign by doing the opposite of the operations represented by the terms:

- Keep equations in balance. Always perform inverse operations on both sides of the equation.
- Move positive terms by subtracting them, and move negative terms by adding them:

$$7x - 2 = 3x + 6$$
$$7x - 2 - 3x = 3x + 6 - 3x$$
$$4x - 2 = 6$$
$$4x - 2 + 2 = 6 + 2$$
$$4x = 8$$
$$\frac{4x}{4} = \frac{8}{4}$$
$$x = 2$$

SOLVING EQUATIONS

- First combine like terms on each side of the equals sign if necessary.
- Then use inverse operations so the variable terms are on one side of the equals sign and the numerical terms are on the other.

- Then remove coefficients and/or denominators so that the variable is the only term on its side of the equal sign.
- Maintain balance throughout the process by applying inverse operations to both sides of the equation:

$$7x - 2 = 3x + 6$$
$$7x - 2 - 3x = 3x + 6 - 3x$$
$$4x - 2 = 6$$
$$4x - 2 + 2 = 6 + 2$$
$$4x = 8$$
$$\frac{4x}{4} = \frac{8}{4}$$
$$x = 2$$

MULTIPLE VARIABLES

Equations frequently involve more than one variable:

$$4x + 3y = 6x + y + 2$$

These equations can be evaluated if we're given (or we assume) a value for one of the two variables. Assume that $y = 6$ in the equation below:

$$4x + 3y = 6x + y + 2$$
$$4x + 18 = 6x + 8$$
$$10 = 2x$$
$$x = 5$$

Simultaneous Equations

Multivariable equations are sometimes presented in pairs, called simultaneous equations or systems of equations:

$$y = 3x - 1$$
$$y = x + 5$$

These equations can be set equal to one another:

$$3x - 1 = x + 5$$

Next, solve for x:

$$2x = 6, \text{ so } x = 3$$

Substitute the value of x into both equations:

$$y = 3(3) - 1, \text{ so } y = 8$$
$$y = 3 + 5, \text{ so } y = 8$$

The solution to the system is expressed as an ordered pair (x,y): (3, 8)

You can also add or subtract the equations:

$$y = 3x - 1$$
$$\underline{-y = x + 5}$$
$$0 = 2x - 6$$

$$2x = 6, \text{ so } x = 3$$

EXTRANEOUS SOLUTIONS

An extraneous solution is a solution that is based on valid algebra but doesn't satisfy the original equation. One situation in which these can occur is when squaring both sides of a radical equation:

- Start with the equation $x = \sqrt{x+2}$
- Square both sides: $x^2 = x + 2$
- Subtract x from both sides: $x^2 - x = 2$
- Subtract 2 from both sides: $x^2 - x - 2 = 0$
- Factor the left side (reverse FOIL): $(x - 2)(x + 1) = 0$
- This leads to two solutions: 2 and −1

These solutions are both based on valid algebra, but that doesn't mean that they are both valid solutions to the original equation. To verify them, we need to substitute each of them into the original equation:

- $2 = \sqrt{2+2} = \sqrt{4}$
- $-1 = \sqrt{-1+2} = \sqrt{1}$

This substitution process shows that only 2 is a valid solution to the original equation, because only 2 creates a true statement: 2 does equal $\sqrt{4}$. The other solution, −1, is an extraneous solution because it creates a false statement: −1 does not equal $\sqrt{1}$ (because $\sqrt{1}$ refers to the nonnegative root).

QUADRATIC EQUATIONS

A quadratic equation is a polynomial equation in the form $ax^2 + bx + c = 0$. The symbols a and b represent coefficients, and c represents a constant. a, b, and c are real numbers and x cannot be zero. The solutions (or roots) of a quadratic equation are values for x that produce zero when the quadratic expression is evaluated. These solutions are also called zeros.

Finding the Zeros

The polynomial side of a quadratic equation can be factored:

$$x^2 - 2x - 15 = 0$$
$$(x - 5)(x + 3) = 0$$

The factored form of the equation shows that the product of two terms is equal to 0. This means that one of the two terms must be equal to 0. (If $ab = 0$, then $a = 0$ or $b = 0$.)

- If $x - 5 = 0$, then $x = 5$.
- If $x + 3 = 0$, then $x = -3$.
- This means that there are two zeros: 5 and –3

COMPLETING THE SQUARE

In some cases, it is possible to make a quadratic equation easier to factor by manipulating it.

1. Move the constant term c across the equal sign.
2. Divide the coefficient of b by 2 and square the result.
3. Add the square to the equation. Do this on both sides to maintain balance and avoid changing the relationship between the sides.
4. The left side will be an easily factored quadratic expression (a perfect square). Factor it.
5. Take the square root of both sides of the equation.
6. Solve for x.
7. Plug the solutions into the equation to verify them.

For example, we can use this to solve $x^2 - 8x + 7 = 0$:

Move the constant:	$x^2 - 8x = -7$
Add the square of half of the coefficient:	$x^2 - 8x + 16 = -7 + 16$
Factor the left side:	$(x - 4)^2 = 9$
Take the square root of both sides:	$x - 4 = \pm 3$
Solve for x:	$x = 7, 1$
Verify 7:	$7^2 - 8(7) + 7 = 49 - 56 + 7$
	$= -7 + 7 = 0$
Verify 1:	$1^2 - 8(1) + 7 = 1 - 8 + 7 = 0$

THE QUADRATIC FORMULA

The quadratic formula is:

$$x = \frac{-b \pm \sqrt{b^2 - 4ac}}{2a}$$

It can be used to find the zeros (or roots) of a quadratic equation. The values for a, b, and c come from the standard form of the equation ($ax^2 + bx + c = 0$). For example, in the equation $2x^2 - 12x + 16 = 0$, $a = 2$, $b = -12$, and $c = 16$:

$$x = \frac{12 \pm \sqrt{-12^2 - 4(2)(16)}}{2(2)}$$

$$x = \frac{12 \pm \sqrt{144 - 128}}{4}$$

$$x = \frac{12 \pm \sqrt{16}}{4}$$

$$x = \frac{12 \pm 4}{4}$$

$$x = \frac{16}{4}, \frac{8}{4}$$

$$x = 4, 2$$

LESSON 3: GRAPHING EQUATIONS

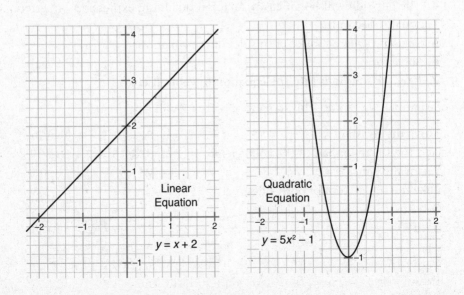

Linear Equation

$y = x + 2$

Quadratic Equation

$y = 5x^2 - 1$

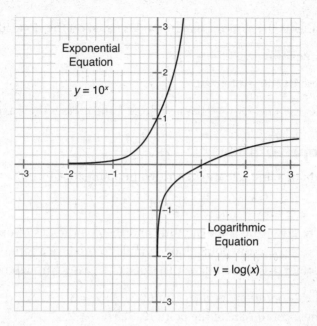

In the figures on page 172 and above, we can see that each of these kinds of equations has a recognizable shape when graphed. Linear equations produce straight lines that can slope up or down. Quadratic equations create "U-shaped" curves called parabolas, which can open upwards or downwards. Exponential equations create a "hockey stick" shape, and logarithmic equations create a reversed (or reflected) version of that shape. (This makes sense since logarithms invert exponent operations.)

STANDARD FORM

The standard for a linear equation (the equation of a line) is $ax + by = c$, where a, b, and c are all real numbers.

Slope-Intercept Equation

The equation of a line can be written in other ways. One of the most common methods is the slope-intercept equation:

$$y = mx + b$$

The slope-intercept formula for a line, or $y = mx + b$, includes 4 variables: y, m, x, and b

- x represents the x-coordinate of a point on the line.
- y represents the y-coordinate of a point on the line.

- m represents the slope of the line and is based on the slope formula $\frac{\Delta y}{\Delta x}$.
  The slope formula is $\left(\frac{y_2-y_1}{x_2-x_1}\right)$.
- b represents the y-intercept.

For example, the line $y = x - 4$ has a slope of 1 and crosses the y-axis at $(0, -4)$.

Point-Slope Formula

The equation of a line can also be written in point-slope form:

$$y - y_1 = m(x - x_1)$$

When you're given the slope of a line and the coordinates of one point on the line, you can use the point-slope formula to produce a formula in slope-intercept format. Assume a line with a slope of 2 passes through point $(2, 3)$:

- y_1 is the y-coordinate of the point $(2, 3)$, so $y_1 = 3$.
- x_1 is the x-coordinate of the point $(2, 3)$, so $x_1 = 2$.
- m is the slope of the line, so $m = 2$.

$$y - 3 = 2(x - 2)$$

- Rearrange the terms

$$y - 3 = 2x - 4 \rightarrow y = 2x - 1$$

RATE OF CHANGE

Whether a line on a graph is straight or curved depends on the equation's rate of change in y. If the change in y is constant from one point to another, the line will be straight. If the change in y increases or decreases from one point to another, the line will curve.

The average rate of change between two points on a line is equivalent to the *slope* of the line between those points. The things to remember about slope or rate of change are:

- Positive change goes up from left to right.
- Negative change goes down from left to right.
- "Steeper" lines indicate larger (faster) rates of change.
- "Flatter" lines indicate smaller (slower) rates of change.
- A flat horizontal line indicates no change.
- Rate of change = $\frac{y_2 - y_1}{x_2 - x_1}$ or $\frac{f(a) - f(b)}{a - b}$ (using function notation).

Linear equations have a constant rate of change, and they produce straight lines. There is no increase or decrease in the rate of change, so the line never becomes "steeper" or "flatter." It maintains a constant slope.

DISTANCE FORMULA

The distance formula can be used to determine the distance (d) between two points on the coordinate plane:

$$d = \sqrt{(x_2 - x_1)^2 + (y_2 - y_1)^2}$$

For example, if point X is at (2, 2) and point Y is at (12, 18), then we can find the distance between them with the distance formula:

$$d = \sqrt{(12-2)^2 + (18-2)^2} = \sqrt{100 + 256} = \sqrt{356} \approx 18.867962$$

In cases where you are given a graphed line and asked for the distance between points, it is likely that you will also be able to use Pythagorean theorem ($a^2 + b^2 = c^2$) to find the distance. Use the given line as the hypotenuse of a right triangle and extend straight lines from the endpoints until they intersect, which will form the triangle's legs. Count the units on the graph to determine the lengths of the legs and then use the theorem to find the hypotenuse.

EQUATION OF A CIRCLE

A circle with center (h, k) and radius (r) can be defined with an equation:

$$(x - h)^2 + (y - k)^2 = r^2$$

LESSON 4: INEQUALITIES

When we use phrases like "greater than" and "less than" to compare and order numbers, we are speaking in terms of *inequalities*. An inequality is a statement about a range of possible values for an unknown number relative to a known number, such as "a number greater than 5." Instead of identifying one specific value for the unknown number, we are identifying numbers that the unknown could equal. We're doing this by talking about numbers that the unknown does not equal. A number greater than 5 is not equal to 5. This is how inequalities got their name.

INCLUSIVE AND EXCLUSIVE INEQUALITIES

Inequalities define a range (or domain) of possible values starting with a specific, known number called an endpoint. An inclusive range includes the endpoint, and an exclusive range does not. Look at the following examples.

Inclusive: A number 4 or smaller

- It could be 3.99999, 2, 0.4, 0, –1, or any smaller number.
- It could be 4.
- The endpoint is included in the domain of possible values.
- Inclusive inequalities use greater than or equal to (GTE) and less than or equal to (LTE) comparisons.

Exclusive: A number greater than 5

- It could be 6, 7, 8, or any larger number.
- It could also be 5.1 or 5.2. It could even be 5.00000000001.
- It could not be 5, 4.9999999, or any smaller number.
- The endpoint is excluded from the domain of possible values.
- Exclusive inequalities use greater than (GT) and less than (LT) comparisons.

INEQUALITY SYMBOLS

$\neq$	Not equal to
$>$	Greater than
$<$	Less than
$\geq$	Greater than or equal to
$\leq$	Less than or equal to
$\bullet$	Inclusive endpoint
o	Exclusive endpoint

SIMPLE AND COMPOUND INEQUALITIES

SIMPLE INEQUALITY This is an inequality made up of a single comparing statement. An example is "a number less than 7."

COMPOUND INEQUALITY This is an inequality made up of two comparing statements joined by the word *and* or by the word *or*: One example is "a number greater than 2 **and** less than 8." Another is "a number less than or equal to 3 **or** greater than 6."

INEQUALITIES AND THE NUMBER LINE

Drawing inequalities on the number line means plotting the endpoint and then using arrows or line segments to describe the domain.

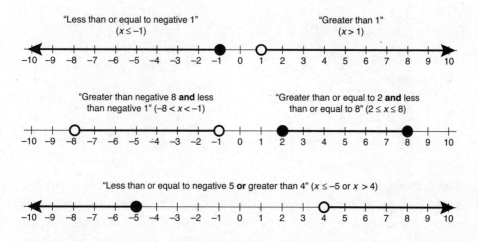

MANIPULATING INEQUALITIES

All of the rules for manipulating equations apply to inequalities as well:

$$2x + 5 > 21$$
$$2x > 16$$
$$x > 8$$

The rules apply for all inequality operators: $>$, $<$, $\geq$, and $\leq$.

One special case that applies only to inequalities relates to negative coefficients and negative denominators. When multiplying or dividing to simplify these sorts of inequalities, you must reverse the inequality sign:

$$-3x < 21$$

$$\frac{-3x}{-3} > \frac{21}{-3}$$

$$x > -7$$

$$\frac{x}{-5} \leq 4$$

$$\frac{-5}{1} \bullet \frac{x}{-5} \geq 4 \bullet -5$$

$$x \geq -20$$

GRAPHING INEQUALITIES

Inequalities in one or two variables can be graphed on the coordinate plane using lines and shaded regions:

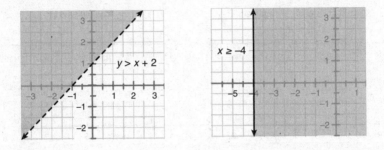

The shaded region indicates all the points that satisfy the inequality. The line represents the boundary of that region. Note the difference in the lines based on the operators. A "greater than" or "less than" will use a dotted line, because the inequality does not include the values that are represented by the line. A "greater than or equal to" or "less than or equal to" will use a solid line, because it does include those values.

LESSON 5: FUNCTIONS

A *function* is an expression that contains one variable: $3x - 2$. In *function notation* this would be expressed as $f(x) = 3x - 2$.

A given value for the variable x (input) will produce one and only one value for the function $f(x)$ (output):

Input (x)	Operation ($3x - 2$)	Output $f(x)$
0	$3(0) - 2 = -2$	-2
1	$3(1) - 2 = 1$	1
2	$3(2) - 2 = 4$	4
3	$3(3) - 2 = 7$	7
4	$3(4) - 2 = 10$	10
5	$3(5) - 2 = 13$	13

Since the value of the function depends on the value of the variable, the value of the function is called the *dependent variable*. The value of the variable is called the *independent variable*. These concepts play an important role in interpreting and graphing scientific data.

DOMAIN AND RANGE

DOMAIN The set of all allowed values for the variable in a function is the domain. Consider the function below:

$$f(x) = \frac{x+2}{x}$$

One of the laws of mathematics says that a rational expression may not have zero as a denominator. As a result, the domain of values for the function above is all real numbers except 0: $x \neq 0$

RANGE The set of possible values of the function, based on using all the values in the domain, is called the range.

MANIPULATING FUNCTIONS

Functions are represented with symbols. The most common symbol is the $f(\ )$ symbol, as seen in $f(x)$ or $f(y)$. These symbols can be treated like more familiar variables (x, y, z) when they appear in algebraic equations or expressions.

For example, if $f(x) = 25$, then we can evaluate $\frac{f(x)}{5} + 3$ by doing algebra. Divide 25 by 5 to get 5, then add 3 to get 8: $\frac{f(x)}{5} + 3 = 8$.

This can also work in the other direction. If $\frac{2}{3}f(x) - 4 = 20$, we can solve for $f(x)$ by using inverse operations as we do with other variables. Add 4 to both sides, then multiply by $\frac{3}{2}$.

$$f(x) = 36$$

LINEAR FUNCTIONS

A linear function is one in which the change in $f(x)$ is constant when the change in x is constant:

$$f(x) = 3x - 2$$

x	$f(x)$	change in $f(x)$
0	−2	—
1	1	3
2	4	3
3	7	3
4	10	3

Note that when x increases by 1, $f(x)$ increases by 3. This constant change in $f(x)$ is the sign of a linear function.

QUADRATIC FUNCTIONS

A quadratic function is one in which the change in $f(x)$ increases by a fixed amount when the change in x is constant:

$$f(x) = x^2 + 3x - 2$$

x	$f(x)$	change in $f(x)$
−3	−2	—
−2	−4	−2
−1	−4	0
0	−2	2
1	2	4
2	8	6
3	16	8

Note that when x increases by 1, $f(x)$ increases by 2 more than the previous row's increase. This sequential adding of 2 to the change in $f(x)$ is the sign of a quadratic function.

EXPONENTIAL FUNCTIONS

An exponential function is one in which the change in $f(x)$ increases proportionally (i.e., is multiplied by a fixed amount) when the change in x is constant:

$$f(x) = 5(2^x)$$

x	$f(x)$	change in $f(x)$
0	5	—
1	10	5
2	20	10
3	40	20
4	80	40

Note that when x increases by 1, $f(x)$ increases by double the previous row's increase. This sequential multiplication of the change in $f(x)$ is the sign of an exponential function.

INVERSE FUNCTIONS

An inverse function inverts or "reverses" the original function by producing the original function's inputs when applied to the original function's outputs. The notation for an inverse function is $f^{-1}(x)$ where $f(x)$ is the original function.

The table below shows the inputs and outputs for function $f(x) = 3x - 2$:

x	$f(x)$	change in $f(x)$
0	–2	—
1	1	3
2	4	3
3	7	3
4	10	3

The function $f(x)$ multiplies by 3 and subtracts 2. The inverse function would add 2 and divide by 3:

$$f^{1}(x) = \frac{x+2}{3}$$

x	$f^{-1}(x)$	change in $f^{-1}(x)$
0	$\frac{2}{3}$	—
1	1	$\frac{1}{3}$
2	$\frac{4}{3}$	$\frac{1}{3}$
3	$\frac{5}{3}$	$\frac{1}{3}$
4	2	$\frac{1}{3}$

Note that the change in $f^{-1}(x)$ is the inverse of the change in $f(x)$. $\frac{1}{3}$ is the inverse of 3.

LESSON 6: GRAPHING FUNCTIONS

Functions can be graphed using x for the x-coordinate and using $f(x)$ for the y-coordinate. This is expressed as $y = f(x)$, and each point has the coordinates $(x, f(x))$. To identify coordinates, perform the operations defined as $f(x)$ on a series of values for x (inputs) and record the resulting values for $f(x)$ (outputs).

- These ordered pairs become the (x, y) coordinates of points on the graph.
- Once the pairs are plotted, a line can be drawn to connect the points.
- Some lines are straight (linear equations), and some are not (quadratics, some functions).

GRAPHS OF FUNCTIONS

The graph below shows the function $y = f(x)$. It shows the values of $f(x)$ for a range of values for x from –3 to 3. The range of x-values graphed is called an *interval*.

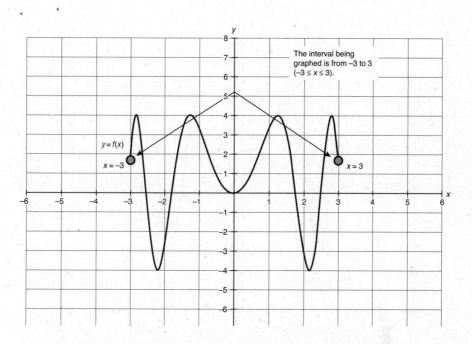

The interval being graphed is from –3 to 3 ($-3 \leq x \leq 3$).

$y = f(x)$

$x = -3$

$x = 3$

Even though we may not know what expression $f(x)$ represents, we can analyze the graph and draw some conclusions about some of the characteristics of the function based on things that we already know about the coordinate plane:

- y-coordinates above the x-axis are positive.
- y-coordinates below the x-axis are negative.
- y-coordinates on the x-axis are equal to zero.
- The highest point reached on the y-axis is the maximum (max) value for the y-coordinate.
- The lowest point reached on the y-axis is the minimum (min) value for the y-coordinate.

OPERATIONS ON FUNCTIONS (TRANSFORMATIONS)

The graph below shows $y = f(x)$. A reference point has been added at the center of the graph. Basic arithmetic functions can be applied to functions and/or to the variable within the function. These operations will affect either the curve's position or its shape.

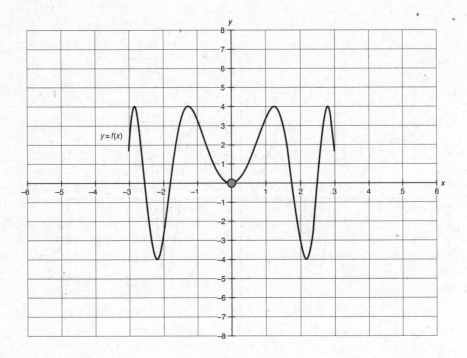

ADDING AND SUBTRACTING

Adding and subtracting affect the position of the function on the graph but leave the shape of the function unchanged. These operations can be performed on the function $f(x)$ or on the variable x.

Operations on the function $f(x)$ are applied outside the parentheses:

$$y = f(x) + 2$$

- Adding outside the parentheses causes a vertical shift in an upward direction.
- Subtracting outside causes a vertical shift in a downward direction.
- The shifts are vertical (along the y-axis), because an operation on $f(x)$ affects the value of the y-coordinate.

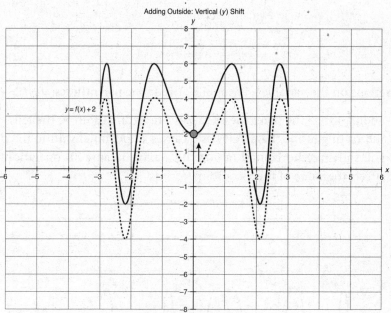

Adding Outside: Vertical (y) Shift

$y = f(x) + 2$

Reference Point moves +2 units (up)

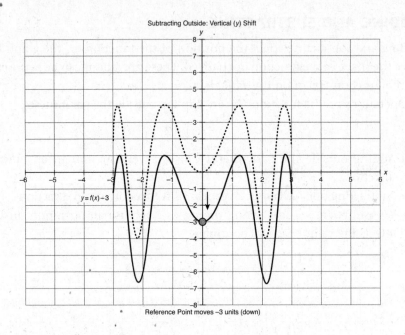

Subtracting Outside: Vertical (y) Shift

Reference Point moves –3 units (down)

Operations on the variable x are applied inside the parentheses: $y = f(x - 3)$

- Adding inside the parentheses causes a horizontal shift to the left.
- Subtracting inside the parentheses causes a horizontal shift to the right.
- The shifts are horizontal (along the x-axis) because an operation on x affects the value of the x-coordinate.

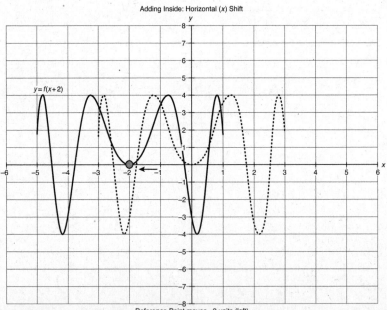

Adding Inside: Horizontal (x) Shift

Reference Point moves –2 units (left)

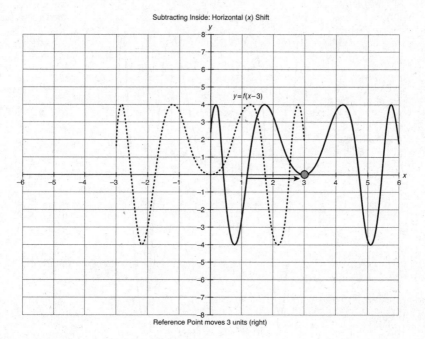

Subtracting Inside: Horizontal (x) Shift

$y = f(x-3)$

Reference Point moves 3 units (right)

MULTIPLYING AND DIVIDING

Multiplying and dividing affect the shape of the curve without changing the location of the center. Operations on $f(x)$ affect the height (or vertical range) of the curve. Operations on x affect the width of the curve:

- Multiplying outside the function causes vertical stretching.
- Dividing outside the function causes vertical compression.

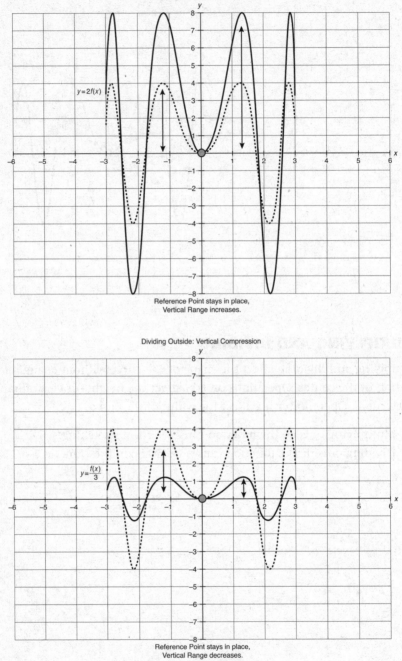

Multiplying Outside: Vertical Stretch

$y = 2f(x)$

Reference Point stays in place,
Vertical Range increases.

Dividing Outside: Vertical Compression

$y = \dfrac{f(x)}{3}$

Reference Point stays in place,
Vertical Range decreases.

- Multiplying inside the function causes horizontal compression.
- Dividing inside the function causes horizontal stretching.

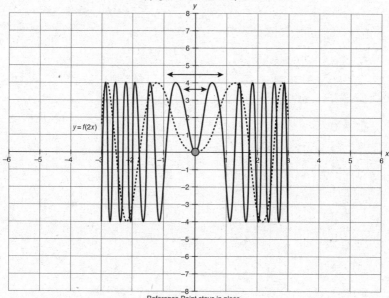

Multiplying Inside: Horizontal Compression

$y = f(2x)$

Reference Point stays in place,
Horizontal Range decreases.

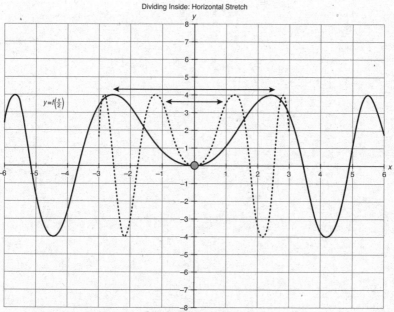

Dividing Inside: Horizontal Stretch

$y = f\left(\frac{x}{2}\right)$

Reference Point stays in place,
Horizontal Range increases.

Review Test

1. Translate and graph the following simple inequalities using the letter y for the unknown number. If needed, reverse the inequality so that y is always on the left side:

    a. y is less than or equal to 3

    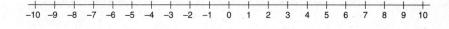

    b. 7 is greater than y

    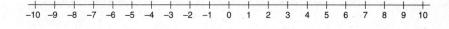

    c. −2 is less than y

    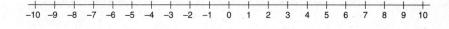

2. In the inequality "y is less than or equal to 5 and is greater than or equal to −2," the product of the endpoints will be which of the following?
    (A) odd
    (B) positive
    (C) negative
    (D) None of the above

191

QUESTIONS 3 AND 4 REFER TO THE FOLLOWING 3 EQUATIONS:

$$x = q^{11} \qquad y = q^7 \qquad z = q^{-2}$$

3. Which of the following expresses $\left(\dfrac{x}{y}\right)^3$ in terms of q?

   (A) q^{12}
   (B) q^{33}
   (C) q^{54}
   (D) q^{64}

4. Which of the following is equivalent to zx?

   (A) q^{13}
   (B) q^9
   (C) q^{-9}
   (D) q^{-13}

_____

5. $\sqrt{397}$ is between which numbers?

   (A) 18 and 19
   (B) 19 and 20
   (C) 20 and 21
   (D) 21 and 22

6. Simplify the following:

   a. 0.14×0.14

   b. $0.00225 \div 0.015$

7. Which of the following is equivalent to $(2.3 \times 10^{19}) \times (4.8 \times 10^{-14})$?

   (A) 11.04×10^6
   (B) 1.104×10^6
   (C) 71×10^6
   (D) 7.1×10^6

8. The graph below shows the values of the 8 points listed in the table.

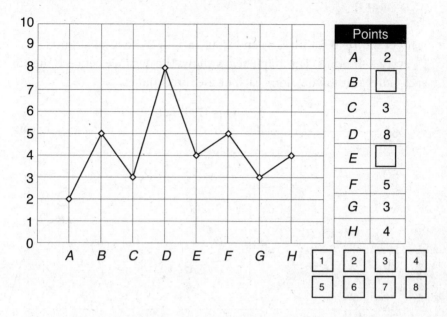

The values for two points, points *B* and *E*, are missing from the table.
Write numbers in the empty boxes to correctly complete the table.

QUESTIONS 9 AND 10 REFER TO THE FOLLOWING INFORMATION
AND GRAPH:

A hotel shuttle bus travels to and from each of three local airports (A, B, and
C) every four hours. The graph below shows the distance between the bus and
each hotel as it travels along each of the three routes.

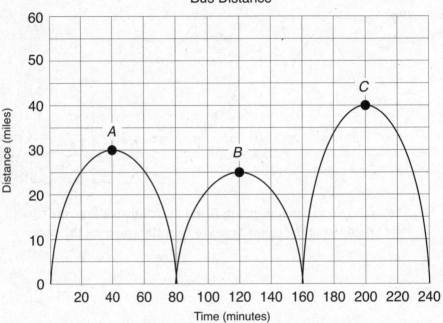

9. What is the distance, in miles, of the longest trip from the hotel to one
    of these three airports and back? Write your answer in the space below.
    Your answer may contain numbers, a negative sign, and/or a decimal
    point.

10. What is the average speed, in miles per hour, of the bus over the whole
    4-hour period? Write your answer in the space below. Your answer may
    contain numbers, a negative sign, and/or a decimal point.

11. In a cookie baking contest, the final score is weighted. Ratings from four pastry chef judges make up $\frac{3}{4}$ of the score, and a rating from one amateur cookie baker makes up $\frac{1}{4}$ of the score. A contestant's ratings from the pastry chef judges were 3.5, 4.0, 4.5, and 4.0. Her rating from the amateur cookie baker was a 5.0. In the equation below, use the numbers provided to write in the numbers in the empty boxes that correctly complete the expression needed to calculate the contestant's final score.

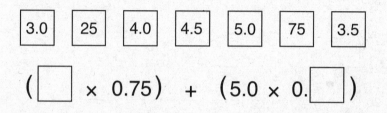

12. The graph below shows the values of the 8 points listed in the table. The names of two points are missing from the table. Write the missing letters in the empty boxes to correctly complete the table.

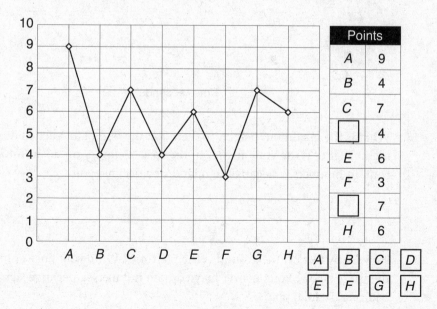

QUESTIONS 13 AND 14 REFER TO THE FOLLOWING INFORMATION
AND GRAPH:

A pumpkin is fired upward from a ground-level catapult into a basket on a
raised platform. The graph below shows the pumpkin's height, in feet, as it
travels.

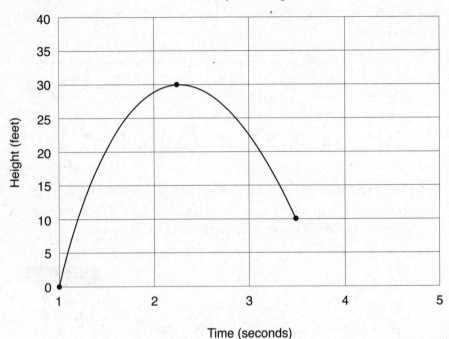

13. What is the maximum height, in feet, that the pumpkin reached dur-
    ing its flight? Write your answer in the space below. Your answer may
    contain numbers, a negative sign, and/or a decimal point.

14. How many feet off the ground is the platform? Write your answer in
    the space below. Your answer may contain numbers, a negative sign,
    and/or a decimal point.

15. A parking lot owner wanted to create a break schedule for her parking attendants based on the busier and slower times during the morning shift. She counted the number of vehicles coming in each hour between 5 A.M. and 12 P.M. and calculated that an average of 20 vehicles came into the lot each hour. She started to create a chart of incoming vehicles for each hour, but she didn't get a chance to finish it. Two vehicle counts are missing.

Choose two numbers, from the list of numbers below the chart, that could be the missing vehicle counts for the 6–7 A.M. and 10–11 A.M. slots respectively. Write your answers in the empty boxes to correctly complete the chart. Note that there may be more than one correct answer for each empty box.

Incoming Vehicles						
5–6 am	6–7 am	7–8 am	8–9 am	9–10 am	10–11 am	11 am–12 pm
10	☐	18	36	20	☐	26

14   30   20   16   34   10

Answers Explained

1. a. $y \leq 3$

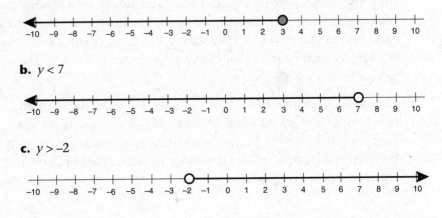

b. $y < 7$

c. $y > -2$

2. (C) When multiplying numbers with different signs, the product will be negative: $5 \times -2 = -10$

3. (A) Remember the rules for exponents with the same base: Multiplication means add the exponents together. Division means subtract the exponents. Raising a power to a power means multiply the exponents: $11 - 7 = 4 \rightarrow 4 \times 3 = 12$. The result is q^{12}.

4. (B) Remember the rules for exponents with the same base: Multiplication means add the exponents together. Division means subtract the exponents. Raising a power to a power means multiply the exponents: $11 + (-2) = 9$. The result is q^9.

5. (B) 397 is between 361 (19^2) and 400 (20^2).

6. a. 0.0196 When multiplying decimals, first multiply as usual. Then account for all decimal places in both factors by moving the decimal in the product to the left, adding zeros to the left end as needed.

b. 0.15 When dividing, move the decimal point in the divisor to the right until it is an integer. Then move the decimal point of the dividend the same number of places to the right. Divide as usual.

7. (B) Multiply the decimal numbers as usual: $2.3 \times 4.8 = 11.04$. Since this is multiplication, add the exponents of 10: $19 - 14 = 5$. Scientific notation conventionally puts the decimal point next to the units digit, which means we need one additional exponent of 10 to move the decimal point one place to the left: $11.04 \times 10^5 = 1.104 \times 10^6$

8. **B is 5 and E is 4** Use the scale on the vertical axis to determine the value of each point on the horizontal axis. Move up from B until it meets the graphed line, and then move left to the vertical axis to find the missing value. Repeat these steps for E.

9. **80** The longest of the three trips is the trip to Airport C, which is 40 miles away from the hotel. If it is a round trip (to the airport and back to the hotel), then the total length of the trip is double the distance, or 80 miles.

10. **47.5** The total distance traveled in the four-hour period is the sum of the three trips (60 miles + 50 miles + 80 miles), which equals 190 miles. The distance divided by the 4 hours of time (190 ÷ 4) gives 47.5 miles per hour.

11. **4.0 and 25** The contestant's average rating among the pastry chef judges is 4.0. This counts for 75% of the weighted average (three-fourths is equivalent to 0.75). The amateur cookie baker's rating, 5.0, counts for 25% of the weighted average (one-fourth is equivalent to 0.25). To calculate the weighted average, multiply the parts of the weighted average by the decimal equivalent of the weights, and then add the results together, as shown in the expression $(4.0 \times 0.75) + (5.0 \times 0.25)$.

12. **D and G** This question is similar to question 8, but this time you need to work in reverse. Compare the labels on the horizontal axis with the letters in the first column of the table to identify the two letters that are missing from the table. Verify each missing letter by comparing the value in the second column with the location of that point on the graph. The line reaches 4 on the vertical axis at points B and D. Since point B is already listed in the table, the missing value for 4 must be point D. The line reaches 7 on the vertical axis at points C and G. Since point C is already listed in the table, the missing value for 7 must be point G.

13. **30** The top (highest point) of the curve, which represents the pumpkin's height, is at 30 feet on the vertical axis.

14. **10** The curve, which represents the pumpkin's height, stops at 10 feet on the vertical axis. This stopping point is the time at which the pumpkin landed in the basket, which is on the platform, and stopped moving.

15. **20 and 10** or **16 and 14** The owner calculated the daily average to be 20 incoming vehicles per hour. This means that the total number of incoming vehicles for all 7 hours between 5 A.M. and 12 P.M. must be

140 incoming vehicles (7 × 20 = 140). The sum of the numbers on the chart (10 + 18 + 36 + 20 + 26) is 110. This means that the sum of the two missing numbers must be 30 (140 − 110 = 30). Any pair of numbers, from the list of numbers, that adds to 30 is a possible pair of values for the chart.

UNIT 3:
SOCIAL STUDIES

Social Studies Skills | 10

The GED® test tests your ability to read, interpret, and respond to social studies texts, maps, charts, graphs, and political cartoons. Five different types of items will be used to evaluate your literacy skills in social studies:

→ **MULTIPLE-CHOICE**

→ **DROP-DOWN**

→ **FILL-IN-THE-BLANK**

→ **DRAG-AND-DROP**

→ **HOT SPOT**

The following skills will be covered in this unit:

Lesson 1: Drawing Conclusions and Making Inferences

Lesson 2: Identifying Central Ideas and Drawing Conclusions

Lesson 3: Analyzing Events and Ideas

Lesson 4: Analyzing Language

Lesson 5: Integrating Content Presented in Different Ways

Lesson 6: Evaluating Reasoning and Evidence

LESSON 1: DRAWING CONCLUSIONS AND MAKING INFERENCES

Reading a social studies document is much like reading any other type of document. It requires the reader to be able to identify elements that are stated or implied by the text and to make reasonable assumptions based on the supplied information.

Details

Specific pieces of information in social studies documents, such as dates, locations, incidents, and so on, are known as details. The details are what support the larger idea of the passage. In other words, details are the proof in an argument and the happenings in the larger event.

Summaries

A way to be an active reader who summarizes is to think like a detective. When a crime takes place, the detective's job is to determine what has happened. While the detective is piecing together what transpired, he or she tries to find answers to the 5 Ws and 1 H. The 5 Ws and 1 H are:

Who?
What?
When?
Where?
Why?
How?

The answers to the above questions will outline the most important information in the passage. A summary is defined as a short restatement of the most important ideas in the passage. If you're able to assemble these answers into a sentence or two, you have just effectively summarized a passage.

Unstated Assumptions, Implications, and Inferences

Although some answers to questions can be found directly in the passages and excerpts, questions will often require the reader to determine what is suggested by the passage. In other words, you will have to read between the lines to answer these questions. You will have to make assumptions.

If you're reading an article about how the Constitution was adopted in Philadelphia, Pennsylvania, chances are the author is not going to explain that Pennsylvania is a state located on the East Coast of the United States of America. The author is going to assume that you already know this and therefore require no further explanation.

Another way passages convey information without directly stating it is through implication. An implication is when an author uses information to suggest something or indicate a particular belief. The author does not directly state the item or belief.

Although assumptions and implications are more about what the author does with the information at hand, inferences are more about what you as the reader do with the information. Making an inference requires the reader to look at the available information and data and then determine what reasonable conclusion can be made.

Evidence to Support Inference Analyses

When making inferences, you must be able to back up your belief with evidence. In other words, go with your gut but make sure that you have the solid facts to back it.

LESSON 2: IDENTIFYING CENTRAL IDEAS AND DRAWING CONCLUSIONS

Central Ideas

The central idea of a social studies passage is the central idea of the paragraph or passage; it is the main point that the author is trying to convey. All the other elements in the passage are known as supporting details. Details are pieces of evidence that support the central idea.

Think of the central idea as the roof of a house and the supporting details as the beams. The central idea covers all the supporting details like a roof covers the beams. The supporting details uphold the central idea like the beams support and hold up the roof.

The central or main idea can be found in various places. Most of the time, it is located in the first sentence or two. Sometimes it is at the end of the passage. Occasionally, it is not stated at all.

Drawing Conclusions

Drawing a conclusion utilizes many of the components we've already discussed. After you recognize the details and central idea and have asked yourself the 5 Ws and 1 H, you can look at the evidence and ask, "What does this mean?" Like a detective, the evidence is put together to form a conclusion about what the evidence means.

LESSON 3: ANALYZING EVENTS AND IDEAS

Compare and Contrast

Comparing and contrasting have different meanings. Very often people say "compare" when they really mean "contrast." When we compare two things, we describe the ways in which they are similar. For example, both a dog and a cat have four legs and fur. When we contrast two things, we describe the ways in which they are different. For example, a dog barks, but a cat purrs. Make sure you distinguish between questions that are asking you to compare and questions that are asking you to contrast.

Cause and Effect

A cause is an action, and an effect is what happens as a result of that action. Although this may seem simple and straightforward, cause-and-effect relationships can often be confusing because an effect of one action may be the cause of another action.

Chronological Order and Sequence

Chronological order means putting things in time order. Sequence simply means putting things in the order in which they belong. In terms of your ability to read well, understand social studies passages, and write well, you must be able to think sequentially. In order to understand a situation fully, you need to understand the order in which the events took place.

LESSON 4: ANALYZING LANGUAGE

Bias and Propaganda

Authors don't always write objectively. Sometimes they want to push an agenda. They try to convince others of something in order to achieve some objective. Bias exists when an author does not give a balanced, objective description of an issue. This may be intentional or unintentional. Propaganda is material that is purposefully misleading. It is usually used to promote a particular political agenda.

Credibility

How do we know if the individual who has authored a passage is credible? Unfortunately, determining an author's credibility is often difficult without doing further research. However, you can look for certain things in the writing to determine the author's credibility:

- Has the author cited facts?
- Has the author avoided using his or her opinion as evidence?
- Has the author given data from a reputable source?
- Is the author affiliated with a reputable organization?

If the answer to all of these questions is "yes," there is a good chance that the material is credible and that the information is likely to be objective.

Meaning of Symbols, Words, and Phrases

Whether in fiction or in nonfiction, symbols, words, and phrases very often have meanings not found in a dictionary. You must analyze these symbols, words, and phrases in order to fully understand the meaning of the text. For example, if the author writes, "That's water under the bridge," he or she is not talking about either water or bridges. That phrase means the topic or subject is over and cannot be changed.

LESSON 5: INTEGRATING CONTENT PRESENTED IN DIFFERENT WAYS

ANALYSIS OF MAPS, GRAPHIC ORGANIZERS, TABLES, AND CHARTS

When analyzing maps, graphic organizers, tables, and charts, it is important to look at all of the information available. First, look for any headings or titles as they can provide a concise overview of the data. Second, look at any labels. They will indicate the specific type of data being displayed. Third, look to see if there is a key of some type. It will define any symbols you may encounter. Finally, look at the big picture and ask yourself, "What is the central idea of this information?" Following these steps will help you fully analyze and understand what is being displayed.

TRENDS IN DATA

The exam is going to test your ability, not only to locate specific pieces of data, but to identify trends as well. The word *trend* simply refers to the direction in which something is moving. If housing costs are trending upward, this means the costs are increasing.

MAPS

When analyzing maps, examine all the information provided. See if there is a title, a legend or key, and labels. Additionally, make sure you read all passages that correspond with the map as they may contain valuable information and help you further analyze the map.

TABLES

Look at the table below. What sort of information is it giving you? Look at the title, the column headings, and the units. If a question asked you to find how many billions of dollars of Chinese imports came into the U.S. in 2004, you would go to the column heading labeled "China Imports" and go down to the year 2004. The table indicates that $44.66 billion in Chinese imports came into the U.S. in 2004.

Statistical Discrepancy of Westbound Trade

Year	U.S. Exports	China Imports	Bilateral Discrepancy	Discrepancy in Percentage
2000	16.25	22.36	6.11	27.3%
2004	34.72	44.66	9.94	22.3%
2006	55.22	59.21	3.99	6.7%

Unit: Billions of U.S. Dollars

Source: "Research Report on the Statistical Discrepancy of Merchandise Trade between the United States and China." *United States Census Bureau.* Last accessed September 7, 2016. *www.census.gov/foreign-trade/aip/recon_china_000406.pdf.*

POLITICAL CARTOONS

One unique graphic you will be asked to interpret and analyze is a political cartoon. Carefully review each symbol, name, and characteristic in the image. Often, political figures are drawn with exaggerated features. The artist uses one or more of the following techniques to convey his or her opinion about the subject: analogy, labels, symbolism, irony, and/or exaggeration.

Analogy

With an analogy, the artist compares two objects, people, or situations that are not alike. For example, the artist may draw a bonfire with piles of money to represent wasteful spending.

Labels

Labels are a more direct way to identify objects or people in the cartoon. The artist simply writes the name of a person, object, document, or place to clearly identify it in the cartoon.

Symbolism

Just as symbolism is found in literature, an artist uses an object or symbol to represent an idea in his or her cartoon. Sometimes these symbols are labeled, which makes analyzing the cartoon even easier, but most of the time they are not. For example, an artist may use a donkey to represent a Democrat and an elephant to represent a Republican in the cartoon.

Irony

Usually humorous, irony uses words or images to describe the exact opposite. For example, a team of scientists with the label "Global Warming Research" may be wearing heavy coats in a snow storm and have shocked looks on their faces. They expected warmer temperatures but discovered the exact opposite. That's irony.

Exaggeration

Probably the most common technique artists use to make a point is exaggeration. Almost every political cartoon depicting a president exaggerates a facial feature to make the president recognizable.

LESSON 6: EVALUATING REASONING AND EVIDENCE

When an author writes about a particular topic, the author often reveals a great deal about himself or herself. The passages that you'll encounter on the Social Studies subject test will be informational texts. However, they may not be objective. The author may shed light on his or her values by using both fact and opinion to make a point.

Fact and Opinion

The differences between a fact and an opinion can be confusing. You must consider the choices carefully when encountering a question that deals with a fact and an opinion. Remember that a fact has objective truth. In other words, a fact can't be argued about. In contrast, an opinion is how someone feels about a fact. For example, it is a fact that the stock market crashed in 1929. However, it is an opinion that the government should have done something to prevent the crash. One cannot argue that the stock market didn't crash in 1929. However, one could argue that the United States government should have done more to prevent the crash.

Reasoned Judgment

When a person makes a reasoned judgment, he or she is using both fact and opinion in the argument. Reasoned judgment involves taking one side of an argument by using facts to support that position.

Unsupported Claims and Informed Hypotheses

We've all heard the old adage, "Don't believe everything you hear." This holds true for the passages you will read on the Social Studies subject test. Secondary sources, such as editorials, may take one side or the other on a particular issue and make certain claims. Instead of using reasoned judgment, though, they make a claim and do not provide the needed evidence to support the claim.

In contrast to an unsupported claim, an informed hypothesis is rooted in fact. Sufficient evidence is provided to support the hypothesis.

Review Test

▀▄▀▄▀▄▀▄▀▄▀▄▀▄▀▄▀▄▀▄▀▄▀▄▀▄▀▄▀▄▀▄▀▄▀▄

> **DIRECTIONS:** This practice exam contains passages, maps, charts, graphs, and political cartoons, which you will need to analyze in order to answer the questions that follow.

QUESTIONS 1 THROUGH 3 ARE BASED ON THE FOLLOWING PASSAGE:

PRESS RELEASE ANNOUNCING
U.S. RECOGNITION OF ISRAEL (1948)

In 1917 Chaim Weizmann, scientist, statesperson, and supporter of the effort to establish a state of Israel, persuaded the British government to issue a statement favoring the establishment of a Jewish national home in Palestine. The statement, which became known as the Balfour Declaration, was, in part, payment to the Jews for their support of the British against the Turks during World War I. After the war, the League of Nations ratified the declaration and in 1922 appointed Britain to rule Palestine.

This course of events caused Jews to be optimistic about the eventual establishment of a homeland. Their optimism inspired the immigration to Palestine of Jews from many countries, particularly from Germany when Nazi persecution of Jews began. The arrival of many Jewish immigrants in the 1930s awakened Arab fears that Palestine would become a national homeland for the Jews. By 1936 guerrilla fighting had broken out between the Jews and the Arabs. Unable to maintain peace, Britain issued a white paper in 1939 that restricted Jewish immigration into Palestine. The Jews, feeling betrayed, bitterly opposed the policy and looked to the United States for support.

While President Franklin D. Roosevelt appeared to be sympathetic to the Jewish cause, his assurances to the Arabs that the United States would not intervene without consulting both parties caused public uncertainty about his position. When Harry S. Truman took office, he made clear that his sympathies were with the Jews and accepted the Balfour Declaration, explaining that it was in keeping with former President Woodrow Wilson's principle of "self-determination." Truman initiated several studies of the Palestine situation that supported his belief that, as a result of the Holocaust, Jews were oppressed and also in need of a homeland. Throughout the Roosevelt and Truman administrations, the Departments of War and State, recognizing the possibility of a Soviet-Arab connection and the potential Arab restriction on oil supplies to this country, advised against U.S. intervention on behalf of the Jews.

Britain and the United States, in a joint effort to examine the dilemma, established the "Anglo-American Committee of Inquiry." In April 1946 the committee submitted recommendations that Palestine not be dominated by either Arabs or Jews. It concluded that attempts to establish nationhood or independence would result in civil strife; that a trusteeship agreement aimed at bringing Jews and Arabs together should be established by the United Nations; that full Jewish immigration be allowed into Palestine; and that two autonomous states be established with a strong central government to control Jerusalem, Bethlehem, and the Negev, the southernmost section of Palestine.

British, Arab, and Jewish reactions to the recommendations were not favorable. Britain, anxious to rid itself of the problem, set the United Nations in motion, formally requesting on April 2, 1947, that the UN General Assembly set up the Special Committee on Palestine (UNSCOP). This committee recommended that the British mandate over Palestine be ended and that the territory be partitioned into two states. Jewish reaction was mixed—some wanted control of all of Palestine; others realized that partition spelled hope for their dream of a homeland. The Arabs were not at all agreeable to the UNSCOP plan. In October the Arab League Council directed the governments of its member states to move troops to the Palestine border. Meanwhile, President Truman instructed the State Department to support the UN plan, and it reluctantly did so. On November 29, 1947, the partition plan was passed by the UN General Assembly.

At midnight on May 14, 1948, the Provisional Government of Israel proclaimed a new State of Israel. On that same date, the United States, in the person of President Truman, recognized the provisional Jewish government as de facto authority of the Jewish state (de jure recognition was extended on January 31, 1949). The U.S. delegates to the UN and top-ranking State Department officials were angered that Truman released his recognition statement to the press without notifying them first. On May 15, 1948, the first day of Israeli Independence and exactly one year after UNSCOP was established, Arab armies invaded Israel and the first Arab-Israeli war began.

Source: "Press Release Announcing U.S. Recognition of Israel (1948)." *Our Documents*. Last accessed July 27, 2016. *www.ourdocuments.gov/doc.php?doc=83*.

1. According to the passage, the establishment of Israel was _____.

2. The passage suggests that the United States supported which of the following?
   (A) the Arabs
   (B) the Jews
   (C) the Soviets
   (D) the Palestinians

3. Which of the following was the initial catalyst for the formation of a Jewish state?
   (A) President Truman's recognition of Israel
   (B) the British government's support of the creation of a Jewish state
   (C) President Roosevelt's policies
   (D) UNSCOP

QUESTIONS 4 THROUGH 6 ARE BASED ON THE FOLLOWING PASSAGE AND CHART:

SUSTAINABILITY AND THE EPA

Sustainability is based on a simple principle: Everything that we need for our survival and well-being depends, either directly or indirectly, on our natural environment. Sustainability creates and maintains the conditions under which humans and nature can exist in productive harmony, that permit fulfilling the social, economic and other requirements of present and future generations.

Sustainability is important to making sure that we have and will continue to have, the water, materials, and resources to protect human health and our environment.

Sustainability has emerged as a result of significant concerns about the unintended social, environmental, and economic consequences of rapid population growth, economic growth and consumption of our natural resources. In its early years, EPA acted primarily as the nation's environmental watchdog, striving to ensure that industries met legal requirements to control pollution. In subsequent years, EPA began to develop theory, tools, and practices that enabled it to move from controlling pollution to preventing it.

Today EPA aims to make sustainability the next level of environmental protection by drawing on advances in science and technology to protect human health and the environment, and promoting innovative green business practices.

Energy Efficiency	Reduce energy intensity 30 percent by 2015, compared to an FY 2003 baseline.
Greenhouse Gases	Reduce greenhouse gas emissions through reduction of energy intensity 30 percent by 2015, compared to an FY 2003 baseline.
Renewable Power	At least 50 percent of current renewable energy purchases must come from new renewable sources (in service after January 1, 1999).
Building Performance	Construct or renovate buildings in accordance with sustainability strategies, including resource conservation, reduction, and use; siting; and indoor environmental quality.
Water Conservation	Reduce water consumption intensity 16 percent by 2015, compared to an FY 2007 baseline.
Vehicles	Increase purchase of alternative fuel, hybrid, and plug-in hybrid vehicles when commercially available.
Petroleum Conservation	Reduce petroleum consumption in fleet vehicles by 2 percent annually through 2015, compared to an FY 2005 baseline.
Alternative Fuel	Increase use of alternative fuel consumption by at least 10 percent annually, compared to an FY 2005 baseline.
Pollution Prevention	Reduce use of chemicals and toxic materials and purchase lower risk chemicals and toxic materials.
Procurement	Expand purchases of environmentally sound goods and services, including biobased products.
Electronics Management	Annually, 95 percent of electronic products purchased must meet Electronic Product Environmental Assessment Tool standards where applicable; enable Energy Star® features on 100 percent of computers and monitors; and reuse, donate, sell, or recycle 100 percent of electronic products using environmentally sound management practices.

Source: "Sustainability and the EPA." *United States Environmental Protection Agency.* Last accessed July 27, 2016. *www.epa.gov.*

4. Indoor environmental quality relates to [Select ∨] .

   (A) procurement
   (B) vehicles
   (C) building performance
   (D) energy efficiency

5. Which of the following does NOT have to do with oil conservation?
   (A) water conservation
   (B) alternative fuel
   (C) electronics management
   (D) renewable power

6. Sustainability has to do with the protection of the _____.

QUESTIONS 7 AND 8 ARE BASED ON THE FOLLOWING PASSAGE:

THE TRUMAN DOCTRINE (1947)

. . . I am fully aware of the broad implications involved if the United States extends assistance to Greece and Turkey, and I shall discuss these implications with you at this time.

One of the primary objectives of the foreign policy of the United States is the creation of conditions in which we and other nations will be able to work out a way of life free from coercion. This was a fundamental issue in the war with Germany and Japan. Our victory was won over countries which sought to impose their will, and their way of life, upon other nations.

To ensure the peaceful development of nations, free from coercion, the United States has taken a leading part in establishing the United Nations. The United Nations is designed to make possible lasting freedom and independence for all its members. We shall not realize our objectives, however, unless we are willing to help free peoples to maintain their free institutions and their national integrity against aggressive movements that seek to impose upon them totalitarian regimes. This is no more than a frank recognition that totalitarian regimes imposed on free peoples, by direct or indirect aggression, undermine the foundations of international peace and hence the security of the United States.

The peoples of a number of countries of the world have recently had totalitarian regimes forced upon them against their will. The Government of the United States has made frequent protests against coercion and intimidation, in violation of the Yalta agreement, in Poland, Rumania, and Bulgaria. I must also state that in a number of other countries there have been similar developments.

At the present moment in world history nearly every nation must choose between alternative ways of life. The choice is too often not a free one.

One way of life is based upon the will of the majority, and is distinguished by free institutions, representative government, free elections, guarantees of individual liberty, freedom of speech and religion, and freedom from political oppression.

The second way of life is based upon the will of a minority forcibly imposed upon the majority. It relies upon terror and oppression, a controlled press and radio; fixed elections, and the suppression of personal freedoms.

I believe that it must be the policy of the United States to support free peoples who are resisting attempted subjugation by armed minorities or by outside pressures.

I believe that we must assist free peoples to work out their own destinies in their own way.

I believe that our help should be primarily through economic and financial aid which is essential to economic stability and orderly political processes. . . .

Source: "The Truman Doctrine (1947)." *Our Documents.* Last accessed July 27, 2016. *www.ourdocuments.gov/doc.php?doc=81&page=transcript.*

7. The main goal of the United Nations is to

Select ∨
(A) ensure lasting peace
(B) remain aligned with the United States
(C) prevent the spread of communism
(D) ensure that all people of the world have some of the same rights

8. President Truman states, "One way of life is based upon the will of the majority, and is distinguished by free institutions, representative government, free elections, guarantees of individual liberty, freedom of speech and religion, and freedom from political oppression." Which of the following is a philosophy NOT expressed in this statement?
    (A) democracy
    (B) natural rights
    (C) totalitarianism
    (D) independence

QUESTIONS 9 AND 10 ARE BASED ON THE FOLLOWING MAP, GRAPH, AND PASSAGE:

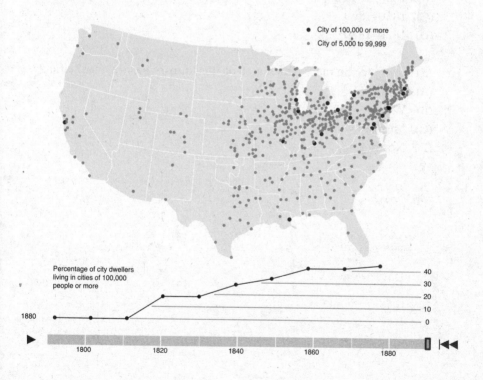

The number and size of cities increased dramatically between 1790 and 1890 as the country's population grew and became increasingly urban. By 1890, people living in cities of 100,000 or more made up a larger proportion of all urban dwellers. This reflected a shift from a rural, agrarian society to one focused on industrial production, especially in the Northeast and around the Great Lakes.

Source: "Percentage of City Dwellers from 1790 to 1890." *United States Census Bureau.* Last accessed July 28, 2016. *www.census.gov.*

9. According to the map, graph, and passage, during which period of time did the nation see the greatest increase in urban population?
   (A) 1810–1820
   (B) 1830–1840
   (C) 1850–1860
   (D) 1870–1880

10. According to the map, which area of the country has the most cities?
   (A) South
   (B) West
   (C) Midwest
   (D) Northeast

QUESTION 11 IS BASED ON THE FOLLOWING POLITICAL CARTOON:

11. What opinion is being expressed in the political cartoon above?
    (A) Income tax reform has made filing confusing.
    (B) You need to work with many numbers when filing your taxes.
    (C) Some people will owe as much as $6 billion.
    (D) There are few provisions for income taxes.

QUESTIONS 12 AND 13 ARE BASED ON THE FOLLOWING TABLE:

Consumer Price Index—Average Price Data
Original Data Value

Series Id: APU000074712

Area: U.S. city average

Item: Gasoline, leaded regular (cost per gallon/3.8 liters)

Years: 1981 to 1991

Year	Jan	Feb	Mar	Apr	May	Jun	Jul	Aug	Sep	Oct	Nov	Dec
1981	1.238	1.321	1.352	1.344	1.333	1.324	1.315	1.310	1.305	1.299	1.297	1.293
1982	1.285	1.260	1.206	1.148	1.166	1.242	1.263	1.254	1.236	1.219	1.207	1.181
1983	1.150	1.099	1.064	1.131	1.177	1.197	1.207	1.203	1.189	1.172	1.156	1.146
1984	1.131	1.125	1.125	1.145	1.154	1.147	1.129	1.116	1.120	1.127	1.124	1.109
1985	1.060	1.041	1.071	1.119	1.144	1.153	1.154	1.143	1.129	1.117	1.123	1.123
1986	1.107	1.034	0.894	0.815	0.852	0.885	0.822	0.778	0.797	0.771	0.762	0.764
1987	0.806	0.848	0.856	0.879	0.888	0.906	0.921	0.946	0.940	0.931	0.928	0.912
1988	0.881	0.859	0.850	0.883	0.911	0.910	0.923	0.945	0.933	0.910	0.904	0.885
1989	0.876	0.886	0.907	1.047	1.098	1.093	1.075	1.034	1.007	1.001	0.975	0.961
1990	1.006	1.011	0.999	1.027	1.044	1.077	1.089	1.198	1.297	1.354	1.351	1.335
1991	1.246	1.137	1.047	1.062								

12. From 1982 to 1986, gas prices were relatively _____.

13. What was the average price per gallon for regular gasoline in July 1989?
     (A) $1.075
     (B) $1.089
     (C) $1.062
     (D) $0.961

QUESTIONS 14 AND 15 ARE BASED ON THE FOLLOWING PASSAGES:

CHECK FOR THE PURCHASE OF ALASKA (1868)

In 1866 the Russian government offered to sell the territory of Alaska to the United States. Secretary of State William H. Seward, enthusiastic about the prospects of American Expansion, negotiated the deal for the Americans. Edouard de Stoeckl, Russian minister to the United States, negotiated for the Russians. On March 30, 1867, the two parties agreed that the United States would pay Russia $7.2 million for the territory of Alaska.

For less than 2 cents an acre, the United States acquired nearly 600,000 square miles. Opponents of the Alaska Purchase persisted in calling it "Seward's Folly" or "Seward's Icebox" until 1896, when the great Klondike Gold Strike convinced even the harshest critics that Alaska was a valuable addition to American territory.

The check for $7.2 million was made payable to the Russian Minister to the United States Edouard de Stoeckl, who negotiated the deal for the Russians. . . . [T]he Treaty of Cession, signed by Tzar Alexander II, . . . formally concluded the agreement for the purchase of Alaska from Russia.

Source: "Check for the Purchase of Alaska (1868)." *Our Documents.* Last accessed July 27, 2016. *www.ourdocuments.gov/doc.php?doc=41.*

JOINT RESOLUTION TO PROVIDE FOR ANNEXING THE HAWAIIAN ISLANDS TO THE UNITED STATES (1898)

In the 1890s, the efforts of the Hawaiian people to preserve their national sovereignty and native heritage ran headlong into the unstoppable force of American expansionism. Throughout the 19th century, westerners—particularly Americans—came to dominate Hawaii's economy and politics. When Queen Liliuokalani assumed the throne in 1891 and tried to reassert the power of the throne and the will of Native Hawaiians, she was deposed by a small group of American businessmen, with the support of the American diplomats and the U.S. Navy.

Although even President Cleveland challenged the legitimacy of this takeover, it did stand. To a nation poised to take its place as a world power, the control of Hawaii, strategically located to serve as a mid-Pacific naval installation, seemed crucial. In 1898, with a naval base firmly established at Pearl Harbor, the United States officially annexed Hawaii.

Source: "Joint Resolution to Provide for Annexing the Hawaiian Islands to the United States (1898)." *Our Documents.* Last accessed July 27, 2016. *www.ourdocuments.gov/doc.php?doc=54.*

14. Which of the following is a benefit of the purchase of Alaska that Seward could NOT have foreseen?
    (A) During the Cold War, the United States had territory strategically close to the Soviet Union.
    (B) Many organizations would protest drilling for oil in the arctic.
    (C) Ice manufacturers would relocate to Alaska.
    (D) Many species of animals indigenous to Alaska would become endangered.

15. How did the acquisition of Alaska differ from the acquisition of the Hawaiian Islands?
    (A) Alaska was purchased, whereas Hawaii was taken by force.
    (B) Sums of money were paid for both.
    (C) In both cases, the United States doubled its total area.
    (D) Alaska was acquired through war, whereas Hawaii was purchased.

Answers Explained

1. **"Controversial"** or any similar word would be the best answer.

2. **(B)** According to the passage, the United States supported the Jews. Choices A, C, and D are incorrect. While the passage mentions all of these groups, it does not indicate that the United States supported them.

3. **(B)** The first paragraph states that Chaim Weizmann was able to persuade the British government to favor the creation of a Jewish state. Choices A, C, and D are incorrect because no evidence is provided to support these answers.

4. **(C)** The chart indicates that building performance has to do with, among other things, indoor environmental quality. Choice A is incorrect because procurement has to do with purchasing. Choice B is incorrect because vehicles have to do with the way cars are built. Choice D is incorrect because energy efficiency has to do with the overall performance of machinery.

5. **(A)** Water conservation is not directly part of oil conservation. Choices B, C, and D all are directly involved with oil conservation.

6. **"Environment"** or any similar word would be the best answer.

7. **(A)** The third paragraph states the main goal of the United Nations. Choices B, C, and D are incorrect because these are not the main goals of the United Nations.

8. **(C)** Totalitarianism is complete control by a ruler. That philosophy is not expressed in President Truman's statement. Choices A, B, and D are incorrect because they are all expressed in the statement.

9. **(A)** The steepest part of the graph is from 1810 to 1820, indicating the most rapid growth. Choices B, C, and D are incorrect.

10. **(D)** The highest concentration of dots, which indicates cities, is in the Northeast.

11. **(B)** The swirling numbers and pieces of scrap paper indicate that people have to work with many numbers when filing their taxes. Choices A, C, and D are incorrect because no evidence supports these answers.

12. **"Stable"** or any similar word would be acceptable.

13. **(A)** According to the table, regular gasoline averaged $1.075 per gallon in July 1989.

14. **(A)** During the Cold War, the proximity of Alaska to the Soviet Union was advantageous for the United States. Choice B is incorrect. Protesters are not advantageous. Choices C and D are incorrect because no evidence supports these answers.

15. **(A)** The first passage states the amount that the United States paid for Alaska. The second passage states that American diplomats and the U.S. Navy deposed Queen Liliuokalani. Choices B, C, and D are not supported by both passages.

UNIT 4:
SCIENCE

Science Overview

11

The GED® test is an assessment of reasoning skills. It values your ability to explain your reasoning much more than it values your ability to repeat recalled (remembered) information. In other words, the test is much more about how you think than which facts you know. The test will provide source materials for you to review and will ask you questions based on them. You'll answer the questions and support your answers using evidence (facts) from the source materials. The Science subject test contains the following question types:

→ **MULTIPLE-CHOICE**
→ **FILL-IN-THE-BLANK**
→ **DROP-DOWN**
→ **HOT SPOT**
→ **DRAG-AND-DROP**
→ **SHORT-ANSWER**

The following sections will be covered in this unit:

Life Science

Physical Science

Earth and Space Science

Understanding Science

SCIENTIFIC REASONING: THINK LIKE A SCIENTIST

The Science subject test measures scientific reasoning. This means that the materials and questions will be related to subjects in science. To do well on the Science subject test, you'll need to use science-related source materials to answer questions the way a scientist would. The lessons in this unit of the book will help you learn to think like a scientist.

Remember that you will not have to learn four years' worth of science facts in order to be ready for the exam. Keep this point in mind when you're looking over the subject matter. You are expected to have a *general* understanding of science topics, not a detailed understanding. Always focus on the big picture. You just need to be familiar enough with the concepts that you can use when they are presented on the exam.

Be Analytical

Analytical skills are critically important on the Science subject test. "Analysis" is a formal word that describes a process of careful examination. It answers the question "What does this information tell me?" To analyze something means to:

- Look at it closely and break it down into its components (parts).
- Identify the relationships among the parts, such as cause and effect.
- Compare multiple items and identify relationships, similarities, and differences.

Scientists analyze everything. They analyze measurements and other observations, looking for structures, patterns, trends, and other relationships. They use this analysis to help them develop questions, answers, and experiments. They analyze work done by other scientists, including the data and experimental design. They do all this to see if the data could be useful in their own work and to see if they agree with the other scientists' conclusions.

In many cases, analysis requires scientists to work with information from more than one source. Therefore, scientists must compare these sources to identify relationships, similarities, and differences. The comparison may be between the findings of two different scientists, the results from two different experiments, or the design of experiments themselves. The ability to compare and contrast information from multiple sources is an important analytical skill.

SUBJECT MATTER

The Science subject test will include source materials from three areas of science:

- Life Science (40%)
- Physical Science (40%)
- Earth and Space Science (20%)

Life science includes biology and related subjects. It focuses on the study of living things, from simple, single-celled organisms to mammals and other more complex forms of life.

Physical science includes chemistry and related subjects. It focuses on the physical materials (sometimes called "matter").

Earth and space science includes geology and related subjects. It focuses on the study of our planet, our solar system, and the galaxy and universe beyond.

Major Themes

Throughout the Science subject test, questions will be related to two major themes:

- Human life/living things
- Energy systems

When examining source information, questions, or answer choices, pay attention to any references to these themes. Information related to how living things interact or how energy is transferred within systems will usually be contained in the correct answer.

Life Science 12

LESSON 1: ORGANISMS

Living things are called **organisms**. There are many different types of organisms. Some are very large and complex (like humans), and some are smaller and simpler (like bacteria). What makes something alive? For the purposes of the Science subject test, something is alive if it meets all of the following requirements.

- It maintains a balanced internal environment. This is called **homeostasis**, and humans do it when we sweat to maintain a steady body temperature.

- It has an **organized structure** consisting of one or more **cells**. In humans, these cells are grouped into **tissues**, which form the basis for **organs** (like the heart, liver, or kidneys). Organs are collected into **systems**, like the **respiratory** system that supports breathing. Bacteria are much simpler, consisting of simply one cell.

- It can **transform energy** into a form it can use to sustain itself. Plants do this when they convert sunlight to nutrients during **photosynthesis**. Humans do this when we eat and **digest** food.

- It **grows**, meaning that its systems and individual parts increase in size. Plants grow.

- It can respond to changes in its external environment. This is often indicated by the ability to move. Plants turn to face the sun. Humans react to things we see, hear, feel, taste, or touch. Changes in the external environment are called **stimuli**.

- It can produce new organisms and pass on genetic material through a **replication** (copying) process called **reproduction**. In some cases, reproduction involves a single parent. That is called **asexual** reproduction. For example, bacteria reproduce asexually. In other cases, reproduction involves two parents who both contribute genetic material to the **offspring**. That is called **sexual** reproduction. Humans reproduce sexually.

- It can **adapt** to its external environment by changing over time. The **theory of evolution** states that humans and all other living things have done this over very long periods of time.
- Unfortunately, a living thing can also die, proof that something is an organism.

CELLS

All organisms are made up of fundamental units (or building blocks) called **cells**. Cells are made up mostly of water and carbon taken from a simple sugar called **glucose**. Cells are living things because they carry out all or most of the functions listed earlier. Cells maintain homeostasis. They have an organized structure consisting of parts called **organelles** and **membranes**. They break down food and use its energy to sustain themselves through **photosynthesis** and **respiration**. They grow, reproduce through **mitosis** or **meiosis**, and respond to stimuli. Cells can adapt over time.

Cells are self-contained, meaning that they are surrounded by some form of outer shell, like a capsule, **cell wall**, or other **membrane**. These are intended to act as barriers that can regulate the flow of material (food, oxygen, waste products) into and out of the cell. Membranes allow necessary materials to flow in while preventing any unneeded or harmful materials from entering the cell. They also allow waste products to flow out. (This process is called **excretion**.) For example, plant cells use a process called **osmosis** to maintain a balance of water between their internal environment and the external environment.

Virtually all living things are made up of cells. Some are **unicellular** (one cell). Some—like humans, animals, and plants—are **multicellular** (more than one cell, many cells). Some cells have a fairly simple organization. They have several surrounding layers (capsule, cell wall, and cell membrane) that protect a loosely packed mixture of genetic material and other cellular components. These cells are called **prokaryotes**. Other cells, called **eukaryotes**, have a more complex organization. Humans are made of eukaryotic cells. These cells have an external cell membrane that regulates the flow of materials in and out. However, they also have a number of internal components, called **organelles**, that are surrounded by their own membranes.

Organelles are responsible for the more complex cellular functions required by many highly complex forms of life. The most important organelle is the **nucleus**, which is a central membrane-bound container of the cell's **genetic material** (called **chromatin**). This material is made up of the cell's **chromosomes** as well as supporting **proteins**. The chromosomes carry the cell's

DNA. Other organelles are involved in breaking down food to produce energy and transporting energy and other materials within or out of the cell.

The molecules of **DNA** found in a cell's chromosomes provide the "blueprints" for everything in an organism that is made from cells. At a molecular level, DNA molecules interact with amino acids to form proteins, and these proteins are the basis for many critical processes and functions within cells.

Chromosomes

A cell's chromosomes contain its **genes**, which carry all the genetic information for the **traits** (like eye color) an organism will develop. In humans and many other living things, chromosomes exist in **homologous pairs**. For example, most human cells have 46 chromosomes, organized into 23 pairs that determine various physical characteristics (height, weight, complexion, eye color, hair color, and so on). Cells with pairs of homologous chromosomes are called **diploid**. Humans are diploid organisms because almost all of our cells have pairs of chromosomes. One specialized type of cell, called a **gamete**, carries only one-half of each homologous pair. These are called **haploid** cells. Haploid gametes are a very important part of sexual reproduction and of the science of **genetics**, which studies the inheritance of traits from parents to **offspring**.

CELL DIVISION AND DIFFERENTIATION

Cells reproduce through **cell division**. In this process, a **parent** cell splits into two or more **daughter** cells. The genetic material and other components in the parent cell are shared equally between the daughter cells. A process called **cytokinesis** physically separates the halves into two membrane-bound individuals by pinching or closing off the middle of the cell.

In prokaryotic cells, the process of cell division is called **binary fission** and results in two identical offspring. The cell's DNA is replicated (copied). The resulting duplicate chromosomes are separated within the cell. Then the cell membrane closes off one-half of the cell from the other.

Mitosis creates the new cells needed for an organism to grow. Even though each cell contains all the genetic information for all types of cells in an organism's body, cells usually demonstrate (or **express**) only a portion of that information. This leads to the development of different types of cells that are appropriate for different purposes in the body of a complex organism, such as nerve cells, blood cells, lung cells, or brain cells. This process of developing specialized cells is called **differentiation**.

For most eukaryotic cells, cell division includes a process called **mitosis**. The membrane-bound nucleus of the cell separates into two identical **nuclei** (plural of nucleus). This requires the replication of the cell's DNA, followed by the separation of the chromosomes into two identical sets, followed by the closing of the **nuclear membrane** to form separate nuclei. This duplication of the nucleus must happen before the cell itself can complete dividing its organelles and physically separating. Mitosis occurs in several phases in which the cell prepares itself, replicates important genetic information, divides up organelles and chromosomes, and then physically separates in half.

Gametes and Sexual Reproduction

Gametes are specialized cells involved in sexual reproduction. In humans, each gamete carries half of the homologous pairs required for human cells to grow and sustain life. When a **sperm** cell from a male parent and an **egg** cell from a female parent are combined, the resulting **zygote** (new diploid cell or offspring) contains homologous pairs of chromosomes. Half of the chromosomes are from one parent and half from the other. In humans, this means that 23 of the chromosomes are from the mother and 23 are from the father.

Gametes are created from diploid cells through a process called **meiosis**. During meiosis, homologous pairs of chromosomes exchange **genes**, which define human traits. As a result the **gene sequences** in each chromosome are different from the sequences in each parent's chromosome. Virtually all genes from the parent are still present, but they are combined into new sequences. The parent cell then divides, creating two diploid cells whose chromosomes are different from those in the parent's other cells. The new chromosome pairs in the daughter cells then separate. The daughter cells divide again, each receiving one-half of each new pair. This creates 4 haploid cells, each with half a pair of chromosomes that represents a new combination of the parent's genetic code.

Meiosis

Meiosis allows the offspring of humans, other animals, and plants to inherit physical characteristics from their parents without being identical copies of their parents. These new combinations of inherited traits lead to the family resemblance we see among members of a family. For example, fair-skinned parents usually have fair-skinned offspring. These same combinations can also determine whether or not a child has a genetic ability or disability.

ENERGY AND RESPIRATION

All living things, including cells, require **energy** to sustain them. This energy comes from some external source. One characteristic of a living thing is the ability to transform energy from an external form into one that can be used to support life. One method that cells use is called **cellular respiration**. This is not to be confused with breathing (which we also call respiration). Cellular respiration is a process that takes place inside cells. In eukaryotic cells, specialized organelles called **mitochondria** are able to convert a substance called **pyruvate** into **ATP**. ATP is a form of chemical energy that can be transported around the cell and used to power the various cellular life functions. ATP can be extracted from simple sugars (like **glucose**) and other basic **nutrients** in food.

Several types of respiration occur. However, the one most common type among humans, animals, and plants requires oxygen and is called **aerobic respiration**. Cells use a series of chemical reactions called **glycolysis** to break glucose down into pyruvate. The pyruvate then enters the mitochondria, and additional chemical reactions extract the ATP for use by the cell. The overall process requires the presence of **oxygen**, and it produces waste in the form of **carbon dioxide** and **water**. Respiration also releases energy that maintains the body's temperature.

In humans and other complex organisms, the cellular respiration process is supported by some important organ systems. The **respiratory system**, which includes the lungs, nasal cavity, and other organs, brings oxygen into the body for use in aerobic respiration and transports carbon dioxide out of the body. We call this **breathing**. The **digestive system**, which includes the mouth, esophagus, stomach, intestines, and other organs, breaks food down into a simple form (glucose) for use in aerobic respiration. It also transports waste products out of the body through **excretion**. The **circulatory system**, which includes the heart, blood, blood vessels, and other organs, supports aerobic respiration by moving oxygen from the lungs and glucose from the digestive system to the cells. It also returns the waste products created by respiration back to these systems for transport out of the body.

Some living things are able to acquire and transform energy through a process that does not require oxygen. This process is called **anaerobic respiration**; **fermentation** is an example. Even so, the purpose of fermentation is to extract ATP by breaking down substances like pyruvate, which is often produced by glycolysis.

PHOTOSYNTHESIS

Plants don't really eat. They "eat" sunlight using a process called **photosynthesis**. Plant cells have specialized organelles called **chloroplasts**. Sunlight shines onto chloroplasts, which convert the sunlight into chemical energy that can be stored by the plant's cells. Photosynthesis produces glucose. The plant can then use aerobic respiration to extract energy from the glucose to sustain itself. Photosynthesis converts sunlight, carbon dioxide, and water into glucose and oxygen. The glucose is stored in the plant's cells, and the oxygen is released into the atmosphere.

LESSON 2: ECOSYSTEMS

ECOSYSTEMS AND THE FOOD CHAIN

An **ecosystem** is a collection of living things that occupy a common environment and interact with each other as part of a system in which nutrients and energy flow from **producers** (plants) to **consumers** (animals). Energy usually enters the system as sunlight, which is converted and captured by plants using photosynthesis. For this reason, plants are called producers. The plants are then eaten by herbivores (primary consumers), many of whom are then eaten by carnivores (secondary consumers). Some organisms (tertiary consumers) eat the secondary consumers. Still others (omnivores like humans) often get food from multiple levels of this **food chain**.

Food chains from producers to consumers are often interconnected into more complex **food webs** in which a number of different plants provide a variety of food sources to a group of consumers, who in turn provide variety to other consumers, and so on. This ensures that each type of consumer has diverse food sources in order to survive.

All the energy and physical material (matter) that an organism uses to live and grow comes from its food sources. When an organism consumes food, the matter and energy it takes in will either be used to sustain life and growth in the organism, or it will be stored in the organism's cells. If that organism becomes food for another organism, the stored energy and some of the physical matter is transferred into the consuming organism. Since no new matter or energy is created, only the consumed portions are transferred. The energy that was needed to sustain the consumed organism is not transferred, nor is the matter from any part of its body that was discarded. In fact, each time a plant or animal is consumed, only about 10% of its matter and energy are transferred to the consumer.

This steady reduction in the amount of energy available at different levels of a food chain is called the **pyramid of energy**. It dictates that only a small fraction of the total energy captured from sunlight will reach secondary or tertiary consumers. This leads to some similar phenomena like the **pyramid of numbers** and **pyramid of biomass (matter)**. As we move from the lowest level of a food chain, which consists of the producers (plants), to the higher levels, we can observe the population getting smaller and the individual size of the organisms getting larger. In other words, there are many more plants than animals. Plus most carnivores are larger than most herbivores.

Carrying Capacity

Each ecosystem has a **carrying capacity**, which is the overall population of organisms that it can sustain without exhausting resources like food, water, and space to live (or **habitat**). Since living things have a tremendous capacity for reproduction, and their numbers can grow quite large very quickly, limits to growth are needed in order to keep populations in line with an ecosystem's carrying capacity. Without these limits, a population could completely consume the ecosystem's available resources.

Ecosystems have natural limits in place that work to keep them balanced in terms of population and resources. Fundamentally, the resources themselves can act as limits to population through supply and demand, because many resources in an ecosystem participate in cycles that restore their supply. The water cycle refills rivers, lakes, and streams with supplies of fresh water. New plants grow from the seeds and roots of other plants. New animals are born. Many of these cycles are constant or repeat rather quickly (i.e., once a year). As a result, it is more likely that a resource will be temporarily rather than permanently exhausted.

In some cases the population interacts to limit itself, as when one group in a food chain or web consumes another. This occurrence between animals is called **predation**. The consumer is a **predator** and the consumed animal is the **prey**. Predation naturally limits the prey population. Another limit, called **competition**, occurs when organisms in one or more species rely on a common limited resource. If two different species of predator share the same prey, and one species is more successful in hunting it, there will be less of it available to the less successful species. Without sufficient food, some members of that species will not survive. A third limit to population that occurs in nature is **disease**.

In response to these limits, species of animals have developed **group** and **cooperative behaviors** that help increase their chances of survival. Prey species travel together in groups called **herds**, **flocks**, and **schools** to make them less vulnerable to predators. Predators cooperate while hunting to increase their ability to capture prey. Many types of animals travel in large groups in response to seasonal changes, as when birds **migrate** to warmer locations during winter.

The natural limits to population in an ecosystem are usually effective at maintaining balance (or **equilibrium**) between population and resources. When the ecosystem is disrupted, like a disease or drought that quickly reduces population, it is usually able to return to carrying capacity over a period of time as the population recovers.

This is not always the case, however. Some disruptions are extreme enough or permanent enough that the ecosystem cannot return to its original state. Instead, a new ecosystem may develop with a population that is better able to survive in the new conditions. Species that are no longer able to survive in the new conditions will either be **displaced** (forced to move), or die out completely (go **extinct**) if no ecosystem is available where the affected species could go.

Extreme disruptions can be natural. Volcanic eruptions, changes to the earth's orbit, tectonic events, and collisions with objects in space are all capable of destroying or permanently changing ecosystems. It is also possible for human activity to disrupt ecosystems in extreme or unrecoverable ways. Human development of land causes **habitat destruction** that leaves species with no place to live. The **pollution** that accompanies human ways of life can poison an ecosystem's land, water, and air, making it impossible for living things to survive there. Humans can also introduce **invasive species** into an ecosystem. These are species from a different ecosystem that can consume the new ecosystem's prey but have no natural predator there. Ecosystems can also be disrupted by the **climate change** from human activity.

LESSON 3: HEREDITY

A species is the lowest and most specific grouping of living things. Organisms within a single species are able to breed together and produce viable offspring that are themselves capable of reproduction. Individuals within a species may have considerable variation in their physical characteristics (or **characters**). For example, all dogs are a single species. However, different dogs vary greatly in their shape, size, and color. These are **inheritable variations** within a species, and each variation is called a **trait**. The passing of inheritable traits from parents to offspring within a species is called **heredity**. Many of the traits present in a species are **inherited**, meaning that they are passed from parent to offspring through sexual reproduction.

GREGOR MENDEL

The combination of parental traits in offspring has been recognized for thousands and thousands of years, long before a science called **genetics** was developed. In the mid-19th century, a monk and scientist named Gregor Mendel found that traits are passed on in a very structured way. In the process, he changed the way that we understand the inheritance of traits.

Mendel spent a great deal of time cultivating many varieties of pea plants. He became increasingly interested in the various traits that pea plants have and how these traits were passed on from generation to generation. The garden setting gave Mendel a lot of control over the breeding process. He began to experiment with controlled breeding to try to learn more about the way traits are inherited.

Pea Plant Experiment

One trait that Mendel worked with is the trait for the color of the flower that grows on the pea plant. Some pea plants grow purple flowers, and some grow white flowers. Mendel began by breeding plants with the same colors over many generations. If offspring of the other color were produced, they were removed. Over time, these plants produced offspring with flowers of only the parent color. These were called **true-breeding** plants. Mendel then crossed a true-breeding purple-flowered plant with a true-breeding white-flowered plant. These parent plants were members of the **parent generation (P)**. All of the offspring that resulted from crossing the parent generation produced only purple flowers. The offspring were called the **F1 generation**. The plants in the F1 generation were then bred together. The colors of the flowers in the next generation (called the **F2 generation**) were analyzed. In the F2 generation, 75% of the plants produced purple flowers, but 25% produced white flowers.

The presence of white flowers in the F2 generation suggested that the trait for white flowers was preserved in the F1 generation and passed to the F2 generation, even though none of the members of the F1 generation manifested the trait. It also suggested that the purple trait was somehow stronger than the white trait since a cross between true purple and true white always produced purple. This recognition that traits could be preserved as they moved from generation to generation set the stage for the science of genetics.

DOMINANT AND RECESSIVE TRAITS

Mendel went on to identify many other traits that behaved in a similar way in both pea plants and other organisms. Over time, he developed the concept of Mendelian inheritance, which in turn became our modern science of genetics. When we talk about inheritance, we talk about traits that are passed from parent to offspring. These traits are transmitted through **genes** and **alleles**. Many traits are defined by a single pair of alleles, and offspring receive one allele from each parent during reproduction. Traits (and alleles) are either **dominant** or **recessive**. These terms refer to how the traits appear in a group of offspring. When both parents pass on the dominant trait, the offspring shows the dominant trait. When both parents pass on the recessive trait, the offspring shows the recessive trait. When one parent passes on the dominant trait and the other passes on the recessive trait, the offspring will show the dominant trait.

Pea plant flowers can be either purple (dominant) or white (recessive). Mendel observed that when a true-breeding purple-flowered plant is crossed with a true-breeding white-flowered plant, the offspring will always produce purple flowers. The physical appearance of a trait is called the **phenotype**. Mendel also observed that some of the offspring of the F1 generation, the F2 generation, would produce white flowers. This means that at least some of the F1 purple-flowered plants carried the alleles for white flowers even though they themselves produced only purple flowers. The set of actual genes or alleles present in an individual's genetic material is called the **genotype**. As Mendel observed, identifying an organism's genotype based on its phenotype is not always easy. Some purple-flowering pea plants carry no alleles for white flowers and will always produce purple-flowering offspring. Other purple-flowering pea plants carry alleles for white flowers and will produce some white-flowering offspring. Both kinds of plants produce purple flowers (same phenotype) but they don't have the same alleles (different genotypes).

DNA

Deoxyribonucleic acid (**DNA**) is the vehicle that carries our genetic information. It is responsible for the development of all of our physical traits. It is the foundation for genetic inheritance and also for adaptation and speciation resulting from natural selection.

DNA resides in the chromosomes contained in the nucleus of each cell. When cells divide, each cell receives a complete set of DNA from the parent cell. The exception to this is in gametes (sperm and egg cells), which contain half as many chromosomes as other kinds of human cells. DNA is organized in a very complex **double helix** structure. However, it can be more easily visualized as having a shape similar to a ladder. An even better analogy is the zipper that is used to seal various kinds of clothing. Both a ladder and a zipper are organized with two parallel vertical sides that are joined in the middle. In the case of the ladder, the sides are joined by rungs. In the case of the zipper, the two sides are joined by a connection between the teeth on each side.

A DNA molecule is composed of two vertical **strands** joined at regular intervals by pairs of bases. The sequences of these paired bases make up the genes and alleles responsible for the development of new cells and for the genetic inheritance of traits. The bases are like the teeth in the zipper. At times, they are connected. At other times, they can separate and then reconnect.

DNA Bases

There are four types of bases in DNA:

adenine (A)
cytosine (C)
guanine (G)
thymine (T)

DNA strands are joined when the bases attached to one strand pair up with the bases on the other strand to form **bonds**. There are two categories of bases: **purines** and **pyrimidines**. These different categories of bases differ in size. The bases also differ in terms of the hydrogen bonds that they can form with other bases. The bonds that can be formed are determined by the number of locations that a base has available to form hydrogen bonds with another base. Some bases have 2 bond locations, and some have 3.

Bases can appear along one strand in any sequence, but they form pairs according to certain rules.

1. First, each pair must contain both a purine and a pyrimidine.
2. Second, a base can pair only with a base that has the same number of available bond locations.
3. Third, a base cannot pair with itself (for example, adenine cannot pair with another adenine).

The table below shows information about these DNA bases.

Base	Type	Number of Bond Locations	Base It Bonds With
Adenine (A)	Purine	2	Thymine (T)
Cytosine (C)	Pyrimidine	3	Guanine (G)
Guanine (G)	Purine	3	Cytosine (C)
Thymine (T)	Pyrimidine	2	Adenine (A)

LESSON 4: EVOLUTION

When scientists examine the DNA of the many species of organisms on Earth, they find that much of the genetic information is similar, suggesting that the species are related. Since genetic variation is constant in organisms that reproduce sexually, each generation has the potential to be slightly different from the one before. Over time, as variation continues, it is possible for accumulated differences to result in a new species. This is called **speciation** (or **evolution**).

Using the similarities and differences between the genes of different species, it is possible to develop a timeline for the evolution of new species. Moving backwards in time, the many different species that exist today converge into smaller groups of "ancestor" species. This can be visualized as a branching "family tree," in which branches are created when new species emerge. When variations in these species cause more new species to emerge, new branches are created. Similar species (like dogs and cats) reside on recent branches and species that are different (like cats and birds) reside on branches that diverge much earlier.

The evidence for **common ancestry** goes beyond the similarities in DNA. When the **body structures** of various species are examined, many similarities are found among them as well. For example, the structure of the human arm and leg is very similar to that of the limbs of other organisms, like birds and cats. This suggests that the structures were present in a common ancestor and were preserved when new species developed. There are also many similarities in the unborn **embryos** of related species. At early stages of development, the human embryo is very similar to those of many other species, from fish to birds to other land animals.

NATURAL SELECTION

The natural limits present in ecosystems can contribute to a process where, based on genetic variation within the species, some members of a species of organisms are more likely to survive than other members. An individual organism's survival depends on its ability to successfully compete for resources and (in some cases) avoid predators. Some physical traits can increase the chances for success, and other traits can decrease those chances. Over time, the more successful individuals will survive and reproduce in greater numbers, and the less successful individuals will not. As a result, the future generations of that species will be much more likely to inherit the successful traits. Since this change in the frequency of traits occurred in response to the need for natural resources from the ecosystem, it is said that the ecosystem helped choose the successful trait. This is called **natural selection**.

ADAPTATION

Ecosystems can change. As an ecosystem changes, the traits that increase chances of survival can also change. When this happens, the natural selection process can cause a species to change (or **adapt**) in order to survive under the new conditions. If these adaptations cause enough change in the members of a species, a new species may develop.

THEORY OF EVOLUTION

The **theory of evolution** seeks to explain the apparent common ancestry of living things and the diversity of species. It states that the current diversity of species in the natural world was the result of natural selection and adaptation as life developed and multiplied over time. As the planet and its ecosystems changed, species of organisms adapted to the change by developing new traits and, eventually, by developing into new species. Those species whose traits were not suited to changing conditions went extinct. This theory was developed and put forward in a book called *The Origin of the Species*, written by Charles Darwin and published in 1859.

Charles Darwin

As part of a survey expedition to South America, Charles Darwin collected fossils and live specimens of plants and animals from many places, including from each of the Galapagos Islands. He documented their various characteristics. Among the animal species he documented were several species of finches (birds) that seemed to have descended from a common species. The common ancestor was the species of finch that had first arrived on the islands from the mainland. All of the finch species were related to this single ances-tor, but each was different in some observable ways from both the common ancestor and from one another. The different species had beaks with different shapes (long, short, pointed, blunt, large, small) and different food sources. In general, Darwin observed that the differences were beneficial to the species because they gave the finches access to a local source of food.

For example, some new species had larger, stronger beaks well suited to cracking nuts. These species lived in an area where nuts were plentiful. The original ancestor did not have a beak suited for cracking nuts. Another new species had a long, narrow beak well suited for digging into cactus fruit. This species lived in an area where cactus fruit was available. Darwin imagined that the ancestor species had likely included some individuals that were born with unusual beak shapes but that these shapes were probably not suited to the sources of food in the original environment. Without access to food, the individuals would likely not survive to reproduce. The traits for these unusual beak shapes would remain rare in the population.

Darwin then imagined the effect of migration to the new environment in the Galapagos. Different ecosystems presented different sources of food, and the original beak shapes might not have been well suited to any of them. Instead, he reasoned, the unusual shapes that had been a disadvantage before might provide an advantage in the new environment, as in the case of the nut-cracking and cactus-eating beaks. In this new setting, the individuals with unusual beak shapes would have sources of food for which there was little competition; thus, greatly increasing their survival rates. Further, if the indi-viduals with the original beak shapes weren't able to find a viable food source, the trait for those beak shapes might eventually be reduced or eliminated in that community of finches. The natural environment, by providing various sources of food and other challenges to survival, would select the individuals with the traits that were best suited for survival. Over time, those traits would become the dominant traits within that species.

This realization provided the basis for an understanding of the fossil record, which showed clear evidence of adaptation and speciation over long periods of time. It also agreed with the ideas that Mendel and others were develop-ing. In the years that followed, scientists would find a great deal of additional evidence to support and extend the ideas in these central theories. One of the most important of these findings was the work done by Watson, Crick, and other scientists to develop our knowledge of the existence and function of DNA.

Physical Science

Physical Science 13

LESSON 1: MATTER

The fundamental unit of all the material in our physical world, including all living things and nonliving objects and substance, is called an **atom**. Atoms make up all forms of **matter**, including solids, liquids, gases, and plasma. Atoms are made up of three types of components called **particles**: **protons**, **neutrons**, and **electrons**. Atoms are identified by the number of protons and neutrons they have. The number of protons determines the **chemical element** (hydrogen, carbon, oxygen, and so on). The number of neutrons determines the specific variation of the element, called the **isotope**.

Atoms have an internal structure that organizes the particles. Protons and neutrons make up the **nucleus** (or center) of the atom. The electrons move around the nucleus in regions called principal energy levels (or **shells**). You can think of these shells as being similar to "rings" or "orbits" around the nucleus at different distances, although this is a bit of a generalization. Usually, there is one electron for each proton in an atom, although it is possible for an atom to gain or lose an electron in some situations. Some atomic particles carry an **electrical charge**. Protons have a positive electrical charge. Neutrons have no electrical charge. Electrons have a negative electrical charge. Atoms can also have an electrical charge. If an atom has the same number of protons and electrons, it is neutrally charged. If it has more protons than electrons, it has a net positive charge. If it has more electrons than protons, it has a net negative charge. An atom with an electrical charge is called an **ion**.

Elements differ in the number of protons present in the nucleus. Each element has an **atomic number** that indicates the number of protons present in the nucleus of an atom of that element. The atomic number is sometimes called the **proton number**. Some elements have very few protons, like **hydrogen (H)**, which has only 1. Others have many protons, like **gold (Au)**, which has 79.

Since the number of protons is related to the number of electrons, a larger number of protons has an effect on the number of electron shells present

245

in atoms of a given element. The first electron shell can hold up to 2 electrons. Atoms with 2 or fewer electrons have only one shell. Only hydrogen and helium (He) have a single electron shell. Each shell between the first and outermost shells can hold an increasing number of electrons. The outermost electron shell can hold a maximum of 8 electrons. Electrons in the outer shell of an atom are called **valence electrons**.

Period \ Group	1	2	3	4	5	6	7	8	9	10	11	12	13	14	15	16	17	18
1	1 H																	2 He
2	3 Li	4 Be											5 B	6 C	7 N	8 O	9 F	10 Ne
3	11 Na	12 Mg											13 Al	14 Si	15 P	16 S	17 Cl	18 Ar
4	19 K	20 Ca	21 Sc	22 Ti	23 V	24 Cr	25 Mn	26 Fe	27 Co	28 Ni	29 Cu	30 Zn	31 Ga	32 Ge	33 As	34 Se	35 Br	36 Kr
5	37 Rb	38 Sr	39 Y	40 Zr	41 Nb	42 Mo	43 Tc	44 Ru	45 Rh	46 Pd	47 Ag	48 Cd	49 In	50 Sn	51 Sb	52 Te	53 I	54 Xe
6	55 Cs	56 Ba	57 La	72 Hf	73 Ta	74 W	75 Re	76 Os	77 Ir	78 Pt	79 Au	80 Hg	81 Tl	82 Pb	83 Bi	84 Po	85 At	86 Rn
7	87 Fr	88 Ra	89 Ac	104 Rf	105 Db	106 Sg	107 Bh	108 Hs	109 Mt	110 Ds	111 Rg	112 UUb	113 Uut	114 Uuq	115 Uup	116 Uuh	117 Uus	118 Uuo

Lanthanides	57 La	58 Ce	59 Pr	60 Nd	61 Pm	62 Sm	63 Eu	64 Gd	65 Tb	66 Dy	67 Ho	68 Er	69 Tm	70 Yb	71 Lu
Actinides	89 Ac	90 Th	91 Pa	92 U	93 Np	94 Pu	95 Am	96 Cm	97 Bk	98 Cf	99 Es	100 Fm	101 Md	102 No	103 Lr

THE PERIODIC TABLE

The **Periodic Table of Elements** (shown on page 246) organizes the elements into rows of increasing atomic number, with a new row (or **period**) for each collection of elements with the same number of electron shells. The table currently contains elements with up to 7 shells. Each column (or **group**) in the table represents a collection of elements with the same number of valence electrons in their outer shells, increasing from left to right. For example, nitrogen (N) and oxygen (O) both have two electron shells. However, oxygen has 6 valence electrons but nitrogen has only 5. Oxygen and sulfur (S) both have 6 valence electrons. However, sulfur has 3 electron shells while oxygen has only 2.

Atoms are also described using a **mass number**, which is the total number of particles in the nucleus (protons and neutrons) since those particles contribute the most to an atom's mass. Subtracting the atomic number from the mass number will yield the number of neutrons in an atom, which is called the neutron number. Different isotopes of the same element are often distinguished using their mass numbers since the number of neutrons determines the particular isotope of an element.

Elements can form connections, or **bonds**, with one another. When elements of different types bond together, they form **compounds** (or **molecules**). Many of the more familiar substances in our world are compounds made up of bonded elements. Water is a combination of atoms of hydrogen and oxygen. Carbon dioxide is a combination of carbon and oxygen. Glucose (a sugar) is made up of carbon, hydrogen, and oxygen.

Molecules are represented using a combination of letters and numbers indicating which elements it contains and how many of each atom. For example, water is symbolized as H_2O, which means it has 2 atoms of hydrogen (H) and 1 atom of oxygen (O). Carbon monoxide (CO) consists of 1 atom of carbon (C) and 1 of oxygen (O). Carbon dioxide (CO_2) has 1 atom of carbon and 2 of oxygen.

BONDS

Covalent bonds are formed when two atoms share a pair of valence electrons. Covalent bonds can be single (one shared pair), double (two shared pairs), or triple (three shared pairs). The more unpaired electrons in the valence shell, the greater the number of different bonds it can form with other atoms. Covalent bonds tend to form between elements with similar numbers of electrons.

Ionic bonds form between atoms with larger differences in the numbers of their electrons. The number of electrons in an atom has an impact on its

electronegativity, which describes how powerfully an atom pulls on shared electrons. Some atoms actually pull electrons from other atoms into their own shells, increasing their negative charge. The other atom's charge is made more positive by the loss of the electron. Since opposite charges attract, the two atoms are bonded through the differences in their charges.

MATTER AND MATERIALS

The various states of matter describe how close together the atoms and molecules are. In solids, atoms and molecules are not able to move because they are packed closely together. In liquids, they are close enough to touch but have some ability to move around each other. In gases, they are separated by space and free to move.

Matter can be transformed from one state to another by **melting** or **boiling**. When a given type of material reaches its **melting point**, it will transition from solid to liquid. When it reaches its **boiling point**, it will transition from liquid to gas. In general, the higher the temperature required to melt or boil a material, the stronger the bonds are between the atoms and molecules that make up that material. This strength is indicated in the amount of energy (heat) required to modify the structure of the material.

CHEMICAL REACTIONS

Just as bonds can form between atoms, bonds between atoms can also be broken. Once the existing bonds have been broken, new bonds can form between the newly separated atoms. In general, the breaking of bonds requires the presence of some other element. The process of breaking bonds between atoms and then forming new compounds is called a **chemical reaction**.

The molecules that exist prior to the reaction are called **reagents** (or **reactants**), and the new molecules that are formed after the reaction are called **products**. Most reactions require that some energy, like heat or light, be introduced because energy is usually required to break the bonds that exist between atoms. That energy is called **activation energy** because it activates the reaction. Reactions that don't require additional energy are **spontaneous** reactions.

LESSON 2: MOTION AND FORCES

MOTION

Motion, as demonstrated by the swing of the pendulum, can be defined as a change in an object's position or location. Motion has several properties that can be described quantitatively. One familiar property is called **speed**. Speed indicates the rate of change in an object's position without describing the direction of motion. When you say that a car is traveling at 55 miles per hour, you are discussing its speed. You are describing the rate of change in position but not describing the direction of that change. The description of motion that includes both the **magnitude** (amount) of the change and the **direction** of the change is called **velocity**. If you say that a car is traveling north at 55 miles per hour, you are discussing the car's velocity.

A change in velocity is called **acceleration**. Even though we typically associate that word with something that makes an object move faster (like the accelerator in a car), acceleration can cause an object to slow down as well as speed up. It can also make an object start moving from a stationary position (or **at rest**). Instead, acceleration can stop a moving object and cause it to become stationary. Slowing down or stopping is sometimes called **deceleration**. Acceleration can also act to change an object's direction as opposed to changing its speed.

Moving objects have **momentum**, which is the product of their mass and velocity. Momentum describes the object's tendency to resist deceleration. Heavy moving objects resist deceleration more than light ones. Momentum is conserved, which means that the total amount in a system of multiple objects will stay the same. If a rolling shopping cart collides with a stationary shopping cart, the first cart may stop abruptly, but the second cart will roll away because the first cart's momentum has been transferred to the second cart.

FORCE

Acceleration is an example of the result of **force** acting on an object. Anything that can cause a change in an object's shape/structure, direction, or movement is considered a force. There are several different kinds of force, but they can all be classified as either push or pull. Push forces **repel** another object. Pull forces **attract** another object. Gravity, which is a force that pulls all objects near Earth toward Earth's core, is an example of a force that pulls on objects.

When a force is applied in the direction of motion, the moving object accelerates. When a force is applied in the direction opposite the direction of motion, the moving object decelerates (accelerates in reverse). When a force is applied at an angle to the direction of motion, the object's direction changes (accelerates in a different direction). If all the forces applied to an object are balanced in opposite directions, the object's motion stops. This is because there is no **net force** or **unbalanced force** working on the object. When we jump off a chair, gravity causes us to move until we encounter the floor. The floor essentially acts like a force because it provides support against the pull of gravity. The floor balances the pull of gravity because it is strong enough to do so. If the floor were made from cardboard, gravity would be a **net force** on us and we would continue moving through the floor.

THE LAWS OF MOTION

Sir Isaac Newton studied motion extensively and articulated three laws of motion as part of the science of mechanics, which is now known as classical mechanics. Learn Newton's three laws of motion:

First law: "An object at rest will tend to stay at rest, and an object in motion will tend to stay in motion." If no unbalanced force acts on an object, that object's velocity will remain constant. If the object is moving, it will continue to move in the same direction at the same rate (same velocity). If it is not moving, it will continue to not move.

Second law: "The force required to accelerate an object is directly proportional to the object's mass. The amount of acceleration a force can produce in an object is inversely proportional to the object's mass." This is usually expressed as $F = ma$, where F is the force, m is the mass, and a is the acceleration. This law also states that acceleration occurs in the direction of the force applied.

Third law: "For every action, there is an equal and opposite reaction." Forces are balanced. When one object applies force to another, that second object applies an equal force to the first object in the opposite direction. This can be understood in terms of standing on the floor. Most of us know that when we stand on a floor, our weight applies force to the floor. What Newton's third law explains is that the floor also applies a force of equal strength to us but in the opposite direction. While we're pushing down on the floor, it's pushing up on us. Think about how it feels to ride an elevator when the car speeds up and slows down. As the speed of the car changes, the force pushing up on us changes, and we feel the floor shift under our feet.

LESSON 3: ENERGY

Chemical bond energy and heat energy are good examples of two categories of energy: **potential energy** and **kinetic energy**. The combined amount of potential and kinetic energy in a moving object is called **mechanical** energy. Potential energy, like chemical energy, is a form of stored energy. Kinetic energy, like heat, is energy related to the motion of a physical object. Heat is related to the motion of the particles in a substance, and always moves toward an equilibrium between warmer and cooler objects. This is the reason that a metal spoon in a cup of warm liquid becomes warm.

Consider a pendulum at rest. The pendulum hangs at the end of the string, not moving. No energy is in this system. Now if we pull the pendulum up to one side, we have introduced potential energy into the system. By holding the pendulum against the weight of gravity, we have positioned the pendulum so that it has the potential to move.

When we release the pendulum, the potential energy is converted to kinetic energy as the pendulum begins to swing. The amount of potential energy begins to decrease as the speed of the swing increases. However, as the pendulum starts to swing upward, the speed of the swing slows. This decreases the amount of kinetic energy. As the swing takes the pendulum farther away from the pull of gravity, the potential energy related to its position begins to increase again. When the swing stops and reverses, the cycle repeats itself.

Earth and Space Science

14

LESSON 1: EARTH'S PLACE IN THE UNIVERSE

EARTH AND THE SOLAR SYSTEM

Let's start at the beginning. Unless there have been some very big and recent changes, you are reading this on **Earth**. Earth is a physical object in space called a **planet**. A planet is one kind of **astronomical object** (or "celestial body"). An astronomical object is an object in space that is composed of naturally occurring materials and held together by gravity and other forces. A planet is a round astronomical object that is moving around another object called a **star.** Our star is called the **sun**, and Earth's path around the sun is called an **orbit**. Earth is one of eight planets orbiting the sun at various distances. From closest to farthest, the sun's planets are: Mercury, Venus, Earth, Mars, Jupiter, Saturn, Uranus, and Neptune.

Some of you may be thinking, "What happened to Pluto? Isn't Pluto a planet?" Not anymore. These days Pluto has been re-classified as a "dwarf planet," making it one of many non-planetary objects that are orbiting the sun. There are many others. For example, Earth has a **moon**. The moon is a **satellite**, which is a round astronomical object that orbits a planet or other object. Several of the other planets have moons. Mars has only two, but Neptune has around thirteen, Uranus has around twenty-seven, and Jupiter and Saturn have around *sixty* each.

Earth is a **terrestrial planet**, which means that it is made up of mostly solid materials like rocks and metals. It has a **core** with two layers, consisting of a solid iron center surrounded by a layer of liquid iron. The core of Earth is very hot (which explains the liquid iron). Surrounding the core are layers of rocky material. These layers are all relatively solid, but the **mantle**, which is the layer above the liquid core, is not totally rigid. It's more like an extremely thick liquid that can move in response to pressure. Earth's **crust**, which is the layer above the mantle, is much more solid and rigid. It is the outermost solid layer of Earth, and we live on the **surface** of Earth, which is the outside of the crust.

Mercury, Mars, and Venus are also terrestrial planets. The other planets are called **giants** because they are much larger than the terrestrial planets. Jupiter and Saturn are **gas giants**, and Uranus and Neptune are **ice giants**. These names come from the materials that these planets are made of. Giants are composed mostly of hydrogen, helium, oxygen, and carbon, rather than the rock and metal making up the terrestrial planets.

The planets, their satellites, and a few types of other objects orbit the sun in a structure called the **solar system**. The sun is very close to the center of the system, and the planets and other objects move in round (but not circular) paths around the sun. Even though it consists of multiple objects, the solar system is considered an astronomical object because it is held together by gravity.

GRAVITY

The force of **gravity** (or **gravitational force**) draws physical objects and materials (or **matter**) together. The effect of gravitational force is stronger when objects are closer together, and it is stronger when objects have more **mass**, which is the amount of matter the object contains. The more mass an object has, the more it will be affected by gravity, making it "heavier."

Gravity plays an important role in the formation of astronomical objects. In space, clouds of matter in the form of "gas" and "dust" are pulled closer together over time. As the matter gets closer together, it gets more **dense**, which means that the amount of empty space between pieces is reduced. Eventually the matter will form a fairly dense and solid core, and the gravitational force of that core will continue to attract more matter. Depending on the kind of matter involved, this process may eventually form a star, a planet, or another round object. Since temperature usually increases as matter becomes denser and experiences more pressure, the core of an object formed by gravity is often extremely hot.

In space, gravity also pulls "lighter" objects into orbit around "heavier" objects. The moon orbits Earth because Earth is heavier. Earth orbits the sun because the sun is heavier. Systems or structures like these, where objects are held in orbit around a center with strong gravity, are "gravitationally bound" systems, and they are considered astronomical objects themselves.

STARS

The sun is another kind of astronomical object called a **star**. A star produces energy that we call **light**. This energy is called **electromagnetic radia-**

tion, and it travels through space in **waves**. On Earth, humans and other living things mostly experience this energy as **heat** (or **infrared** or **thermal**) energy or as **visible light**.

Stars are large balls of material called **plasma**, made up mostly of hydrogen and helium. The pressure at the dense core of the star is so great that it pushes (or **fuses**) atoms together to form new atoms. This process is called **nuclear fusion**, and it converts one **chemical element** (hydrogen) to another (helium). This conversion releases electromagnetic energy. During nuclear fusion, hydrogen in the core of a star is converted into helium, and the energy produced flows to the surface of the star and is released into space in every direction. The amount of energy a star produces is not constant. For example, there is an 11-year cycle of solar activity in which the frequency of solar phenomena like **sunspots** and **solar flares** rises and falls.

Stars have **life cycles**. The specific steps and stages vary a bit because there are different kinds of stars out there, but there are some general phases that many stars, including the sun, go through as they "age." They are formed (or "born"), they develop (or "live and grow"), and then they either collapse or explode (or "die"). This cycle can take billions of years to complete. Our sun is estimated to be little less than halfway through a 10 billion year life cycle.

GALAXIES AND BEYOND

Stars travel in groups. Our sun is one of a large group of stars in a gravitationally bound system called a **galaxy**, where stars orbit a common center with strong gravitational pull. Our sun is in a very long orbit around the center of our galaxy, as are all of the other stars in our galaxy. We call our galaxy the Milky Way.

Galaxies also travel in gravitationally-bound groups called **clusters**. Clusters are, in turn, grouped into **superclusters**, and superclusters are grouped into even larger structures called **filaments** separated by large areas of empty space called **void**. Think of a "web" or a "net," with strands of galaxy clusters separated by large areas of space. This pattern of structure and void continues for as far as we can see in every direction in the space we call the **universe**.

LOTS OF SPACE OUT THERE . . .

The universe is extremely large, and the distances between objects in space are very large in human terms. To begin, the distance around the circumference of Earth is just a bit more than 40,000 kilometers (km). The moon, which is the closest natural object to Earth, is almost 385,000 km away. The sun is almost 150,000,000 (one hundred fifty *million*) km away from Earth, which is almost 40 times the distance to the moon. That's about 400 times around Earth, and these objects are considered "very close" to Earth.

Obviously these distances are huge when we think of them in terms of our everyday units of measurement, so larger units are required to describe them. One common unit of measure in space is the light year, which is the distance that light travels in a year. The speed of light is just under 300,000 km per second, which translates to roughly 10 trillion km in a year. Light years make distances in space a bit more manageable. For example, the average distance between stars in the Milky Way becomes 5 light years.

LIGHT, ELECTROMAGNETIC RADIATION, AND WAVES

The "light" produced by the sun and other stars is a result of a process called nuclear fusion. This process generates a form of energy called electromagnetic radiation, which travels through space in shapes called waves. A wave is like a line that curves up and down as it moves, going between a highest point ("crest" or "top") and lowest point ("trough" or "bottom"). The straight-line distance the line travels as it moves (or "oscillates") through the cycle from the top to the bottom of a wave is called a **wavelength**.

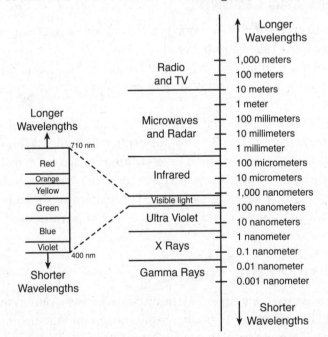

Electromagnetic radiation consists of much more than the **visible light** that humans see. It includes radio waves, microwaves, infrared (heat), visible light, ultraviolet rays, X-rays, and gamma rays, among others. All of these different types of waves have different wavelengths. Some, like radio and microwaves, have longer wavelengths than visible light. Others, like ultraviolet radiation, have shorter wavelengths. This variation in wavelength is also present in visible light.

Visible Light and Color

Visible light consists of a range (or **spectrum**) of different colors that vary by wavelength. The order of colors is red, orange, yellow, green, blue, indigo, and violet. Red has the longest wavelength and violet has the shortest wavelength. When light shines on an object, some colors of light travel into (or are **absorbed** by) the object and some colors bounce off (or are **reflected** by) the object. Different materials (metals, stones, chemical elements, etc.) absorb and reflect different colors of light. This pattern of absorption and reflection, combined with the way that our eyes work, determines the color that an object appears to have when we look at it.

THE BIG BANG

Where did the universe come from? How did it get to be this way? What will happen to it in the future? Questions like these, that deal with the origin, structure, and development of the universe, are **cosmological** questions. The possible answers and explanations are **cosmological models**, and the most widely accepted model for the origin and development of our universe is called the **Big Bang** theory.

Let's Keep it Simple

The Big Bang theory starts in the first instant of our universe, more than 13 billion years ago. According to this theory, everything that currently exists in the universe, including all matter and all space, was packed together in an incredibly dense, incredibly small, and incredibly hot state. At the moment of the Big Bang, there was a sudden expansion, which resulted in a larger space filled with an extremely hot "cloud" of energy. This expansion continued, and as the energy spread out, it cooled until it was cool enough to form some of the first chemical elements, hydrogen and helium. This led to the formation of stars and galaxies, which in turn led to the creation of other elements.

Over billions of years, gravity caused clouds of these elements to collapse into planets and other astronomical objects.

Simple, right? Everything started in a hot, dense, tiny thing that suddenly started to expand and cool; the galaxies, stars, and planets we see in the universe were formed during this cooling. Not so complicated at first, but then we come to the idea that the "everything" that was contained in that initial tiny thing included *space*, too.

According to this theory, at the moment of the Big Bang, absolutely everything in the universe, *including space*, was contained in a single, tiny thing that many believe to have been much smaller than a grain of sand. When the Big Bang occurred, the expansion that followed was an expansion of *space itself*, rather than just an explosion of physical matter, and that expansion has been occurring continually since then. The expansion of space is one idea in the Big Bang theory that can be initially hard to imagine.

LESSON 2: SYSTEMS OF EARTH

Earth is divided into a variety of systems called **spheres.** The **lithosphere** ("the rocks") consists of the cooler and more rigid layers of mantle and crust that make up the planet's tectonic plates. The lithosphere is constantly changing. Different parts of the system (like plates) interact with each other, and these interactions cause change (rifting, subduction, oceans, mountains, etc.).

In addition to the lithosphere, Earth has a **hydrosphere** ("the water"), consisting of all the water in the oceans, lakes, rivers, and other bodies of water found on Earth's surface. The areas where the water is in solid form (ice or snow) are part of the **cryosphere** ("the ice"). Earth has an **atmosphere** ("the air"), which is a layer of gas (which we call **air**) that surrounds the planet in an area above Earth's surface, and a **biosphere** ("life"), which consists of all living things (including humans). These systems interact with one another, and the interactions can cause change. For example, several systems interact during the **water cycle** and **rock cycle** and cause significant change to the surface of Earth.

Water Cycle

During the water cycle, water in the oceans is heated by incoming sunlight until it **evaporates** into **water vapor** in the air. It rises into the air and cools, until it **condenses** back into drops of liquid water in **clouds**. Eventually, changes in the conditions in the atmosphere will cause these drops to fall out of the clouds in the form of **precipitation** (rain, snow, sleet) that falls over land. Some of this water will fall on very cold parts of Earth and remain there as **glacial ice**, but a lot of the water that falls on land as precipitation finds its way back to the oceans. Some flows over the surface of Earth as **runoff**, ending up in **streams** or **rivers** that lead back to the oceans. Similar things happen to water that flows into and under Earth's surface. Some is absorbed by plants or consumed by other living things and then is released back into the air through various biological processes. During the various phases of this cycle, water changes its form from salt water in the ocean to vapor; to fresh water in rain, streams, and rivers; or to ice in the glaciers.

Rock Cycle

The water cycle also plays a major role in the rock cycle, which traces the various forms of rock that can exist in Earth's crust. Rocks generally begin the cycle in a liquid form, as magma near the surface of Earth. This magma cools and solidifies, hardening into **igneous rock**. In some cases, this magma reaches the surface of Earth (where we call it **lava**) and hardens into igneous rock. This is the point where the rock cycle and water cycle intersect, because water and ice have a destructive effect on rock. **Weathering** occurs when wind and precipitation break down surface rock. **Frost wedging** can break rock below the surface; when liquid water seeps in and then freezes, it causes the rock to expand and crack. **Erosion** occurs when rock is worn down by the motion of water against it. Over time, the effects of water break down the igneous rock into small grains of **sediment**, which is like sand. This sediment can be moved by water or wind, and **deposited** in another location. As more and more sediment is deposited in a given location, layers form, and the lower layers solidify into **sedimentary rock**. This layered rock will be affected by tectonic forces like subduction and continental collision, and the tremendous pressure involved will cause changes to its internal structure, creating **metamorphic rock**.

Carbon Cycle

Carbon is a very important element. It's one of the fundamental elements present in all living things; it's a key ingredient in photosynthesis, and its presence in the atmosphere helps keep the planet warm enough to support human life. As is the case with other essential materials, like water, carbon moves through Earth's systems in a cycle called the **carbon cycle**. In this cycle, carbon moves from the atmosphere into other systems, where it is stored for differing lengths of time. After these periods of storage (or **sequestration**), the carbon is released back into the atmosphere. One role of the carbon cycle is to regulate the amount of carbon dioxide in the atmosphere, which in turn regulates the amount of heat the atmosphere can hold. In this way, the carbon cycle plays a critical role in the climate system.

The cycle works on land and in the ocean, and while the details differ, the basic concept of how the cycle works is the same. Carbon is taken out of the atmosphere. Some is returned and some is stored. On land, the carbon dioxide in the atmosphere is consumed by plants during photosynthesis. Some is returned to the atmosphere when the plants breathe (or **respirate**), converting oxygen to carbon dioxide. More carbon is returned to the atmosphere by the respiration of other kinds of living things, including humans. Some of the carbon consumed by plants is incorporated into the physical structure of the plants (or **plant biomass**), but some also flows through plants and into the soil, where it is absorbed and stored. Some of this stored carbon can remain in the ground for a long time. In some cases, it collects in pools of material we call **fossil fuels**. (**Oil** is a fossil fuel.) Over the ocean, the photosynthesis takes place in small plants called **phytoplankton**, and the stored carbon is captured in water instead of soil, but the effect is the same. Large amounts of carbon are stored deep in the ocean as well as in the ground.

LESSON 3: HUMAN ACTIVITY

The modern human population is large. There are billions of us, and we consume a lot of natural resources. Many of us live in cities and have a modern lifestyle that includes electricity, transportation systems, consumer goods, and many other conveniences. We practice agriculture on a huge scale, operating giant farms that produce the crops and livestock we prefer to eat. We've covered large portions of Earth with cities, farms, roads, and the many other things we construct. To provide the energy that powers our civilization, we extract and burn fossil fuels.

The large-scale consumption of natural resources that results from human activity has many significant (and often negative) effects on Earth. Humans take up a lot of space, which takes living space away from other living things. This is called a **loss of habitat**. We eat a lot of plants and animals, and this can dramatically reduce their populations. These effects combine to cause many species to become extinct, which reduces the variety of life (or **biodiversity**) present on Earth. We cut down a lot of trees to make room for us to live and farm, and this **deforestation** is harmful to many of the planet's systems. We produce a lot of **waste**, which enters the planet's systems in the form of **pollution** and can have very damaging effects to living things (including ourselves). We also burn a lot of coal, oil, and natural gas (fossil fuels), and this increases the amount of carbon dioxide in the atmosphere. Increases in carbon dioxide can increase atmospheric temperatures and cause acid rain.

CLIMATE CHANGE

All of the effects described here are worthy of real concern because they demonstrate the harm that human activity is capable of doing to our planet. Among these, however, the increase in atmospheric carbon dioxide that comes from the large-scale consumption of fossil fuels is of particular significance. This is due to the potential for feedback in the systemic changes that are caused by the increase in this greenhouse gas. The warmer temperatures that are caused by the increase in carbon dioxide can have effects on other systems that can, in turn, increase or accelerate this warming trend.

Carbon dioxide in the atmosphere captures heat. The more carbon dioxide that is present, the warmer the atmosphere can become. When temperatures increase, ice in the colder regions of the planet begins to melt. This transfer of water from the cryosphere to the hydrosphere can contribute to further warming in several ways.

First, ice reflects sunlight, which reduces the amount of solar radiation that enters Earth's surface. As more ice melts, less is present to reflect sunlight, and a greater amount of light will enter Earth and be released back into the atmosphere as heat. This can increase surface temperatures.

In addition, the frozen soil under the ice near the poles holds a lot of stored carbon dioxide. When the melting ice uncovers this soil and the soil thaws, the stored carbon dioxide is released into the atmosphere. More carbon dioxide means more captured heat, and therefore a greater increase in surface temperatures.

Melting ice also increases the liquid water in the hydrosphere. As temperatures increase, more of this water is evaporated into water vapor, which is also a greenhouse gas. This increase in the amount of moisture in the atmosphere enables the capture of even more heat, leading to even more potential for increased temperatures. Another sobering result of this change is an increase in global sea levels, which leads to the erosion or flooding of coastal areas.

Prior to the industrial period, the carbon cycle was able to maintain an effective balance between the amount of carbon dioxide entering and leaving the atmosphere. The amounts were almost equal, with a small amount being stored underground and deep in the ocean. Since the development of industry, however, the burning of fossil fuels has returned stored carbon dioxide to the atmosphere, leading to a measurable increase in the amount present. Over the same time frame, there has been a **global warming** trend in average temperatures. While high and low temperatures may vary from place to place, season to season, or year to year, there is an identifiable upward trend in average global temperatures. As a result of this warming, the amount of glacial ice is shrinking, and scientists believe that this is creating feedback in the warming trend. It has also contributed to an increase in global sea levels, and all of these trends are expected to continue as long as human activity continues to consume fossil fuels.

Scientists project significant consequences for our planet, including more violent storms and weather events, more extreme seasons, and the widespread flooding of coastal areas. Other effects could include an increase in infectious disease and a decrease in the availability of food and fresh water. The potential impact on human civilization could be severe, to say the least, and some scientists believe that we are already seeing the early effects today.

Needless to say, it is in humanity's best interest to reduce our impact on our planet. To accomplish this, we need to be attentive to our consumption of natural resources by increasing our reliance on **renewable** resources and reducing our consumption of **non-renewable** ones. We need to develop ways of living that are **sustainable** over long periods of time and produce less **pollution**. Efforts to reduce the amount of carbon dioxide we return to the atmosphere (or our **carbon footprint**) are particularly important.

Understanding Science

15

LESSON 1: SCIENTIFIC THEORIES

Most of the knowledge developed by scientists is organized into **theories**. Theories offer proposed answers or explanations for the questions scientists ask. In everyday life, when we say "that's just a theory," we usually mean that a given idea is just an unproven opinion. However, that definition doesn't apply to science. In science, a theory is a strongly supported and reliable idea that is accepted as fact.

Examples of well-known scientific theories include:

- **Heliocentric model of the solar system**—This theory states that the sun is the center of the **solar system** and that the planets move in orbit around it.
- **Cell theory**—This theory states that all living things are composed of **cells**.
- **Atomic theory**—This theory states that all physical material (matter) is made up of particles called atoms.
- **Theory of evolution**—This theory states that natural selection is responsible for adaptation (adjustment to the environment) and speciation (the development of species).

Characteristics of a Scientific Theory

For a theory to be accepted as a theory, it has to have certain characteristics:

- It is able to predict future events accurately across many areas of scientific investigation.
- It is supported by a large body of evidence originating from multiple independent sources rather than from a single source. This is called **independent verification**.
- It agrees with preexisting theories and data.
- It can be adjusted to account for new information without becoming inconsistent.
- It is simple. A simple theory is sometimes called "elegant."

263

INFERENCES AND EVIDENCE

An inference represents the start of a process of scientific discovery, not the end. Inferences are carefully tested and retested before they become part of accepted theory. Even so, scientists have to be careful to keep their inferences cautious. Every inference involves an intuitive leap from data to explanation. In science, though, it is important not to jump too far. Even an inference must be based on some evidence, and it must use the evidence in a reasonable way.

A good inference is cautious and is supported by evidence. On the Science subject test, you will be asked to do the following:

- Cite evidence to support a given inference or generalization.
- Verify claims based on given evidence.

LESSON 2: READING AND INTERPRETING SCIENTIFIC FINDINGS

The ability to read and understand scientific findings is one of the most critical skills in science. It is also one of the most important skills you should develop to do well on the Science subject test. The majority of questions will refer to scientific information presented in various forms. You will have to read, understand, and apply that information when answering the questions. On the Science subject test, you will need to do the following:

- Interpret information presented as text.
- Interpret information presented in symbolic form (equations and formulas).
- Interpret information presented in graphic form (graphs, charts, and diagrams).
- Relate and integrate information from different sources.

Symbols and Terms

The Science subject test will measure your ability to work with scientific ideas, words, and symbols as they appear in source material. Keep in mind that working with this kind of information is not the same as remembering this information. You will never be asked to define a specialized science term without the test first providing supporting source material that contains the term's meaning. Instead, you may need to work out the meaning of a word or symbol based on other information in a source, or you might be asked to apply a given definition or formula to a new situation.

You will be asked to do the following on the test:

- Determine the meaning of symbols and terms in context.
- Apply scientific terms, concepts, and formulas.

INTERPRETING GRAPHIC DATA PRESENTATIONS AND MODELS

Analyzing Structure

Structure refers to the way something (like an apartment building) is constructed or the way that a process (like pedaling a bicycle) works. When analyzing structure in source material, whether it is presented as text or in a graphic form, try to break down the things being described into parts. These parts may be ideas, terms, or actual components. Whatever form they take, though, the next step is to identify the relationships among the parts. Does one part cause another? If one part is changed, how might another part change?

On the Science subject test, you will be asked to do the following:

- **Analyze** the relationships among concepts and elements in given information, including relationships among key terms.
- **Explain** how a change in one variable produces a change in another variable in a given data presentation. A **data presentation** usually takes the form of a table, graph, or chart that shows a relationship between **independent** and **dependent** variables.
- **Predict** the results of additional tests in an **experiment** and predict the future state of a model or system based on given information.

Models

In science, a **model** is a simplified representation of an environment or a process. A **model** is an attempt to describe or simulate a system or process and can take many forms: scatter plot, diagram, formula, equation, and so on. In particular, diagrams are frequently used to model complex processes.

Key Interpretation Concepts

DEPENDENT AND INDEPENDENT VARIABLES

A lot of the data being presented is quantitative data, often laid out in tables or graphs. A key point in understanding these data is the relationship between the **independent variable** (x-axis on a graph) and the **dependent variable** (*y*-axis on a graph). Focus on how a change in the independent variable affects the dependent variable.

CLUSTERS

When data are presented in scatter plots or tables, you must identify intervals of the independent variable where there is a relatively high and dense concentration of dependent variable values. These areas are called **clusters**.

OUTLIERS

When data are presented in scatter plots or tables, you must also identify intervals of the independent variable where there is a relatively low and sparse concentration of dependent variable values. These areas are called **outliers**.

CORRELATION

Scatter plots and graphs can also help model the way that variables are **associated** (or **correlated**). Correlation means the way that a change in the dependent variable relates to a change in the independent variable. If the variables are **strongly correlated**, which means there is a clear relationship between them, the variables may have a cause-and-effect relationship. The key word is "may." Remember that strongly correlated values do not necessarily have a cause-and-effect relationship. Sometimes, though, the data show no correlation between the variables.

CORRELATION AND CAUSATION

It is important to remember that even if two things are **correlated** (happen together), you don't always know that one of them **caused** the other. A familiar phrase says that correlation is not causation. This means that you can't assume cause and effect just because two things occur together. In fact, scientists often have to conduct **investigations** and design **experiments** in order to demonstrate cause and effect reliably.

LESSON 3: PLANNING AND CONDUCTING INVESTIGATIONS

Scientists are investigators. In fact, the word **investigation** is frequently used to describe the work that scientists do. Once they formulate a theory or make an inference, scientists get to work gathering information and evidence for support. This information is called **data,** and the careful collection of data is a major part of science.

Data are collected through **observation** and **measurement**. Scientists observe and measure objects and events. Then they record those observations and measurements. Since supporting data are required for a theory to be accepted, their measurements and observations must be taken precisely and recorded carefully in order to avoid error. Data that have been collected carefully are described as being **valid** or reliable.

Qualitative and Quantitative Data

Qualitative data describe the characteristics or qualities that scientists observe in a group or environment. Examples of qualitative data include a list of the eye and hair color for each member of the family or photographs of color patterns in the feathers of different groups of birds. Information that describes characteristics or attributes (including shapes, colors, and textures) without using numbers is qualitative data.

Quantitative data are made up of numbers or quantities. These numbers usually represent measurements. Examples of quantitative data include a list of the average recorded temperatures for a certain area or a list of the heights and weights of members of a certain group. Information that uses numbers to present or summarize observations or measurements is quantitative data.

Precise Measurements

Scientists use a number of instruments and measurement systems to help them be precise when collecting measurements. The most common measurement system used by scientists is the metric system. However, other nonmetric systems are also sometimes used. Each system is made up of different **units** that are used to measure different physical properties. For example, in the metric system, length is measured with a unit called a **meter**, and mass is measured with the **gram**. In the customary system, a **foot** is used to measure length, and a **pound** is used to measure weight. (Weight and mass are very similar concepts.) Some of the instruments used to take measurements include rulers and measuring tapes for length, scales for weight and mass, and thermometers for temperature.

The units that make up a system can often be divided into smaller units or grouped into larger units. For example, a meter is made up of smaller units called **centimeters**, and meters can be grouped into larger units called **kilo-**

meters. This is similar to the customary system, where feet are made up of **inches** and feet can be grouped into **miles**. Part of taking precise measurements is the use of appropriate units. For example, it wouldn't make sense to measure the distance between a person's eyes using meters or kilometers because these units are too large. Centimeters would be a more appropriate unit of measure.

Experimentation

A lot of scientific observation takes place in the field, which means that it is taken in the natural world. For example, the theory of evolution is based on observations of animals in their natural habitats. Darwin collected his data on the Galapagos Islands.

In some cases, however, the information scientists need cannot be easily obtained through field observation alone. In order to observe or measure certain things, scientists must sometimes recreate (or **simulate**) the conditions or environment in a controlled setting called a **laboratory**. A laboratory is usually used when a specific event is difficult to observe in nature, either because it is unusual or because it only occurs in an environment where observation is difficult. This test performed in a simulated environment is called an **experiment**.

A laboratory approach is also used extensively in physical science where scientists are investigating the origin of the universe and an event called the **Big Bang**. Since scientists cannot yet travel back in time and space to the moment of the huge explosion that created the universe, they must simulate those conditions in a laboratory with the help of complex equipment like **particle accelerators** and **colliders**. These machines accelerate tiny atomic particles up to incredibly high speeds and then smash them together. These collisions cause the particles to fly apart, revealing a lot of information about their structure and their behavior in explosive conditions. Most of modern physics is based on experimental evidence gathered in a laboratory setting like this.

A Hypothesis

The goal of an experiment is to generate evidence in support of a given theory by testing something called a **hypothesis**. A theory is a broad and general statement about the natural world that answers a broad and general question. A hypothesis, in contrast, is a much more specific statement that answers a specific question about an element of the theory. A good hypothesis focuses on an observable and measurable cause-and-effect relationship between two things. An experiment is then designed to create conditions where the hypothesis can be either confirmed or disproven.

Proving or disproving a hypothesis is part of a chain of "if . . . then . . . therefore" reasoning. This reasoning process starts with making a **prediction**:

If A then B.

The letter A represents the hypothesis, and the letter B represents an event that can be tested or measured. The prediction says that if statement A is true, statement B is also true. If put another way, the prediction means that if the hypothesis is true, the predicted event will occur.

The next step in this reasoning process is the **test** or **experiment**. This step focuses on determining whether the prediction is true or false. The test is performed. The results are recorded. Then the data are analyzed to determine what they say about the prediction. In other words, is the prediction true or false? The answer to this question is then extended to the hypothesis:

- If the experiment shows the prediction to be **true**, the evidence **confirms** the hypothesis.
- If the experiment shows the prediction to be **false**, the evidence **contradicts** the hypothesis.

Applying the experimental results to the hypothesis is called **drawing a conclusion**. This conclusion is the "therefore" step in the chain of reasoning:

- **Confirmation:** If the hypothesis is true, then the predicted event will occur. The event did occur. Therefore, the hypothesis is true.
- **Contradiction:** If the hypothesis is true, then the predicted event will occur. The event did not occur. Therefore, the hypothesis is false.

The outcome of the experiment dictates what will happen next:

- If the experiment contradicted the hypothesis, the next step may be to look for a reason that the experimental results may be wrong. This is called looking for sources of **error** or **bias**.
- If none is found, another hypothesis for the same question may be stated and tested.
- If the hypothesis was **confirmed**, the next step may be to repeat the experiment to see if it produces the same results. This is done to **verify the result**. The more often a given result can be reproduced, the more reliable it is.
- After the result has been verified, another question may be asked and a hypothesis for that question may then be stated and tested.

Designing Controlled Experiments

An experiment is intended to simulate an environment or a process that occurs somewhere in nature. Scientists perform experiments to confirm or contradict hypotheses. These hypotheses often involve a **cause-and-effect** relationship between two things. An experiment is often intended to determine whether one thing causes another. In more formal terms, an experiment tests for a **causal** (cause-and-effect) relationship between two **variables** (things):

- The **cause** is called the **independent variable**.
- The **effect** is called the **dependent** variable because it depends on (or is caused by) the independent variable.
- A good hypothesis focuses on an observable and measurable relationship between an independent variable and a dependent variable.

In order to measure a cause-and-effect relationship properly, it is necessary to eliminate any other possible causes or at least minimize their impact. If more than one potential cause exists for a measured effect, then it is not possible to determine the true cause. Creating an environment where the effect of the independent variable can be reliably measured is called **designing a controlled experiment**.

One familiar example of a controlled experiment is the testing of a new drug. In order to be sure that they are measuring the effect of the drug, scientists create two groups of test subjects: a **control group** and an **experimental group**:

- The members of both groups are as similar as possible in terms of age, gender, diet, and other factors that could affect the test.
- The number of people in each group is as similar as possible, preferably identical.
- The experimental group is given the medication to be tested.
- The control group is not given the medication. Instead, its members are given something that appears to be medication but is, in fact, a harmless substance. This is called a **placebo** and is sometimes referred to as a sugar pill.

The goal of this approach is to create a situation where the only significant difference between the two groups is whether they received the medication or the placebo. This way, if there is a measurable difference between the two groups, it can safely be said that the medication caused the difference.

Verification, Error, and Bias

One way to ensure that the results of an experiment are reliable is to repeat the experiment many times to **verify** the original results. This means the experiment is repeated to see if the new results are similar to the original ones. If the results are similar, they provide additional evidence in support of the conclusion. If the results are not similar, it is possible that some of the data were affected by **error** or **bias**.

LESSON 4: REASONING FROM EVIDENCE

After collecting evidence and analyzing it, scientists must do the following:

- Distinguish among data, inferences, and conclusions.
- Determine if the data support a given conclusion.
- Draw a reasonable conclusion based on existing data.
- Re-evaluate a conclusion given new data.

Determine Central Ideas, Hypotheses, and Conclusions

To show you understand the experimental method, you will be asked to do the following:

- Summarize given information and determine the central idea or conclusion.
- Identify the hypothesis, data, and/or conclusion in a scientific finding.
- Verify evidence and data plus use new data to corroborate or challenge a conclusion.
- Construct valid questions, determine whether questions are valid, and refine hypotheses.

LESSON 5: COMMUNICATING AND EVALUATING SCIENTIFIC FINDINGS

After all of the work involved in designing an experiment and collecting data, scientists need to evaluate their findings. They also must communicate their findings to other scientists. In order to accomplish these tasks, they must do the following:

- Create charts, graphs, diagrams, or other models to present the information.
- State their conclusions and provide supporting evidence.
- Describe the methods and details of their investigation.
- Evaluate the validity of their data and reasoning based on the findings of other scientists.

By now, you should be able to interpret scientific data (whether in text or graphic form) and determine whether they are reliable. You should be able to recognize whether evidence supports a given conclusion. You should understand how experiments work and should also know what goes into a well-designed experiment. On the test, you will be asked to do the following when comparing one source with another:

- Compare multiple scientific findings, and determine whether they support or contradict each another.
- Compare and contrast models or experiments, identifying their strengths and weaknesses.
- Determine whether new data or evidence support or weaken a previous experiment's findings.

Review Test

> **DIRECTIONS:** This review test contains science problems that cover a broad number of skills discussed in this unit.

1. Which of the following is a unit in the customary system?
   (A) mile
   (B) centiliter
   (C) gram
   (D) meter

2. Which of the following choices organizes these units from smallest to largest?
   (A) centiliter, milliliter, liter, deciliter
   (B) centiliter, deciliter, liter, milliliter
   (C) liter, deciliter, centiliter, milliliter
   (D) milliliter, centiliter, deciliter, liter

QUESTIONS 3 THROUGH 6 REFER TO THE FOLLOWING DATA
PRESENTATIONS:

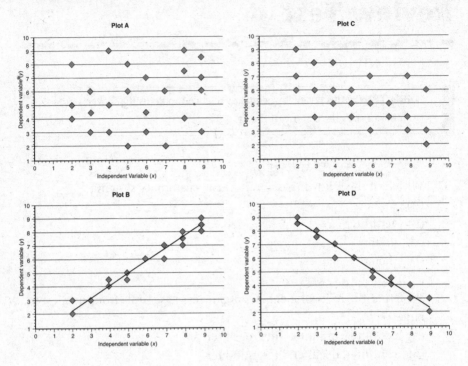

3. Which plot shows a strong positive correlation between variables?
   (A) Plot A
   (B) Plot B
   (C) Plot C
   (D) Plot D

4. Which plot shows a strong negative correlation between variables?
   (A) Plot A
   (B) Plot B
   (C) Plot C
   (D) Plot D

5. What kind of correlation does Plot C show?
   (A) no correlation
   (B) incomplete correlation
   (C) weak negative correlation
   (D) median correlation

6. Which of the plots provides evidence of causation?
   (A) Plot A
   (B) Plot C
   (C) Plots B and D
   (D) None of the plots

_____

7. What is the name of the compound with the formula H_2O?
   (A) water
   (B) dihydrogen dioxide
   (C) methane
   (D) glucose

8. What is the name of the compound with the formula CO_2?
   (A) water
   (B) dicarbon monoxide
   (C) methane
   (D) carbon dioxide

9. How many hydrogen atoms in total are in $C_6H_{12}O_6$ and H_2O?
   (A) 2
   (B) 6
   (C) 12
   (D) 14

QUESTIONS 10 THROUGH 12 REFER TO THE FOLLOWING SET:

Set B: {3, 3, 6, 6, 9, 9, 9}

10. What is the mode in Set B?
    (A) 3
    (B) 6
    (C) 6.4
    (D) 9

11. What is the simple average of the numbers of Set B (rounded to the nearest tenth)?
    (A) 6.4
    (B) 7.5
    (C) 15.0
    (D) 45.0

12. If the numbers equal to the mode of Set B are weighted 75% and all other numbers combined are weighted 25%, what is the weighted average of Set B (rounded to the nearest tenth)?
    (A) 3.9
    (B) 5.6
    (C) 6.4
    (D) 7.9

---

13. Which of the following is a brief definition of cell theory?
    (A) The theory that the sun is the center of the solar system and that the planets orbit around it
    (B) The theory that all complex organisms are composed of small, fundamental, living units
    (C) The theory that all physical material (matter) is made up of extremely small, fundamental particles
    (D) The theory that natural selection is responsible for adaptation (adjusting to the environment) and speciation (the development of species)

14. Which of the following is a brief definition of the theory of evolution?
    (A) The theory that the sun is the center of the solar system and that the planets orbit around it
    (B) The theory that all complex organisms are composed of small, fundamental, living units
    (C) The theory that all physical material (matter) is made up of extremely small, fundamental particles
    (D) The theory that natural selection is responsible for adaptation (adjusting to the environment) and speciation (the development of species)

15. Match the statements below with the role they play in the experimental process using the following vocabulary words:

    question   hypothesis   prediction   test   analysis   conclusion

    a. "If water absorbs less blue light than any other color in the visible spectrum, a reflection of blue light will be brighter than a reflection of any other visible color."
    b. "Water splits visible light into different colors and absorbs different amounts of these various colors of light. Water reflects more blue light than other colors of light."
    c. "Why does water appear blue?"
    d. "All visible-light colors were tested, and the strongest reflection was produced by blue light."
    e. "Water appears blue because it reflects blue light more than it reflects other colors of light."
    f. "Lights of different colors were reflected off of water and onto a light-sensitive panel. The intensity (strength) of each color's reflection was measured."

Answers Explained

1. **(A)** The mile is a customary unit of length. Choice B is incorrect because a centiliter is a metric unit of capacity or volume. Choice C is incorrect because the gram is a metric unit of mass. Choice D is incorrect because the meter is a metric unit of length.

2. **(D)** A milliliter is 10^{-3} liters. A centiliter is 10^{-2} liters. A deciliter is 10^{-1} liters.

3. **(B)** The points in Plot B show a clear positive (upward) trend as the independent variable (x-value) increases. This shows that the dependent variable increases in proportion with the independent variable and suggests the possibility of cause and effect. Choice A is incorrect because Plot A shows no correlation. Choice C is incorrect because Plot C shows a weak negative correlation. Choice D is incorrect because Plot D shows a strong negative correlation.

4. **(D)** The points in Plot D show a clear negative (downward) trend as the independent variable (x-value) increases. This shows that the dependent variable decreases in proportion with the independent variable and suggests the possibility of cause and effect. Choice A is incorrect because Plot A shows no correlation. Choice B is incorrect because Plot B shows a strong positive correlation. Choice C is incorrect because Plot C shows a weak negative correlation.

5. **(C)** Plot C shows a negative (downward) trend, but the organization of the points is too loose to be considered a strong correlation. Choice A is incorrect because the plot shows some correlation. Choices B and D are incorrect because there is no such thing as either an incomplete or a median correlation.

6. **(D)** Correlation refers to two things that happen together and that may be related. Causation, however, refers to a provable cause-and-effect relationship between two things. In causation, one thing clearly and definitely causes the other. Remember, just because two things are correlated does not mean that causation exists between them. Correlation is not causation.

7. **(A)** H_2O is the chemical formula for water. Choice B is incorrect because dihydrogen dioxide is written as H_2O_2 and is commonly called hydrogen peroxide. Choice C is incorrect because the formula for methane is CH_4. Choice D is incorrect because the formula for glucose is $C_6H_{12}O_6$.

8. **(D)** CO_2 is the chemical formula for carbon dioxide. Choice A is incorrect because the formula for water is H_2O. Choice B is incorrect because there is no compound called dicarbon monoxide. If it existed, though, its formula would be C_2O. Choice C is incorrect because the formula for methane is CH_4.

9. **(D)** The subscript numbers in a chemical formula indicate the number of atoms of that element present in the compound. When no subscript is present, a 1 is implied. Add the occurrences of H atoms based on the subscripts: $12 + 2 = 14$

10. **(D)** The mode is the element that appears the most often. There are more 9s in the set than any other element, so the mode is 9.

11. **(A)** The sum of the elements in the set is 45, and there are 7 elements in the set. The arithmetic mean (average) is $45 \div 7 = 6.428571$. Round down because 2 is less than 5. The answer is 6.4.

12. **(D)** The mode is 9. The average of the group of 9s is $27 \div 3 = 9$. Multiply 9 by 0.75 to give this average a weight of 75%: $9 \times 0.75 = 6.75$. The average of the rest of the elements is 4.5. Multiply 4.5 by 0.25 to give this average a weight of 25%: $4.5 \times 0.25 = 1.125$. To find the weighted average, add the $6.75 + 1.125 = 7.875$. Round up since 7 is greater than 5. The answer is 7.9.

13. **(B)** Cell theory states that all complex organisms are composed of small, fundamental, living units.

14. **(D)** The theory of evolution states that natural selection is responsible for adaptation (adjustment to the environment) and speciation (the development of species).

15. **a.** prediction
    b. hypothesis
    c. question
    d. analysis
    e. conclusion
    f. test

MODEL TEST

The following model test is not related to the official GED® test produced and distributed by the American Council on Education® (ACE®) and the GED Testing Service. ACE® and GED Testing Service LLC have not approved, authorized, endorsed, been involved in the development of, or licensed the substantive content of this model test.

ANSWER SHEET
Model Test

REASONING THROUGH LANGUAGE ARTS EXAM

SECTION 1

1. Ⓐ Ⓑ Ⓒ Ⓓ

2. _____

3. Ⓐ Ⓑ Ⓒ Ⓓ

4. Ⓐ Ⓑ Ⓒ Ⓓ

5. _____

6. Ⓐ Ⓑ Ⓒ Ⓓ

7. Use the lines below for your answer.

8. Ⓐ Ⓑ Ⓒ Ⓓ

9. _____

10. Ⓐ Ⓑ Ⓒ Ⓓ

11. Ⓐ Ⓑ Ⓒ Ⓓ

12. Ⓐ Ⓑ Ⓒ Ⓓ

13. Ⓐ Ⓑ Ⓒ Ⓓ

14. Ⓐ Ⓑ Ⓒ Ⓓ

15. Ⓐ Ⓑ Ⓒ Ⓓ

16. Ⓐ Ⓑ Ⓒ Ⓓ

17. _____

18. Ⓐ Ⓑ Ⓒ Ⓓ

19. Ⓐ Ⓑ Ⓒ Ⓓ

20. Ⓐ Ⓑ Ⓒ Ⓓ

7. _____

_____

_____

_____

_____

SECTION 2: Extended Response

_____

_____

_____

_____

_____

_____

_____

_____

_____

_____

_____

_____

_____

_____

_____

_____

_____

ANSWER SHEET
Model Test

REASONING THROUGH LANGUAGE ARTS EXAM

SECTION 3

21. Ⓐ Ⓑ Ⓒ Ⓓ

22. _____

23. Ⓐ Ⓑ Ⓒ Ⓓ

24. Ⓐ Ⓑ Ⓒ Ⓓ

25. _____

26. Ⓐ Ⓑ Ⓒ Ⓓ

27. Ⓐ Ⓑ Ⓒ Ⓓ

28. 1._____

    2._____

    3._____

29. Ⓐ Ⓑ Ⓒ Ⓓ

30. Ⓐ Ⓑ Ⓒ Ⓓ

31. Ⓐ Ⓑ Ⓒ Ⓓ

32. Ⓐ Ⓑ Ⓒ Ⓓ

33. Ⓐ Ⓑ Ⓒ Ⓓ

34. Ⓐ Ⓑ Ⓒ Ⓓ

35. Ⓐ Ⓑ Ⓒ Ⓓ

36. Ⓐ Ⓑ Ⓒ Ⓓ

37. Ⓐ Ⓑ Ⓒ Ⓓ

38. Ⓐ Ⓑ Ⓒ Ⓓ

39. Ⓐ Ⓑ Ⓒ Ⓓ

40. Ⓐ Ⓑ Ⓒ Ⓓ

41. Ⓐ Ⓑ Ⓒ Ⓓ

42. _____

43. Ⓐ Ⓑ Ⓒ Ⓓ

44. Ⓐ Ⓑ Ⓒ Ⓓ

45. Ⓐ Ⓑ Ⓒ Ⓓ

46. Ⓐ Ⓑ Ⓒ Ⓓ

47. _____

48. Ⓐ Ⓑ Ⓒ Ⓓ

49. Ⓐ Ⓑ Ⓒ Ⓓ

50. Ⓐ Ⓑ Ⓒ Ⓓ

51. Ⓐ Ⓑ Ⓒ Ⓓ

ANSWER SHEET
Model Test

REASONING THROUGH LANGUAGE ARTS EXAM

SECTION 3

52. Use the lines below for your answer.

53. Ⓐ Ⓑ Ⓒ Ⓓ

54. Ⓐ Ⓑ Ⓒ Ⓓ

55. Ⓐ Ⓑ Ⓒ Ⓓ

52. _____

_____

_____

_____

_____

REASONING THROUGH LANGUAGE ARTS EXAM

DIRECTIONS: This practice exam contains fiction and nonfiction passages, which you will need to analyze in order to answer the 55 questions and one extended response that follow. Section 1 has 20 questions, and you will be given 35 minutes to complete it. Section 2 includes two passages and an extended-response prompt, which you must complete within 45 minutes. After Section 2, you may take a 10-minute break. Section 3 will contain 35 questions, and you will be given 60 minutes to complete it.

SECTION 1

Section 1 has 20 questions, and you have 35 minutes to complete this section. Set your own timer, and see how long it takes you to complete this section.

QUESTIONS 1 THROUGH 7 ARE BASED ON THE FOLLOWING PASSAGE:

A GIFT

1   The door opened and Jim stepped in and closed it. He looked thin and very serious. Poor fellow, he was only twenty-two—and to be burdened with a family! He needed a new overcoat and he was without gloves.

2   Jim stopped inside the door, as immovable as a setter at the scent of quail. His eyes were fixed upon Della, and there was an expression in them that she could not read, and it terrified her. It was not anger, nor surprise, nor disapproval, nor horror, nor any of the sentiments that she had been prepared for. He simply stared at her fixedly with that peculiar expression on his face.

3   Della wriggled off the table and went for him.

4   "Jim, darling," she cried, "don't look at me that way. I had my hair cut off and sold because I couldn't have lived through Christmas without giving you a present. It'll grow out again—you won't mind, will you? I just had to do it. My hair grows awfully fast. Say 'Merry Christmas!' Jim, and let's be happy. You don't know what a nice—what a beautiful, nice gift I've got for you."

5   "You've cut off your hair?" asked Jim, laboriously, as if he had not arrived at that patent fact yet even after the hardest mental labor.

6   "Cut it off and sold it," said Della. "Don't you like me just as well, anyhow? I'm me without my hair, ain't I?"

7   Jim looked about the room curiously.

8   "You say your hair is gone?" he said, with an air almost of idiocy.

9   "You needn't look for it," said Della. "It's sold, I tell you—sold and gone, too. It's Christmas Eve, boy. Be good to me, for it went for you. Maybe the hairs of my head were numbered," she went on with sudden serious sweetness, "but nobody could ever count my love for you. Shall I put the chops on, Jim?"

10   Out of his trance Jim seemed quickly to wake. He enfolded his Della. For ten seconds let us regard with discreet **scrutiny** some inconsequential object in the other direction. Eight dollars a week or a million a year—what is the difference? A mathematician or a wit would give you the wrong answer. The magi brought valuable gifts, but that was not among them. This dark assertion will be illuminated later on.

11   Jim drew a package from his overcoat pocket and threw it upon the table.

12   "Don't make any mistake, Dell," he said, "about me. I don't think there's anything in the way of a haircut or a shave or a shampoo that could make me like my girl any less. But if you'll unwrap that package you may see why you had me going a while at first."

13   White fingers and nimble tore at the string and paper. And then an ecstatic scream of joy; and then, alas! a quick feminine change to hysterical tears and wails, necessitating the immediate employment of all the comforting powers of the lord of the flat.

14   For there lay The Combs—the set of combs, side and back, that Della had worshipped long in a Broadway window. Beautiful combs, pure tortoise shell, with jeweled rims—just the shade to wear in the beautiful vanished hair. They were expensive combs, she knew, and her heart had simply craved and yearned over them without the least hope of possession. And now, they were hers, but the tresses that should have adorned the coveted adornments were gone.

15   But she hugged them to her bosom, and at length she was able to look up with dim eyes and a smile and say: "My hair grows so fast, Jim!"

16   And then Della leaped up like a little singed cat and cried, "Oh, oh!"

17   Jim had not yet seen his beautiful present. She held it out to him eagerly upon her open palm. The dull precious metal seemed to flash with a reflection of her bright and ardent spirit.

18   "Isn't it a dandy, Jim? I hunted all over town to find it. You'll have to look at the time a hundred times a day now. Give me your watch. I want to see how it looks on it."

19   Instead of obeying, Jim tumbled down on the couch and put his hands under the back of his head and smiled.

20   "Dell," said he, "let's put our Christmas presents away and keep 'em a while. They're too nice to use just at present. I sold the watch to get the money to buy your combs. And now suppose you put the chops on."

Source: Henry, O. Excerpt from *Gift of the Magi.* Reprint of the 1906 Edition, Project Gutenberg, 2015. *www.gutenberg.org/files/7256/7256-h/7256-h.htm.*

1. What is the best meaning of the word "scrutiny" in paragraph 10?
    (A) investigation
    (B) scolding
    (C) meaning
    (D) fault

2. Della can best be described as _____ that Jim won't like her hair.

3. Which of the following is the best characterization of Della?
    (A) self-centered
    (B) devoted
    (C) skeptical
    (D) naive

4. Which of the following literary terms describes the loss of both the hair and the watch?
    (A) simile
    (B) hyperbole
    (C) metaphor
    (D) irony

5. From the choices below, write the action that wakes Jim from his trance, in the box.

> Della tells him that she loves him.
> Della tells him that she cut her hair.
> Della tells him that she has a gift for him.
> Della tells him that she is upset about her hair.

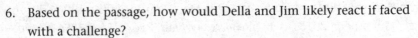

6. Based on the passage, how would Della and Jim likely react if faced with a challenge?
   (A) calmly
   (B) frantically
   (C) wisely
   (D) eccentrically

7. Did Jim react to the loss of his wife's long hair in an appropriate manner? Briefly explain and support your answer.

QUESTIONS 8 THROUGH 13 ARE BASED ON THE FOLLOWING PASSAGE:

COMMON SENSE

1   A government of our own is our natural right: And when a man seriously reflects on the precariousness of human affairs, he will become convinced, that it is infinitely wiser and safer, to form a constitution of our own in a cool deliberate manner, while we have it in our power, than to trust such an interesting event to time and chance. If we omit it now, some, Massanello[1] may hereafter arise, who laying hold of popular disquietudes, may collect together the desperate and discontented, and by assuming to themselves the powers of government, may sweep away the liberties of the continent like a deluge. Should the government of America return again into the hands of Britain, the tottering situation of things, will be a temptation for some desperate adventurer to try his fortune; and in such a case, what relief can Britain give? Ere she could hear the news, the fatal business might be done; and ourselves suffering like the wretched Britons under the oppression of the Conqueror. Ye that oppose independence now, ye know not what ye do; ye are opening a door to eternal tyranny, by keeping vacant the seat of government. There are thousands, and tens of thousands, who would think it glorious to expel from the continent, that barbarous and hellish power, which hath stirred up the Indians and Negroes to destroy us, the cruelty hath a double guilt, it is dealing brutally by us, and treacherously by them.

2   To talk of friendship with those in whom our reason forbids us to have faith, and our affections wounded through a thousand pores instruct us to detest, is madness and folly. Every day wears out the little remains of kindred between us and them, and can there be any reason to hope, that as the relationship expires, the affection will increase, or that we shall agree better, when we have ten times more and greater concerns to quarrel over than ever?

3   Ye that tell us of harmony and reconciliation, can ye restore to us the time that is past? Can ye give to prostitution its former innocence? Neither can ye reconcile Britain and America. The last cord now is broken, the people of England are presenting addresses against us. There are

---

[1] *Thomas Anello, otherwise Massanello, a fisherman of Naples, who after spiriting up his countrymen in the public market place, against the oppression of the Spaniards, to whom the place was then subject, prompted them to revolt, and in the space of a day became king.*

injuries which nature cannot forgive; she would cease to be nature if she did. As well can the lover forgive the ravisher of his mistress, as the continent forgive the murders of Britain. The Almighty hath implanted in us these **unextinguishable** feelings for good and wise purposes. They are the guardians of his image in our hearts. They distinguish us from the herd of common animals. The social compact would dissolve, and justice be extirpated from the earth, or have only a casual existence were we callous to the touches of affection. The robber, and the murderer, would often escape unpunished, did not the injuries which our tempers sustain, provoke us into justice.

4   O ye that love mankind! Ye that dare oppose, not only the tyranny, but the tyrant, stand forth! Every spot of the old world is overrun with oppression. Freedom hath been hunted round the globe. Asia, and Africa, have long expelled her. Europe regards her like a stranger, and England hath given her warning to depart. O! receive the fugitive, and prepare in time an asylum for mankind.

Source: Paine, Thomas. Excerpt from *Common Sense*. Reprint of the 1776 Edition, Project Gutenberg, 2015. *www.gutenberg.org/files/147/147-h/147-h.htm.*

8. What is the main idea of the first paragraph?
   (A) America should be returned to Britain.
   (B) The doors to eternal tyranny must be opened.
   (C) Having a government for the people is a natural right.
   (D) Writing a constitution must be done in a deliberate manner.

9. What is Massanello's occupation? Write the correct answer in the box below.

      Fisherman
      Pundit
      Philosopher
      Doctor

10. What was the most likely purpose of this writing?
    (A) to call people into action
    (B) to calm an agitated group of people
    (C) to make claims about the benefits of tyranny
    (D) to describe liberty

11. What is the best definition for the word "unextinguishable" in the third paragraph?
    (A) unintentional
    (B) thought out
    (C) intense
    (D) unable to quell

12. Based on the third paragraph, how does the author feel about the prospect of returning to an earlier time?
    (A) It is attainable.
    (B) It is impossible.
    (C) There are difficulties associated with it.
    (D) It is the best option.

13. What was the likely catalyst for the author writing this passage?
    (A) an oppressive government
    (B) a desire to move in an unexplored direction
    (C) patriotism
    (D) curiosity

QUESTIONS 14 THROUGH 20 ARE BASED ON THE FOLLOWING PASSAGE:

THE WOODS

1   I went to the woods because I wished to live deliberately, to front only the essential facts of life, and see if I could not learn what it had to teach, and not, when I came to die, discover that I had not lived. I did not wish to live what was not life, living is so dear; nor did I wish to practice resignation, unless it was quite necessary. I wanted to live deep and suck out all the marrow of life, to live so sturdily and Spartan-like as to put to rout all that was not life, to cut a broad swath and shave close, to drive life into a corner, and reduce it to its lowest terms, and, if it proved to be mean, why then to get the whole and genuine meanness of it, and publish its meanness to the world; or if it were sublime, to know it by experience, and be able to give a true account of it in my next excursion. For most men, it appears to me, are in a strange uncertainty about it, whether it is of the devil or of God, and have somewhat hastily concluded that it is the chief end of man here to "glorify God and enjoy him forever."

2   Still we live meanly, like ants; though the fable tells us that we were long ago changed into men; like pygmies we fight with cranes; it is error upon error, and clout upon clout, and our best virtue has for its occasion a superfluous and evitable wretchedness. Our life is frittered away by detail. An honest man has hardly need to count more than his ten fingers, or in extreme cases he may add his ten toes, and lump the rest. Simplicity, simplicity, simplicity! I say, let your affairs be as two or three, and not a hundred or a thousand; instead of a million count half a dozen, and keep your accounts on your thumb-nail. In the midst of this chopping sea of civilized life, such are the clouds and storms and quicksands and thousand-and-one items to be allowed for, that a man has to live, if he would not founder and go to the bottom and not make his port at all, by dead reckoning, and he must be a great calculator indeed who succeeds. Simplify, simplify. Instead of three meals a day, if it be necessary eat but one; instead of a hundred dishes, five; and reduce other things in proportion. Our life is like a German Confederacy, made up of petty states, with its boundary forever fluctuating, so that even a German cannot tell you how it is bounded at any moment. The nation itself, with all its so-called internal improvements, which, by the way are all external and superficial, is just such an **unwieldy** and overgrown establishment,

cluttered with furniture and tripped up by its own traps, ruined by luxury and heedless expense, by want of calculation and a worthy aim, as the million households in the land; and the only cure for it, as for them, is in a rigid economy, a stern and more than Spartan simplicity of life and elevation of purpose. It lives too fast. Men think that it is essential that the Nation have commerce, and export ice, and talk through a telegraph, and ride thirty miles an hour, without a doubt, whether they do or not; but whether we should live like baboons or like men, is a little uncertain. If we do not get out sleepers, and forge rails, and devote days and nights to the work, but go to tinkering upon our lives to improve them, who will build railroads? And if railroads are not built, how shall we get to heaven in season? But if we stay at home and mind our business, who will want railroads? We do not ride on the railroad; it rides upon us. Did you ever think what those sleepers are that underlie the railroad? Each one is a man, an Irishman, or a Yankee man. The rails are laid on them, and they are covered with sand, and the cars run smoothly over them. They are sound sleepers, I assure you. And every few years a new lot is laid down and run over; so that, if some have the pleasure of riding on a rail, others have the misfortune to be ridden upon. And when they run over a man that is walking in his sleep, a supernumerary sleeper in the wrong position, and wake him up, they suddenly stop the cars, and make a hue and cry about it, as if this were an exception. I am glad to know that it takes a gang of men for every five miles to keep the sleepers down and level in their beds as it is, for this is a sign that they may sometime get up again.

Source: Thoreau, Henry David. Excerpt from *Walden, and On the Duty of Civil Disobedience.* Reprint of the 1854 Edition, Project Gutenberg, 2013. *www.gutenberg.org/files/205/205-h/205-h.htm.*

14. At the beginning of the second paragraph, Thoreau writes, "Still we live meanly, like ants." What literary device does he use here?
    (A) analogy
    (B) personification
    (C) juxtaposition
    (D) simile

15. What was the narrator's purpose for going to the woods?
    (A) to face only life
    (B) to seek adventure
    (C) to live like God
    (D) to teach those who lived in the wild

16. Which of the following sums up the author's message?
    (A) Attain luxury.
    (B) Simplify.
    (C) Live meanly.
    (D) Go on excursions.

17. The narrator would most likely _____ living in a city.

18. What does the author mean by, "We do not ride on the railroad; it rides upon us"?
    (A) The railroad crosses many towns.
    (B) Technology has encroached upon us.
    (C) Traveling by railroad is uncomfortable.
    (D) It took many people to build the railroad.

19. Which of the following, in general, does the author find most problematic?
    (A) the pace of life
    (B) the telegraph
    (C) commerce
    (D) gangs

20. What is the best definition of the word "unwieldy" in the second paragraph?
    (A) difficult to carry
    (B) unorganized
    (C) unmade
    (D) displeasing

END OF SECTION 1

SECTION 2: Extended Response

Section 2 has one extended response, and you have 45 minutes to complete this section. Set your own timer, and see how long it takes you to complete this section.

> **DIRECTIONS:** Read and utilize the following passages to construct an extended response to the following prompt:
>
> Do laws such as the Clean Air Act address the specific issues relating to air quality? Cite specific information and examples to support your position and be sure to develop your response fully.

AIR QUALITY

Research has linked air pollution to many effects on ecosystems. Studies have shown that air pollutants such as sulfur can lead to excess amounts of acid in lakes and streams and damage trees and forest soils. Nitrogen in the atmosphere has been found to harm fish and other aquatic life when deposited on surface waters.

Research has helped to understand ozone pollution's ability to damage tree leaves and negatively affect scenic vistas in protected natural areas. Mercury and other heavy metal compounds that are emitted into the air from combustion of fuel and deposited have been found to accumulate in plants and animals, some of which are consumed by people.

Research is conducted to understand the ecological impacts of air pollutants and to support the secondary National Ambient Air Quality Standards (NAAQS), which provide public welfare protection, including protection against decreased visibility and damage to animals, crops, vegetation, and buildings. Deposition modeling tools are developed, air pollution emissions and precursor pollutants (e.g., ammonia) are measured and pollutant deposition on ecosystems is measured and quantified, among other research activities.

Source: "Ecosystems and Air Quality." *United States Environmental Protection Agency.* Last accessed August 4, 2016. *www.epa.gov.*

CLEAN AIR ACT

In 1990, Congress dramatically revised and expanded the Clean Air Act, providing EPA even broader authority to implement and enforce regulations reducing air pollutant emissions. The 1990 Amendments also placed an increased emphasis on more cost-effective approaches to reduce air pollution.

Clean Air Act Roles and Responsibilities

The Clean Air Act is a federal law covering the entire country. However, states, tribes and local governments do a lot of the work to meet the Act's requirements. For example, representatives from these agencies work with companies to reduce air pollution. They also review and approve permit applications for industries or chemical processes.

EPA's Role

Under the Clean Air Act, EPA sets limits on certain air pollutants, including setting limits on how much can be in the air anywhere in the United States. This helps to ensure basic health and environmental protection from air pollution for all Americans. The Clean Air Act also gives EPA the authority to limit emissions of air pollutants coming from sources like chemical plants, utilities, and steel mills. Individual states or tribes may have stronger air pollution laws, but they may not have weaker pollution limits than those set by EPA.

EPA must approve state, tribal, and local agency plans for reducing air pollution. If a plan does not meet the necessary requirements, EPA can issue sanctions against the state and, if necessary, take over enforcing the Clean Air Act in that area.

EPA assists state, tribal, and local agencies by providing research, expert studies, engineering designs, and funding to support clean air progress. Since 1970, Congress and the EPA have provided several billion dollars to the states, local agencies, and tribal nations to accomplish this.

State and Local Governments' Role

It makes sense for state and local air pollution agencies to take the lead in carrying out the Clean Air Act. They are able to develop solutions for pollution problems that require special understanding of local industries, geography, housing, and travel patterns, as well as other factors.

State, local, and tribal governments also monitor air quality, inspect facilities under their jurisdictions and enforce Clean Air Act regulations.

States have to develop State Implementation Plans (SIPs) that outline how each state will control air pollution under the Clean Air Act. A SIP is a collection of the regulations, programs and policies that a state will use to clean up polluted areas. The states must involve the public and industries through hearings and opportunities to comment on the development of each state plan.

Tribal Nations' Role

In its 1990 revision of the Clean Air Act, Congress recognized that Indian Tribes have the authority to implement air pollution control programs.

EPA's Tribal Authority Rule gives Tribes the ability to develop air quality management programs, write rules to reduce air pollution and implement and enforce their rules in Indian Country. While state and local agencies are responsible for all Clean Air Act requirements, Tribes may develop and implement only those parts of the Clean Air Act that are appropriate for their lands.

Source: "A Brief History of the Clean Air Act." *United States Environmental Protection Agency.* Last accessed August 4, 2016. *www.epa.gov/sites/production/files/2015-08/documents/peg.pdf.*

END OF SECTION 2

SECTION 3

Section 3 has 35 questions, and you have 60 minutes to complete this section. Set your own timer and see how long it takes you to complete this section.

QUESTIONS 21 THROUGH 28 ARE BASED ON THE FOLLOWING PASSAGE:

GI BILL

1   While World War II was still being fought, the Department of Labor estimated that, after the war, 15 million men and women who had been serving in the armed services would be unemployed. To reduce the possibility of postwar depression brought on by widespread unemployment, the National Resources Planning Board, a White House agency, studied postwar manpower needs as early as 1942 and in June 1943 recommended a series of programs for education and training. The American Legion designed the main features of what became the Serviceman's Readjustment Act and pushed it through Congress. The bill unanimously passed both chambers of Congress in the spring of 1944. President Franklin D. Roosevelt signed it into law on June 22, 1944, just days after the D-day invasion of Normandy.

2   American Legion publicist Jack Cejnar called it the "GI Bill of Rights," as it offered Federal aid to help veterans adjust to civilian life in the areas of hospitalization, purchase of homes and businesses, and especially, education. This act provided tuition, **subsistence**, books and supplies, equipment, and counseling services for veterans to continue their education in school or college. Within the following 7 years, approximately 8 million veterans received educational benefits. Under the act, approximately 2,300,000 attended colleges and universities, 3,500,000 received school training, and 3,400,000 received on-the-job training. The number of degrees awarded by U.S. colleges and universities more than doubled between 1940 and 1950, and the percentage of Americans with bachelor degrees, or advanced degrees, rose from 4.6 percent in 1945 to 25 percent a half-century later.

3   By 1956, when it expired, the education-and-training portion of the GI Bill had disbursed $14.5 billion to veterans—but the Veterans Administration estimated the increase in Federal income taxes alone

would pay for the cost of the bill several times over. By 1955, 4.3 million home loans had been granted, with a total face value of $33 billion.

Source: "Servicemen's Readjustment Act (1944)." *Our Documents*. Last accessed August 5, 2016. *www.ourdocuments.gov/doc.php?flash=true&doc=76.*

21. The GI Bill
    (A) failed to pass the Senate.
    (B) failed to pass the House of Representatives.
    (C) passed unanimously in both chambers of Congress.
    (D) passed with only a slight majority in both chambers of Congress.

22. From the choices below, choose the best synonym for the word "subsistence," found in the second paragraph of the passage, and write that synonym in the box below.

    Debt
    Support
    Inheritance
    Life

    ┌──┐
    │   │
    │   │
    │   │
    │   │
    └──┘

23. How did the Veterans Administration plan to fund the GI Bill?
    (A) interest from student loans
    (B) sales tax revenue from each state
    (C) cost of living increase
    (D) increase in federal income taxes

24. What was the purpose of the GI Bill?
    (A) to provide for veterans returning home after war
    (B) to increase the risk for a national recession
    (C) to create a housing boom
    (D) to decrease medical insurance availability

25. The anniversary of the Invasion of Normandy is also known as

    _____.

26. When was the Servicemen's Readjustment Act first signed into law?
    (A) 1942
    (B) 1943
    (C) 1944
    (D) 1945

27. What were the most likely long-term effects of the GI Bill?
    (A) Veterans would increase their risk for homelessness.
    (B) Veterans would have a better chance at success after serving active duty.
    (C) Fewer veterans would go to college.
    (D) More veterans would rent homes instead of purchasing them.

28. From the choices below, choose the three problems from everyday civilian life that the Servicemen's Readjustment Act helped returning World War II veterans solve. Write your answers in the box below.

    affording housing
    affording marriage
    affording unemployment insurance
    affording a college education
    affording divorce
    affording childcare

> **DIRECTIONS:** The passages that follow are not complete. You have to select the best sentence or best completion of a sentence from among the A, B, C, or D choices. Choose one.

QUESTIONS 29 THROUGH 33 ARE EMBEDDED IN THE FOLLOWING PASSAGE:

WILLIAM SHAKESPEARE

The father in municipal office.

In July 1564, when William was three months old, the plague raged with unwonted vehemence at Stratford, and his father liberally contributed to the relief of its poverty stricken victims. Fortune still favored him. On July 4, 1565, he reached the dignity of an alderman. From 1567 onwards he was accorded in the corporation archives the honorable prefix of "Mr." At Michaelmas 1568 he attained the highest office in the corporation gift, that of bailiff, and during his year of office the corporation for the first time entertained actors at Stratford. The Queen's Company and the Earl of Worcester's Company each received from John Shakespeare an official welcome.

29.

Select ⌄

(A) On september 5, 1571, he was chief alderman, a post which he retained till september 30 the following year.

(B) He was chief alderman, a post which he retained till September 30 the following year, but that was on September 5, 1571.

(C) On September 5, 1571, he was chief alderman, a post which he retained till September 30 the following year.

(D) He was chief alderman, on September 5, 1571, a post which he retained till September 30 the following year.

In 1573 Alexander Webbe, the husband of his wife's sister Agnes, made him overseer of his will; in 1575 he bought two houses in Stratford, one of them doubtless the alleged birthplace in Henley Street; in 1576 he contributed twelvepence to the beadle's salary. But after Michaelmas 1572 he took a less active part in municipal affairs; he grew irregular in his attendance at the council meetings, and signs were soon apparent that his luck had turned. In

1578 he was unable to pay, with his colleagues, either the sum of fourpence for the relief of the poor or his contribution "towards the furniture of three pikemen, two bellmen, and one archer" who were sent by the corporation to attend a muster of the trained bands of the county.

Brothers and sisters.

30. | Select   ∨ |
     | :-- |
     | (A) Meanwhile his increasing family. |
     | (B) Meanwhile his family are increasing. |
     | (C) Meanwhile his family were increasing. |
     | (D) Meanwhile his family was increasing. |

Four children besides the poet—three sons, Gilbert (baptized October 13, 1566), Richard (baptized March 11, 1574), and Edmund (baptized May 3, 1580), with a daughter Joan (baptized April 15, 1569)—reached maturity. A daughter Ann was baptized September 28, 1571, and was buried on April 4, 1579. To meet his growing liabilities, the father borrowed money from his wife's kinsfolk, and he and his wife mortgaged, on November 14, 1578, Asbies, her valuable property at Wilmcote, for £40 to Edmund Lambert of Barton-on-the-Heath, who had married her sister, Joan Arden. Lambert was to receive no interest on his loan, but was to take the "rents and profits" of the estate. Asbies was thereby alienated forever. Next year, on October 15, 1579, John and his wife made over to Robert Webbe, doubtless a relative of Alexander Webbe, for the sum apparently of £40, his wife's property at Snitterfield.

The father's financial difficulties.

John Shakespeare obviously chafed under the humiliation of having parted, although as he hoped only temporarily, with his wife's property of Asbies, and in the autumn of 1580 he offered to pay off the mortgage; but his brother-in-law, Lambert, retorted that other sums were owing, and he would accept all or none.

31.

Select   ∨

(A) The negotiation, which was the beginning of much litigation,
thus proved abortive.

(B) The Negotiation, which was the beginning of much litigation,
thus proved abortive.

(C) The negotiation which was the beginning of much litigation
thus proved abortive.

(D) The negotiation, which was the beginning off much litigation,
thus proved abortive.

Through 1585 and 1586 a creditor, John Brown, was embarrassingly importunate, and, after obtaining a writ of distraint, Brown informed the local court that the debtor had no goods on which distraint could be levied. On September 6, 1586, John was deprived of his alderman's gown, on the ground of his long absence from the council meetings.

Education.

Happily John Shakespeare was at no expense for the education of his four sons. They were entitled to free tuition at the grammar school of Stratford, which was reconstituted on a medieval foundation by Edward VI. The eldest son, William, probably entered the school in 1571, when Walter Roche was master, and perhaps he knew something of Thomas Hunt, who succeeded Roche in 1577.

32.

Select   ∨

(A) The instruction that he received was mainly confined to the
latin language and literature.

(B) Latin language and literature was the instruction that he
received and was mainly confined to that.

(C) The instruction that he received was mainly confined to the
Latin language and literature.

(D) The instruction that he received, was mainly confined, to the
Latin language and literature.

From the Latin accidence, boys of the period, at schools of the type of that at Stratford, were led, through conversation books like the "Sententiæ Pueriles" and Lily's grammar, to the perusal of such authors as Seneca Terence, Cicero,

Virgil, Plautus, Ovid, and Horace. The eclogues of the popular renaissance poet, Mantuanus, were often preferred to Virgil's for beginners. The rudiments of Greek were occasionally taught in Elizabethan grammar schools to very promising pupils; but such coincidences as have been detected between expressions in Greek plays and in Shakespeare seem due to accident, and not to any study, either at school or elsewhere, of the Athenian drama.

Dr. Farmer enunciated in his "Essay on Shakespeare's Learning" (1767) the theory that Shakespeare knew no language but his own, and owed whatever knowledge he displayed of the classics and of Italian and French literature to English translations. But several of the books in French and Italian whence Shakespeare derived the plots of his dramas—Belleforest's "Histoires Tragiques," Ser Giovanni's "Il Pecorone," and Cinthio's "Hecatommithi," for example were not accessible to him in English translations; and on more general grounds the theory of his ignorance is adequately confuted.

33. **Select** ⌄

(A) A boy with Shakespeares exceptional alertness of intellect, during whose schooldays a training in Latin classics lay within reach, could hardly lack in future years all means of access to the literature of France and Italy.

(B) A boy with Shakespeare's exceptional alertness of intellect, during whose schooldays a training in Latin classics lay within reach, could hardly lack in future years all means of access to the literature of France and Italy.

(C) A boy with Shakespeare's exceptional alertness of intellect, during whose schooldays a training in Latin classics lay within reach, could hardly lack in future years all means of access to the literature of france and italy.

(D) A boy with Shakespeare's exceptional alertness of intellect during whose schooldays a training in Latin classics lay within reach could hardly lack in future years all means of access to the literature of France and Italy.

Source: Lee, Sidney. Excerpt from *A Life of William Shakespeare.* Reprint of the 1899 Edition, Project Gutenberg, 2007. *www.gutenberg.org/files/23464/23464-h/23464-h.htm#page4.*

QUESTIONS 34 THROUGH 38 ARE EMBEDDED IN THE FOLLOWING
PASSAGE:

LIFE AND WORK

WHAT IS THE IDEA?

We have only started on our development of our country—we have not
as yet, with all our talk of wonderful progress, done more than scratch the
surface. The progress has been wonderful enough—but when we compare
what we have done with what there is to do, then our past accomplishments
are as nothing. When we consider that more power is used merely in plowing
the soil than is used in all the industrial establishments of the country put
together, an inkling comes of how much opportunity there is ahead. And
now, with so many countries of the world in ferment and with so much unrest
everywhere, is an excellent time to suggest something of the things that may
be done in the light of what has been done.

34.

Select ⌄
(A) When one speaks of increasing power, machinery, and industry, there comes up a picture of a cold, metallic sort of world in which great factories will drive away the trees, the flowers, the birds, and the green fields.
(B) When one speaks of increasing power, machinery, and industry. There comes up a picture of a cold, metallic sort of world in which great factories will drive away the trees, the flowers, the birds, and the green fields.
(C) When one speaks of increasing power, machinery, and industry, there coming up a picture of a cold, metallic sort of world in which great factories will drive away the trees, the flowers, the birds, and the green fields.
(D) When one speak of increasing power, machinery, and industry, there comes up a picture of a cold, metallic sort of world in which great factories will drive away the trees, the flowers, the birds, and the green fields.

And that then we shall have a world composed of metal machines and human machines.

35.
Select ∨

(A) With all of that I does not agree.
(B) With all of that. I do not agree.
(C) With al of that I do not agree.
(D) With all of that I do not agree.

I think that unless we know more about machines and their use, unless we better understand the mechanical portion of life, we cannot have the time to enjoy the trees, and the birds, and the flowers, and the green fields.

. . .

Power and machinery, money and goods, are useful only as they set us free to live. They are but means to an end. For instance, I do not consider the machines which bear my name simply as machines. If that was all there was to it I would do something else. I take them as concrete evidence of the working out of a theory of business, which I hope is something more than a theory of business—a theory that looks toward making this world a better place in which to live. The fact that the commercial success of the Ford Motor Company has been most unusual is important only because it serves to demonstrate, in a way which no one can fail to understand, that the theory to date is right. Considered solely in this light I can criticize the prevailing system of industry and the organization of money and society from the standpoint of one who has not been beaten by them.

36.
Select ∨

(A) As things are now organized, I could, were I thinking only selfishly, ask for no change.
(B) As things are now organized. I could, were I thinking only selfishly, ask for no change.
(C) As things are now organized, I could, were thinking only selfishly, ask for no change.
(D) As things organized are now, I could, were I thinking selfishly only, ask for no change.

If I merely want money the present system is all right; it gives money in plenty to me. But I am thinking of service. The present system does not permit of the best service because it encourages every kind of waste—it keeps many men from getting the full return from service. And it is going nowhere. It is all a matter of better planning and adjustment.

I have no quarrel with the general attitude of scoffing at new ideas.

37. | Select   ⌄ |
|---|
| (A) Better to be skeptical of all new ideas and to insist upon being shown rather than to rush around in a continuous brainstorm after every new idea. |
| (B) It is better to be skeptical of all new ideas and to insist upon being shown rather than to rush around in a continuous brainstorm after every new idea. |
| (C) It better to be skeptical of all new ideas and to insist upon being shown rather than to rush around in a continuous brainstorm after every new idea. |
| (D) It is better to be skeptical of all new ideas and to insist upon being shown rather than to rush around in a continued brainstorm after every new idea. |

Skepticism, if by that we mean cautiousness, is the balance wheel of civilization. Most of the present acute troubles of the world arise out of taking on new ideas without first carefully investigating to discover if they are good ideas. An idea is not necessarily good because it is old, or necessarily bad because it is new, but if an old idea works, then the weight of the evidence is all in its favor. Ideas are of themselves extraordinarily valuable, but an idea is just an idea. Almost anyone can think up an idea. The thing that counts is developing it into a practical product.

. . .

38. | Select   ⌄ |
|---|
| (A) I are not a reformer. |
| (B) Not being a reformer. |
| (C) I am not a reformer. |
| (D) A reformer not am I. |

I think there is entirely too much attempt at reforming in the world and that we pay too much attention to reformers.

Source: Ford, Henry. Excerpt from *My Life and Work*. Project Gutenberg, 2005. *www.gutenberg.org/cache/epub/7213/pg7213-images.html*.

QUESTIONS 39 THROUGH 44 ARE BASED ON THE FOLLOWING PASSAGE:

TRUNK FULL OF JEWELS

1   MY GOOD MADAM: Not a day passes without our speaking of you. It is our established custom; but there is another reason besides. Just imagine, while washing and dusting the ceilings and walls, Madam Magloire has made some discoveries; now our two chambers hung with antique paper whitewashed over, would not discredit a chateau in the style of yours. Madam Magloire has pulled off all the paper. There were things beneath. My drawing-room, which contains no furniture, and which we use for spreading out the linen after washing, is fifteen feet in height, eighteen square, with a ceiling which was formerly painted and gilded, and with beams, as in yours. This was covered with a cloth while this was the hospital. And the woodwork was of the era of our grandmothers. But my room is the one you ought to see. Madam Magloire has discovered, under at least ten thicknesses of paper pasted on top, some paintings, which without being good are very tolerable. The subject is Telemachus being knighted by Minerva in some gardens, the name of which escapes me. In short, where the Roman ladies repaired on one single night. What shall I say to you? I have Romans, and Roman ladies, and the whole train. Madam Magloire has cleaned it all off; this summer she is going to have some small injuries repaired, and the whole revarnished, and my chamber will be a regular museum. She has also found in a corner of the attic two wooden pier-tables of ancient fashion. They asked us two crowns of six francs each to regild them, but it is much better to give the money to the poor; and they are very ugly besides, and I should much prefer a round table of mahogany.

2   I am always very happy. My brother is so good. He gives all he has to the poor and sick. We are very much cramped. The country is trying in the winter, and we really must do something for those who are in need.

We are almost comfortably lighted and warmed. You see that these are great treats.

3   My brother has ways of his own. When he talks, he says that a bishop ought to be so. Just imagine! the door of our house is never fastened. Whoever chooses to enter finds himself at once in my brother's room. He fears nothing, even at night. That is his sort of bravery, he says.

4   He does not wish me or Madame Magloire feel any fear for him. He exposes himself to all sorts of dangers, and he does not like to have us even seem to notice it. One must know how to understand him.

5   He goes out in the rain, he walks in the water, he travels in winter. He fears neither suspicious roads nor dangerous encounters, nor night.

6   Last year he went quite alone into a country of robbers. He would not take us. He was absent for a fortnight. On his return nothing had happened to him; he was thought to be dead, but was perfectly well, and said, "This is the way I have been robbed!" And then he opened a trunk full of jewels, all the jewels of the cathedral of Embrun, which the thieves had given him.

Source: Hugo, Victor. Excerpt from *Les Misérables*. Reprint of the 1887 New York Edition, Project Gutenberg, 2015. *www.gutenberg.org/files/135/135-h/135-h.htm.*

39. The reference to Telemachus in the first paragraph is an example of which of the following?
     (A) metaphor
     (B) allusion
     (C) apostrophe
     (D) characterization

40. Which of the following characterizes the speaker's brother?
     (A) selfish
     (B) aloof
     (C) giving
     (D) self-deprecating

41. At the end of the first paragraph, the author states, "They asked us two crowns of six francs each to regild them, but it is much better to give the money to the poor." What is the best definition of the word "crowns"?
    (A) the top of a head
    (B) a slap on the head
    (C) a hat that adorns a king
    (D) money

42. From the choices below, write the emotions that the speaker displays in the box. You may choose more than one emotion.

    anger
    curiosity
    concern
    happiness

    ┌───┐
    │   │
    │   │
    │   │
    │   │
    └───┘

43. The recipient of the letter is thought of
    (A) fondly.
    (B) infrequently.
    (C) scathingly.
    (D) neutrally.

44. The overall tone of the letter is
    (A) positive.
    (B) negative.
    (C) angry.
    (D) neutral.

QUESTIONS 45 THROUGH 50 ARE BASED ON THE FOLLOWING PASSAGE:

WELCOME TO THE CARPATHIANS

1   3 May. Bistritz.—Left Munich at 8:35 P.M., on 1st May, arriving at Vienna early next morning; should have arrived at 6:46, but train was an hour late. Buda-Pesth seems a wonderful place, from the glimpse which I got of it from the train and the little I could walk through the streets. I feared to go very far from the station, as we had arrived late and would start as near the correct time as possible.

2   The impression I had was that we were leaving the West and entering the East; the most western of splendid bridges over the Danube, which is here of noble width and depth, took us among the traditions of Turkish rule.

3   We left in pretty good time, and came after nightfall to Klausenburgh. Here I stopped for the night at the Hotel Royale. I had for dinner, or rather supper, a chicken done up some way with red pepper, which was very good but thirsty. (Mem. get recipe for Mina.) I asked the waiter, and he said it was called "paprika hendl," and that, as it was a national dish, I should be able to get it anywhere along the Carpathians.

4   I found my smattering of German very useful here, indeed, I don't know how I should be able to get on without it.

5   Having had some time at my disposal when in London, I had visited the British Museum, and made search among the books and maps in the library regarding Transylvania; it had struck me that some foreknowledge of the country could hardly fail to have some importance in dealing with a nobleman of that country.

6   I find that the district he named is in the extreme east of the country, just on the borders of three states, Transylvania, Moldavia, and Bukovina, in the midst of the Carpathian mountains; one of the wildest and least known portions of Europe.

7   I was not able to light on any map or work giving the exact locality of the Castle Dracula, as there are no maps of this country as yet to compare with our own Ordnance Survey Maps; but I found that Bistritz, the post town named by Count Dracula, is a fairly well-known place. I shall enter here some of my notes, as they may refresh my memory when I talk over my travels with Mina.

8   In the population of Transylvania there are four distinct nationalities: Saxons in the South, and mixed with them the Wallachs, who are the descendants of the Dacians; Magyars in the West, and Szekelys in the East and North. I am going among the latter, who claim to be descended from Attila and the Huns. This may be so, for when the Magyars conquered the country in the eleventh century they found the Huns settled in it.

9   I read that every known superstition in the world is gathered into the horseshoe of the Carpathians, as if it were the centre of some sort of imaginative whirlpool; if so my stay may be very interesting. (Mem., I must ask the Count all about them.)

10   I did not sleep well, though my bed was comfortable enough, for I had all sorts of queer dreams. There was a dog howling all night under my window, which may have had something to do with it; or it may have been the paprika, for I had to drink up all the water in my carafe, and was still thirsty. Towards morning I slept and was wakened by the continuous knocking at my door, so I guess I must have been sleeping soundly then.

11   I had for breakfast more paprika, and a sort of porridge of maize flour which they said was "mamaliga", and eggplant stuffed with forcemeat, a very excellent dish, which they call "impletata". (Mem., get recipe for this also.)

12   I had to hurry breakfast, for the train started a little before eight, or rather it ought to have done so, for after rushing to the station at 7:30 I had to sit in the carriage for more than an hour before we began to move.

13   It seems to me that the further east you go the more **unpunctual** are the trains. What ought they to be in China?

14   All day long we seemed to dawdle through a country which was full of beauty of every kind. Sometimes we saw little towns or castles on the top of steep hills such as we see in old missals; sometimes we ran by rivers and streams which seemed from the wide stony margin on each side of them to be subject to great floods. It takes a lot of water, and running strong, to sweep the outside edge of a river clear.

15   At every station there were groups of people, sometimes crowds, and in all sorts of attire. Some of them were just like the peasants at home or those I saw coming through France and Germany, with short jackets, and round hats, and home-made trousers; but others were very picturesque.

16   The women looked pretty, except when you got near them, but they were very clumsy about the waist. They had all full white sleeves of some kind or other, and most of them had big belts with a lot of strips of something fluttering from them like the dresses in a ballet, but of course there were petticoats under them.

17   The strangest figures we saw were the Slovaks, who were more barbarian than the rest, with their big cow-boy hats, great baggy dirty-white trousers, white linen shirts, and enormous heavy leather belts, nearly a foot wide, all studded over with brass nails. They wore high boots, with their trousers tucked into them, and had long black hair and heavy black moustaches. They are very picturesque, but do not look prepossessing. On the stage they would be set down at once as some old Oriental band of brigands. They are, however, I am told, very harmless and rather wanting in natural self-assertion.

18   It was on the dark side of twilight when we got to Bistritz, which is a very interesting old place. Being practically on the frontier—for the Borgo Pass leads from it into Bukovina—it has had a very stormy existence, and it certainly shows marks of it. Fifty years ago a series of great fires took place, which made terrible havoc on five separate occasions. At the very beginning of the seventeenth century it underwent a siege of three weeks and lost 13,000 people, the casualties of war proper being assisted by famine and disease.

19   Count Dracula had directed me to go to the Golden Krone Hotel, which I found, to my great delight, to be thoroughly old-fashioned, for of course I wanted to see all I could of the ways of the country.

20   I was evidently expected, for when I got near the door I faced a cheery-looking elderly woman in the usual peasant dress—white undergarment with a long double apron, front, and back, of colored stuff fitting almost too tight for modesty. When I came close she bowed and said, "The Herr Englishman?"

21   "Yes," I said, "Jonathan Harker."

22   She smiled, and gave some message to an elderly man in white shirtsleeves, who had followed her to the door.

23   He went, but immediately returned with a letter:

24   "My friend.—Welcome to the Carpathians. I am anxiously expecting you. Sleep well tonight. At three tomorrow the diligence will start for

Bukovina; a place on it is kept for you. At the Borgo Pass my carriage will await you and will bring you to me.

Source: Stoker, Bram. Excerpt from *Dracula*. Reprint of the 1897 New York Edition, Project Gutenberg, 2013. *www.gutenberg.org/files/345/345.txt.*

45. In the sentence, "It seems to me that the further east you go the more unpunctual are the trains," what is the best definition of the word "unpunctual"?
    (A) not on time
    (B) not punctured
    (C) disrespectful
    (D) precise

46. The first paragraph implies that the speaker is doing which of the following?
    (A) researching Vienna
    (B) working for the train company
    (C) traveling
    (D) interviewing people

47. Transylvania can best be described as which of the following? Write your answer in the box below.

    integrated
    diverse communities
    segregated
    shared space

48. Which quote has a welcoming tone?
    (A) "All day long we seemed to dawdle through a country which was full of beauty of every kind."
    (B) "I feared to go very far from the station, as we had arrived late and would start as near the correct time as possible."
    (C) "My friend.—Welcome to the Carpathians. I am anxiously expecting you. Sleep well tonight."
    (D) "I had to hurry breakfast, for the train started a little before eight, or rather it ought to have done so, for after rushing to the station at 7:30 I had to sit in the carriage for more than an hour before we began to move."

49. What language did the locals speak in Klausenburgh?
    (A) German
    (B) Turkish
    (C) English
    (D) Romanian

50. Who is the speaker?
    (A) Count Dracula
    (B) Jonathan Harker
    (C) Bram Stoker
    (D) The elderly man in white shirtsleeves

QUESTIONS 51 THROUGH 55 ARE BASED ON THE FOLLOWING PASSAGE:

LONG-TERM HEALTH BENEFITS

The *Physical Activity Guidelines for Americans* describes the major research findings on the health benefits of physical activity:

- Regular physical activity reduces the risk of many adverse health outcomes.
- Some physical activity is better than none.
- For most health outcomes, additional benefits occur as the amount of physical activity increases through higher intensity, greater frequency, and/or longer duration.

- Most health benefits occur with at least 150 minutes (2 hours and 30 minutes) a week of moderate intensity physical activity, such as brisk walking. Additional benefits occur with more physical activity.
- Both aerobic (endurance) and muscle-strengthening (resistance) physical activity are beneficial.
- Health benefits occur for children and adolescents, young and middle-aged adults, older adults, and those in every studied racial and ethnic group.
- The health benefits of physical activity occur for people with disabilities.
- The benefits of physical activity far outweigh the possibility of adverse outcomes.

The following are the key Guidelines included in the *Physical Activity Guidelines for Americans*:

. . .

Key Guidelines for Adults

- All adults should avoid inactivity. Some physical activity is better than none, and adults who participate in any amount of physical activity gain some health benefits.
- For substantial health benefits, adults should do at least 150 minutes (2 hours and 30 minutes) a week of moderate-intensity, or 75 minutes (1 hour and 15 minutes) a week of vigorous-intensity aerobic physical activity, or an equivalent combination of moderate- and vigorous-intensity aerobic activity. Aerobic activity should be performed in episodes of at least 10 minutes, and, preferably, it should be spread throughout the week.
- For additional and more extensive health benefits, adults should increase their aerobic physical activity to 300 minutes (5 hours) a week of moderate-intensity, or 150 minutes a week of vigorous-intensity aerobic physical activity, or an equivalent combination of moderate- and vigorous-intensity activity. Additional health benefits are gained by engaging in physical activity beyond this amount.
- Adults should also do muscle-strengthening activities that are moderate or high intensity and involve all major muscle groups on 2 or more days a week, as these activities provide additional health benefits.

Key Guidelines for Older Adults

The Key Guidelines for Adults also apply to older adults. In addition, the following Guidelines are just for older adults:

- When older adults cannot do 150 minutes of moderate-intensity aerobic activity a week because of chronic conditions, they should be as physically active as their abilities and conditions allow.
- Older adults should do exercises that maintain or improve balance if they are at risk of falling.
- Older adults should determine their level of effort for physical activity relative to their level of fitness.
- Older adults with chronic conditions should understand whether and how their conditions affect their ability to do regular physical activity safely.

Source: "2008 Physical Activity Guidelines for Americans Summary." *Office of Disease Prevention and Health Promotion.* Last accessed August 5, 2016. *www.health.gov/paguidelines/guidelines/summary.aspx.*

51. Which statement is true based on the passage?
(A) Adverse health conditions are caused by regular physical activity.
(B) Walking is a high-intensity physical activity.
(C) Some physical activity is better than none.
(D) Health benefits of regular physical activity are only for adolescents.

52. From the choices below, determine which of the groups of people listed will benefit from regular physical activity. Write your answer(s) in the box below. Note that there may be more than one correct answer.

specific ethnic groups only
older adults
infants
people with disabilities
adolescents
young adults

53. Determine the meaning of the word "adverse" as it is used in the following sentence from the passage: "The benefits of physical activity far outweigh the possibility of adverse outcomes."
    (A) negative
    (B) positive
    (C) neutral
    (D) increased

54. How do the Guidelines from the passage differ between adults and older adults?
    (A) Adults should decrease their aerobic physical activity to only 200 minutes per week.
    (B) Older adults should ignore chronic conditions when exercising.
    (C) Adults should do fewer exercises than older adults.
    (D) Older adults should do exercises to improve their balance.

55. What is the purpose of the Guidelines in the passage?
    (A) to explain short-term health benefits from exercise
    (B) to promote weight loss by eating less
    (C) to explain long-term health benefits from exercise
    (D) to compare the exercise needs of adults and older adults

END OF SECTION 3

REASONING THROUGH LANGUAGE ARTS EXAM ANSWERS EXPLAINED

Section 1

1. **(A)** To scrutinize something means to examine or investigate it.

2. Words that would effectively complete the sentence include "**concerned**," "**worried**," and "**nervous**." Any similar word would also work.

3. **(B)** The gesture of Della selling her hair to pay for a Christmas present indicates that she is devoted to Jim. Choice A is incorrect because Della's actions suggest the opposite of being self-centered. Choices C and D are incorrect because no evidence supports these answers.

4. **(D)** Irony is the contrast between what is expected to happen and what actually happens. Choices A and C are incorrect. These literary terms are concerned with comparing unlike things. Choice B is incorrect because a hyperbole is an extreme exaggeration.

5. **Della tells him that she loves him.** When Della tells Jim she loves him, he wakes from his trance.

6. **(A)** At the end, they both calmly moved forward.

7. Answers will vary but need to take a clear stance that is supported by details from the story.

8. **(C)** The main idea is stated in the first sentence. Choices A and B are incorrect because the passage indicates the opposite. Choice D is incorrect. Although the passage mentions the writing of the Constitution, this is not the central idea.

9. **Fisherman** The footnote indicates that Massanello was a fisherman.

10. **(A)** The language used in the passage is aggressive and lends itself to motivating people. Choice B is incorrect because the author does not use calming language. Choice C is incorrect. The author is making the opposite claim. Choice D is incorrect. Although there is some description of liberty, this is not the main purpose of the writing.

11. **(D)** If something is unextinguishable, it cannot be put out or quelled.

12. **(B)** The author clearly states in the third paragraph that it is impossible to go back to an earlier time. Choices A, C, and D are incorrect because nowhere in the passage are any of these options stated.

13. **(A)** The author is speaking out against an oppressive government, so this is the most logical catalyst for writing this passage. Choice C is incorrect because the author is feeling the opposite of patriotism toward Britain. Choices B and D are incorrect because no evidence supports these answers.

14. **(D)** A simile is a comparison of two unlike things using the words "like" or "as." Choice A is incorrect. The author is not inferring that people and ants are similar in numerous respects. Choice B is incorrect. Personification means that an animal is given human characteristics. Choice C is incorrect. The author is not putting together two contrasting things.

15. **(A)** The author indicates that he went into the woods so he would have to deal with only the essentials of life. Choices B, C, and D are incorrect because no evidence supports any of these answers.

16. **(B)** The author indicates in several ways that people should simplify. Choices A and C are incorrect. Although these words do appear in the passage, they do not sum up the author's message. Choice D is incorrect because no evidence supports this answer.

17. The word that would best complete the sentence is "**dislike**," although similar words would be accepted.

18. **(B)** The idea that a railroad rides upon us suggests that technology has encroached upon us. Choices A and D are incorrect because these interpretations are too literal. Choice C is incorrect because no evidence supports this answer.

19. **(A)** The author indicates problems with several things that relate to the pace of life. Choice B is incorrect. Although the author mentions that the telegraph is a contributing factor, it is not the most problematic. Choices C and D are incorrect. Although these words are used within the passage, the author does not indicate that these are great problems.

20. **(B)** The word "overgrown" suggests that "unorganized" is the best definition. Although choice A is a definition of "unwieldy," it does not fit in the context of the sentence. Choices C and D are incorrect.

Section 2

The prompt asks if laws such as the Clean Air Act address the specific issues relating to air quality. You should have chosen a side; either these laws do or do not. You should have clearly articulated your position in the introductory part of your response. Following your introduction, you should have cited specific evidence from both passages that you feel supports your position and you should have explained how and why that evidence supports your position. Finally, you should have restated your position in the conclusion.

Below is a sample, high-scoring extended response for this prompt.

Sulfur, nitrogen, mercury, and other heavy metals have been proven to harm our ecosystem. Without regulations, these pollutants will affect our daily lives. Fortunately, the Clean Air Act has addressed these specific issues and is being enforced by the EPA to protect and improve our air quality.

According to the EPA, our lakes, streams, trees, and soil are all at risk of serious damage by excess amounts of heavy metal compounds. Factories are one of the biggest contributors to this problem. The Clean Air Act, however, has been making progress in limiting the amount of pollutants these factories may release.

According to the "Air Quality" passage, "sulfur can lead to excess amounts of acid in lakes and streams and damage trees and forest soils." Nitrogen has been proven to harm fish once it hits the surface waters. Mercury can accumulate in plants and animals, which both end up being consumed by people, thus tainting our very food supply.

Fortunately, in 1990, Congress gave more authority to the EPA "to implement and enforce regulations reducing air pollutant emissions." Most importantly, the 1990 Amendment emphasized methods to lower the cost of reducing air pollution, making it easier for everyone to promote clean air. This Act ensured that everyone, from the EPA to state and local governments, played some sort of role in cutting down on these types of pollution. The more that the responsibility was shared, the more people that took up this cause.

After performing extensive research, as evidenced in the "Air Quality" passage, the EPA clearly realized that action had to be taken. As a direct result of this research, the EPA outlined a clear path to combat this problem through the Clean Air Act. By establishing clear roles and responsibilities, this Act created a variety of ways to cut down on air pollutants, including setting limits on the emissions of air pollutants from sources like chemical plants, issuing sanctions for state or local governments that do not meet the necessary requirements, and establishing public hearings to comment on the development of state implementation plans to control air pollution. Billions of dollars have been spent under the guidance of the EPA and the Clean Air Act to ensure that future generations will be able to enjoy clean air.

Section 3

21. **(C)** According to the passage, "[t]he bill unanimously passed both chambers of Congress."

22. The best synonym for the word "subsistence" is "**support**." A synonym is a word that means the same thing as the original word. The word "subsistence" in context means monetary or other support that the GI would need after returning home from service in the war.

23. **(D)** According to the passage, "the Veterans Administration estimated the increase in Federal income taxes alone would pay for the cost of the bill several times over."

24. **(A)** The whole purpose of the GI Bill was to provide for veterans after World War II.

25. The Invasion of Normandy in 1944 is widely known as **D-day** and is remembered each June 6.

26. **(C)** The Servicemen's Readjustment Act was signed into law in 1944.

27. **(B)** A long-term effect of this act was to provide veterans with a much better chance at success after their active service ended. The passage indicates that in the ten years after the act was passed, the number of college and university degrees awarded more than doubled.

28. The correct choices are **affording housing**, **affording unemployment insurance**, and **affording a college education**. The passage states that the bill was created "to help veterans adjust to civilian life in the areas of hospitalization, purchase of homes and businesses, and especially, education."

29. **(C)** Choice C is the clearest possible choice. Choice A does not capitalize the "s" in "September." Choices B and D are awkward.

30. **(D)** Choice A is a fragment. Choices B and C have the wrong form of the verb "to be."

31. **(A)** Choice B incorrectly capitalizes the "n" in "negotiation." Choice C is missing commas before "which" and after "litigation." Choice D uses "off" instead of "of."

32. **(C)** Choice A does not capitalize the "l" in "Latin." Choice B is unclear and awkward. Choice D adds unnecessary commas.

33. **(B)** Choice A lacks the possessive form of Shakespeare, and choice C fails to capitalize proper nouns. Choice D is missing commas.

34. **(A)** Choice B uses a period after "industry." Choice C uses "coming" instead of "comes." Choice D uses "speak" instead of "speaks."

35. **(D)** Choice A uses the wrong form of the verb "do." Choice B creates a fragment. Choice C misspells "all."

36. **(A)** Choice B uses a period, instead of a comma, creating a fragment. Choices C and D are unclear.

37. **(B)** Choice A lacks a subject. Choice C lacks a being verb. Choice D uses "continued" instead of "continuous."

38. **(C)** Choice A lacks subject-verb agreement. Choice B is a fragment. Choice D is awkward.

39. **(B)** The author is alluding or making reference to a well-known character from Greek mythology.

40. **(C)** The speaker states, "My brother is so good. He gives all he has to the poor and sick." Therefore, the brother is giving.

41. **(D)** The same sentence also says, "It is much better to give the money to the poor."

42. The speaker displays **concern** (about her brother) and **happiness** (about her life).

43. **(A)** The opening line indicates that not a day goes by that the writer of the letter doesn't speak of the recipient, which implies a fondness.

44. **(A)** The beginning of the second paragraph indicates that the writer of the letter is always happy.

45. **(A)** The previous paragraph states, "I had to sit in the carriage for more than an hour before we began to move," indicating that the train is not running on time.

46. **(C)** The author mentions the train and comments on how Buda-Pesth "seems" like a wonderful place, meaning he is not familiar with it.

47. **Segregated** is the best answer. Paragraph 8 indicates where all the "distinct nationalities" live.

48. **(C)** This quote indicates that the writer is excited to see his friend and has a welcoming tone.

49. **(A)** The speaker says that his "smattering of German [was] very useful here," indicating that the people spoke German.

50. **(B)** At the end of the passage, the speaker indicates that his name is Jonathan Harker.

51. **(C)** According to the passage, "[s]ome physical activity is better than none."

52. The correct answers are **older adults**, **people with disabilities**, **adolescents**, and **young adults**. As described in the passage, all of those groups of people can benefit from regular physical activity. Infants and specific ethnic groups are not mentioned.

53. **(A)** "Adverse" means a negative reaction. This word appears near the end of the first list of health benefits.

54. **(D)** The main difference between the Guidelines for Adults and the Guidelines for Older Adults is that older adults should do exercises that focus on improving their balance since they may be at risk of falling.

55. **(C)** The purpose of these Guidelines is to help people experience long-term health benefits.

SCORING YOUR REASONING THROUGH LANGUAGE ARTS EXAM

In 2016, the GED Testing Service made some adjustments to the "Performance Levels," or score levels, that they use to evaluate GED® test scores. The new structure has three levels based on the existing 100 to 200 score range:

- Passing (145+)—This is the minimum score needed to pass a GED® test.
- College Ready (165+)—A score at or above this level indicates that the student is ready for college-level work.
- College Ready + Credit (175+)—A score at or above this level indicates that the student should qualify for college credit.

Find the number of correct answers on your practice test in the chart below to determine your performance level:

Reasoning Through Language Arts Exam
(Sections 1 and 3)

Score Between	Performance Level
0 and 31	Not Passing
32 and 39	Close to Passing
40 and 47	Likely to Pass
48 and 50	College Ready
51 and 55	College Ready + Credit

Reasoning Through Language Arts Exam— Extended Response Checklist (Section 2)

The score that you receive for your Extended Response in Section 2 of the Reasoning Through Language Arts subject test will be graded by multiple evaluators according to three traits. Those traits are **Creation of Arguments and Use of Evidence**, **Development of Ideas and Organizational Structure**, and **Clarity and Command of Standard English Conventions**. Each trait is worth up to 2 points; the highest score you can receive on your essay is 6 points total. Below is a checklist that can be used to evaluate the extended response that you wrote for this prompt. If you check off all of the following requirements, you most likely would receive a 5 or 6 on your extended response.

☐ My purpose/thesis answers the prompt.

☐ My purpose/thesis is based on the reading passage.

☐ My essay gives specific evidence (direct/indirect quotes) from the reading passages.

☐ My evidence is sufficient and supports my thesis/argument.

☐ My ideas are logical and well-developed and elaborate the main points of my essay.

☐ My essay has an introduction, at least 2–3 body paragraphs, and a conclusion.

☐ I used clear transitions between paragraphs and main points.

☐ I used a formal tone, appropriate to the intended audience.

☐ I used specific vocabulary and/or terms (I avoided vague words like "things" or "stuff").

☐ I used varied sentence structures.

☐ I used proper grammar (with few to no mistakes)—capitalization, punctuation, pronoun usage, subject-verb agreement.

☐ I avoided wordiness and awkward sentences.

☐ I avoided run-ons and sentence fragments.

NOTE: An essay with minor mistakes can still receive a perfect score. Evaluators take into consideration that you are writing a draft under timed circumstances.

ANSWER SHEET
Model Test

MATHEMATICAL REASONING EXAM

PART 1

1. Ⓐ Ⓑ Ⓒ Ⓓ
   Ⓐ Ⓑ Ⓒ Ⓓ
2. Ⓐ Ⓑ Ⓒ Ⓓ
3. Ⓐ Ⓑ Ⓒ Ⓓ
4. Ⓐ Ⓑ Ⓒ Ⓓ
5. Ⓐ Ⓑ Ⓒ Ⓓ

PART 2

6. Ⓐ Ⓑ Ⓒ Ⓓ
7. Ⓐ Ⓑ Ⓒ Ⓓ
8. Ⓐ Ⓑ Ⓒ Ⓓ
9. Ⓐ Ⓑ Ⓒ Ⓓ
10. Ⓐ Ⓑ Ⓒ Ⓓ
11. Ⓐ Ⓑ Ⓒ Ⓓ
12. Ⓐ Ⓑ Ⓒ Ⓓ
13. Ⓐ Ⓑ Ⓒ Ⓓ
14. Ⓐ Ⓑ Ⓒ Ⓓ
15. Ⓐ Ⓑ Ⓒ Ⓓ

16. Ⓐ Ⓑ Ⓒ Ⓓ
17. Ⓐ Ⓑ Ⓒ Ⓓ
18. Ⓐ Ⓑ Ⓒ Ⓓ
19. _____
20. Ⓐ Ⓑ Ⓒ Ⓓ
21. _____
22. _____
23. Ⓐ Ⓑ Ⓒ Ⓓ
24. Ⓐ Ⓑ Ⓒ Ⓓ
25. Ⓐ Ⓑ Ⓒ Ⓓ
26. Ⓐ Ⓑ Ⓒ Ⓓ
27. Ⓐ Ⓑ Ⓒ Ⓓ
28. Ⓐ Ⓑ Ⓒ Ⓓ
29. Ⓐ Ⓑ Ⓒ Ⓓ
30. Ⓐ Ⓑ Ⓒ Ⓓ
31. _____
   _____
   _____

32. Ⓐ Ⓑ Ⓒ Ⓓ
33. Ⓐ Ⓑ Ⓒ Ⓓ
   Ⓐ Ⓑ Ⓒ Ⓓ
34. Ⓐ Ⓑ Ⓒ Ⓓ
35. Ⓐ Ⓑ Ⓒ Ⓓ
36. Ⓐ Ⓑ Ⓒ Ⓓ
   Ⓐ Ⓑ Ⓒ Ⓓ
   Ⓐ Ⓑ Ⓒ Ⓓ
37. Ⓐ Ⓑ Ⓒ Ⓓ
   Ⓐ Ⓑ Ⓒ Ⓓ
   Ⓐ Ⓑ Ⓒ Ⓓ
38. Ⓐ Ⓑ Ⓒ Ⓓ
   Ⓐ Ⓑ Ⓒ Ⓓ
39. Ⓐ Ⓑ Ⓒ Ⓓ
   Ⓐ Ⓑ Ⓒ Ⓓ
40. Ⓐ Ⓑ Ⓒ Ⓓ
41. Ⓐ Ⓑ Ⓒ Ⓓ
42. Ⓐ Ⓑ Ⓒ Ⓓ

MATHEMATICAL REASONING EXAM

> **DIRECTIONS:** This practice exam contains mathematical problems. You will have 115 minutes total to complete the 42 questions in both parts of this exam.

Part 1—Calculators ARE NOT allowed

1. Select the expression that correctly completes the sentence:

    The phrase "Six times the sum of a number (n) plus one is three more than seven times the number" is equivalent to the equation:

Select ∨	=	Select ∨
(A) $6n + 1$		(A) $7n + 3$
(B) $6(n + 1)$		(B) $7(n + 3)$
(C) $6 + n + 1$		(C) $7 + n + 3$
(D) $6(n + 1) + 1$		(D) $3n + 7$

2. What is the correct way of writing "b is greater than or equal to -5 but less than 2"?
    (A) $-5 \geq b > 2$
    (B) $2 < b \leq -5$
    (C) $-5 \leq b < 2$
    (D) $-5 \geq b < 2$

3. Select the number that correctly completes the sentence:

    The total cost in dollars to purchase a one-cup coffee maker and coffee pods can be expressed as an equation, $C = 65.65 + 8.85p$, where C represents the total cost and p represents the number of coffee pods. The total cost of Amit's purchase was \$171.85, and the purchase included

Select ∨	coffee pods.
(A) 9	
(B) 10	
(C) 11	
(D) 12	

4. One thousand three hundred twenty yards is what fraction of a mile?
   (1 mile = 1,760 yards)

   (A) $\dfrac{1}{2}$

   (B) $\dfrac{3}{4}$

   (C) $\dfrac{2}{5}$

   (D) $\dfrac{4}{9}$

5. The first four sprinters to finish in the 200-meter event had the following times:

Sprinter	Time (seconds)
Jay	22.032
Monroe	22.811
Gregory	23.544
Henry	22.524

   Which sprinter finished in second place?
   (A) Jay
   (B) Monroe
   (C) Gregory
   (D) Henry

Part 2—Calculators ARE allowed

6. A seamstress had four pieces of yarn that were the following lengths:

Yarn	Length (feet)
A	$2\frac{3}{4}$
B	$2\frac{1}{4}$
C	$2\frac{3}{8}$
D	$2\frac{11}{16}$

Which piece of yarn is the longest?
(A) Yarn A
(B) Yarn B
(C) Yarn C
(D) Yarn D

7. The teacher told her class that $\frac{1}{4}$ of the class received an "A" grade on the last test. What percentage of the class received an "A"?
(A) 75%
(B) 30%
(C) 45%
(D) 25%

8. A bus has 20 people on board, and 5 of them are women. What is the ratio of men to women?
(A) 3:1
(B) 1:3
(C) 4:5
(D) 1:2

9. In a recent survey, 3 out of 8 people reported that they drink coffee in the morning. If 480 people were surveyed, how many said that they drink coffee in the morning?
   (A) 210
   (B) 475
   (C) 180
   (D) 206

10. Gasoline cost the following over a period of four weeks:
    Week 1: $2.92 per gallon
    Week 2: $3.04 per gallon
    Week 3: $3.16 per gallon
    Week 4: $3.28 per gallon

    If the trend continues, what will the price be in week 5?
    (A) $3.40
    (B) $4.70
    (C) $3.50
    (D) $5.75

11. A family drove 422 miles on 32.5 gallons of gas. To the nearest tenth, how many miles were driven on one gallon of gas?
    (A) 13.0
    (B) 28.3
    (C) 14.7
    (D) 20.8

QUESTIONS 12 AND 13 REFER TO THE FOLLOWING PICTURE:

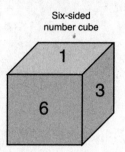

Six-sided
number cube

12. The numbered cube above has six sides, each marked with a different integer from 1 to 6. Suppose you roll the cube above 24 times. How many times are you likely to roll a 1?
    (A) 3
    (B) 16
    (C) 24
    (D) 4

13. What is the probability you will roll a 3 on two successive rolls?

    (A) $\dfrac{1}{9}$

    (B) $\dfrac{1}{36}$

    (C) $\dfrac{1}{64}$

    (D) $\dfrac{1}{2}$

14. Which equation is the result of subtracting 14 from each side of this equation: $\frac{1}{4}x + 16 = 20$?

   (A) $\frac{1}{4}x + 2 = 6$

   (B) $\frac{1}{4}x + 30 = 34$

   (C) $\frac{1}{4}x - 2 = -4$

   (D) $\frac{1}{4}x - 2 = -6$

15. A used car lot announces that all of its cars are on sale for 55% of the original price. If the discounted price of a car is $4,400, what was the original price of the car?
   (A) $8,542
   (B) $4,000
   (C) $7,500
   (D) $8,000

16. Two business partners, John and Cathy, formed a joint business that cost a total of $980 to start. The partners agreed that Cathy would pay $350 more than John because John earns less. How much did John pay to help start the joint business?
   (A) $265
   (B) $155
   (C) $315
   (D) $255

QUESTIONS 17 AND 18 REFER TO THE FOLLOWING GRAPH:

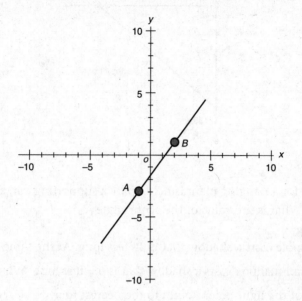

17. What are the coordinates of point *B*?
    (A) (–2, 1)
    (B) (–1, 2)
    (C) (2, –1)
    (D) (2, 1)

18. What is the slope of line *AB*?

    (A) $\dfrac{4}{3}$

    (B) $\dfrac{3}{4}$

    (C) $\dfrac{4}{5}$

    (D) $\dfrac{5}{4}$

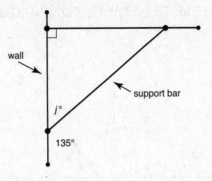

19. A hook for a hanging plant is held up by a supporting bar, as shown above. What is the value of the acute angle *j*?

20. A light pole casts a shadow that is 44 feet long. At the same time, a 3-foot-tall mailbox casts a shadow that is $6\frac{1}{2}$ feet long. What is the height of the light pole? Round to the nearest foot.
    (A) 37 feet
    (B) 20 feet
    (C) 45 feet
    (D) 12 feet

21. △*ABC* is a right triangle with a hypotenuse that is 26 cm long, one leg that is 10 cm long, and another leg that is _____ cm long. Fill in the blank.

22. Mr. Rosenberger is replacing the carpeting in his game room, which is rectangular with an area of 216 square feet. The carpet must cover the entire floor, which is 12 feet wide. The carpet must be _____ feet long. Fill in the blank.

23. What is the measure of an angle whose vertex is at the center of a circle if the two lines that form the angle border an area that is one-eighth of the area of the circle?
    (A) 45 degrees
    (B) 65 degrees
    (C) 90 degrees
    (D) 30 degrees

QUESTIONS 24 THROUGH 26 REFER TO THE FOLLOWING NUMBER LINE:

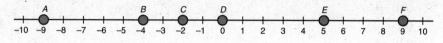

24. What is the value of B minus C?
   (A) –6
   (B) –2
   (C) 2
   (D) 6

25. What is the product of A times E?
   (A) –45
   (B) –14
   (C) –4
   (D) 45

26. Which of the following is true?
   (A) $|A| > |F|$
   (B) $|B| > |E|$
   (C) $-|E| < B$
   (D) $|C| = |D|$

_____

27. If $x = q^5$, $y = q^3$, and $z = q^{-2}$, which of the following expresses $\left(\dfrac{x}{y}\right)^3$ in terms of q?

   (A) q^{24}
   (B) q^{11}
   (C) q^8
   (D) q^6

28. If $x^2 + 5x = 6$, which of these is a possible value of x?
    (A) –1
    (B) 5
    (C) –6
    (D) 11

29. $x^2 + 2xy + y^2$ is equivalent to which of the following?
    (A) $(x + y)(x + y)$
    (B) $(x + y)(x - y)$
    (C) $(x - y)(x - y)$
    (D) $(x + x)(y + y)$

30. Function $z(x)$ is a parabolic function with its vertex at (0, 0). What are the coordinates of the vertex of $z(x) + 3$?
    (A) (0, 3)
    (B) (3, 0)
    (C) (–3, 0)
    (D) (0, –3)

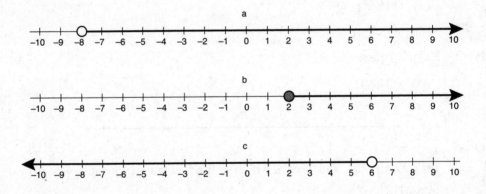

31. Based on the number lines above, provide in the blank the label of the number line that correctly completes the sentence.

    "y is less than 6" is represented by number line _____.
    "y is greater than –8" is represented by number line _____.
    "y is greater than or equal to 2" is represented by number line _____.

32. $\sqrt{156}$ is between which numbers?
    (A) 9 and 10
    (B) 10 and 11
    (C) 11 and 12
    (D) 12 and 13

33. Select the expression that correctly completes the sentence:

    $24x^8 + 48x^3$ divided by $8x^3$ is [Select ⌄] plus [Select ⌄] .

    (A) $3x^5$ (A) 6
    (B) $3x^8$ (B) $6x^3$
    (C) $3x^{11}$ (C) $6x^6$
    (D) $16x^5$ (D) 40

34. $\sqrt{128}$ is equivalent to which of the following?

    (A) $2\sqrt{64}$

    (B) $8\sqrt{2}$

    (C) $4\sqrt{32}$

    (D) 16

35. Which of the following is equivalent to $(1.5 \times 10^{17}) \times (9.3 \times 10^{-12})$?
    (A) 13.95×10^6
    (B) 1.395×10^6
    (C) 0.71×10^6
    (D) 7.1×10^6

QUESTIONS 36 AND 37 REFER TO THE FOLLOWING DRAWING:

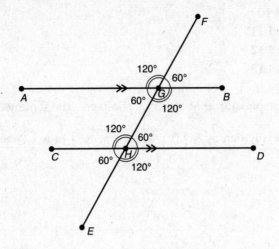

36. Select the word or phrase that correctly completes each sentence:

Angle *FGB* is an ⌈ Select ⌄ ⌉ angle and is

(A) obtuse
(B) acute
(C) interior
(D) right

⌈ Select ⌄ ⌉ angle *AGF*. Angles *AGF* and *FGB*, along

(A) supplementary to
(B) congruent to
(C) complementary to
(D) next to

with angles *CHE* and *EHD*, are ⌈ Select ⌄ ⌉ angles.

(A) exterior
(B) vertical
(C) right
(D) supplementary

37. Select the word or phrase that correctly completes each sentence:

Lines *AB* and *CD* are [Select ∨] lines. Line *EF* is a

(A) parallel
(B) perpendicular
(C) intersecting
(D) similar

[Select ∨], and it intersects lines *AB* and *CD* to form

(A) bisector
(B) ray
(C) transversal
(D) line

[Select ∨] angles.

(A) right
(B) corresponding
(C) complementary
(D) supplementary

38. Select the expression that correctly completes the sentence:

If the polynomial $3x^2 + 2x - 8$ is factored, the two resulting binomial

factors are [Select ∨] and [Select ∨].

(A) $(x + 2)$
(B) $(x - 2)$
(C) $(x + 4)$
(D) $(x - 4)$

(A) $(3x + 4)$
(B) $(3x - 4)$
(C) $(3x + 2)$
(D) $(3x - 2)$

39. Select the number that correctly completes the sentence:

The solutions for the equation $x^2 + 2x - 10 = 5$ are

Select ⌄	and	Select ⌄
(A) 5		(A) 3
(B) –5		(B) –3
(C) –3		(C) 5
(D) 30		(D) –15

40. Solve for x:

$$4x^2 + 11x = -5$$

(A) $\dfrac{-11 \pm \sqrt{201}}{4}$

(B) $\dfrac{-11 \pm \sqrt{41}}{4}$

(C) $\dfrac{-11 \pm \sqrt{201}}{8}$

(D) $\dfrac{-11 \pm \sqrt{41}}{8}$

QUESTIONS 41 AND 42 REFER TO THE FOLLOWING SOLIDS:

(1)

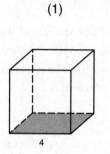

4

(2)

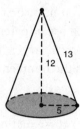

13
12
5

(3)

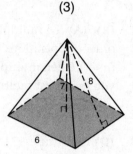

7 8
6

(4)

9
3

(5)

6
14
8

(6)

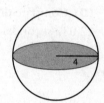

4

41. Which of the pairs listed below includes only solids that require the use
     of π (pi) to calculate their volumes?
     (A) 2 and 3
     (B) 3 and 4
     (C) 4 and 6
     (D) 5 and 6

42. All of the following are true about the cube (1) shown above EXCEPT
     (A) the cube's volume is equal to 64.
     (B) the cube's surface area is 96.
     (C) the cube's edge is equal in length to the sphere's (6) radius.
     (D) the cube's volume is greater than the sphere's (6) volume.

MATHEMATICAL REASONING EXAM ANSWERS EXPLAINED

Part 1

1. **(B), (A)** To multiply a sum, you must first calculate the sum, and the order of operations requires the use of parentheses to contain the sum: $(n + 1)$. Then multiply the sum by 6. To get "three more than" a product, you must first multiply 7 times the number, n, and then add 3.

2. **(C)** The correct answer is $-5 \leq b < 2$.

3. **(D)** Substitute 171.85 for C in the equation and solve for p. Subtract 65.65 from both sides, and then divide by 8.85.

4. **(B)** $1{,}320 \div 1{,}760 = \dfrac{3}{4}$

5. **(D)** Compare digit by digit from left to right. Jay had the fastest time at 22.032 seconds. Henry has the second fastest time at 22.524 seconds.

Part 2

6. **(A)** Since all lengths are between 2 and 3 feet, compare the fractions. Convert the denominators of each fraction to 16, and then compare the numerators:

$$\frac{3}{4} = \frac{12}{16}; \ \frac{1}{4} = \frac{4}{16}; \text{ and } \frac{3}{8} = \frac{6}{16}$$

Since 12 is the largest numerator, $2\dfrac{3}{4}$ is the largest number.

7. **(D)** $\dfrac{1}{4} = 1 \div 4 = 0.25$ and $0.25 = 25\%$

8. **(A)** Find the number of men on the bus (20 people – 5 women = 15 men). The ratio of men to women is 15:5, which simplifies to 3:1.

9. **(C)** Set up a proportion: $\dfrac{3}{8} = \dfrac{x}{480}$. Cross multiply: $8x = (3)(480) = 1{,}440$. Divide both sides by 8 to isolate x: $1{,}440 \div 8$. Therefore, $x = 180$.

10. **(A)** The gas price is increasing by \$0.12 every week: \$0.12 + \$3.28 = \$3.40

11. **(A)** First find the miles per gallon (422 miles ÷ 32.5 gallons = 12.98 miles

per gallon). Then round to the nearest tenth: 13.0

12. **(D)** Your chance of rolling a 1 on each roll is 1 out of 6. Since you roll 24 times, $24 \div 6 = 4$.

13. **(B)** Your chance of rolling a 3 on the first roll is 1 out of 6. Your chance of rolling a 3 on the second roll is also 1 out of 6. To combine these chances, multiply:

$$\frac{1}{6} \times \frac{1}{6} = \frac{1}{36}$$

14. **(A)** Subtract 14 from both sides of the equation: $16 - 14 = 2$ and $20 - 14 = 6$

15. **(D)** Calculate the original price by dividing the new price by the discount. Remember that 55% is 0.55: $\$4,400 \div 0.55 = \$8,000$

16. **(C)** Let c equal what Cathy paid, and let j equal what John paid. Set up your equations: $980 = c + j$ and $c = j + 350$. Substitute $j + 350$ for c in the first equation: $980 = j + 350 + j$. Subtract 350 from each side: $630 = 2j$. Then divide both sides by 2: $j = 315$

17. **(D)** The correct answer is (2, 1).

18. **(A)** Use the points $(-1, -3)$ and $(2, 1)$ in the slope formula: $\frac{1-(-3)}{2-(-1)} = \frac{4}{3}$

19. **45°** The two angles where the support meets the wall are supplementary, which means their sum is 180°. Subtract the known angle from 180° to find angle j: $180° - 135° = 45°$

20. **(B)** Two shadows cast by the same light source (the Sun) will be proportional to the heights of the two objects casting the shadows. Set up the problem as a proportion. Remember to have the actual heights (in feet) in the numerators and the shadow lengths (in feet) in the denominators:

$$\frac{x}{44} = \frac{3}{6.5}$$

Cross multiply: $6.5x = (3)(44) = 132$. Then divide both sides by 6.5 to get $x = 20.31$. Round to the nearest foot: $x = 20$ feet

21. **24** Use Pythagorean theorem $(a^2 + b^2 = c^2)$, and substitute the known side lengths into an equation (the hypotenuse is always c): $10^2 + b^2 = 26^2$ becomes $100 + b^2 = 676$. Subtract 100 from both sides to get $b^2 = 576$. The square root of 576 is 24, so $b = 24$. You should also keep an eye out for common "triplets" and their multiples. One common triplet is

5:12:13. If you recognize that 10 is 5 times 2 and 26 is 13 times 2, then you'll know that this is a 5:12:13 triplet, and that the missing side is 12 times 2 or 24.

22. **18** The formula for the area of a rectangle is $A = lw$ where A is the area, l is the length, and w is the width. Substitute known values into the equation and solve for l: $216 = l(12)$. Divide both sides by 12 to get a result of 18.

23. **(A)** Every circle measures 360°. Since the angle has its vertex at the center, the portion of the circumference that the radii cut equals the portion of 360° cut by the angle. Therefore, divide 360° by 8 to solve: $360° \div 8 = 45°$

24. **(B)** When subtracting a negative, change the operation to addition and change the sign of the second number: $-4 - (-2) = -4 + 2 = -2$

25. **(A)** When the signs are not the same, the product is negative: $(-9)(5) = -45$

26. **(C)** Absolute value makes a number positive. A negative sign outside the absolute value bars makes the absolute value negative: $-5 < -4$

27. **(D)** Remember the rules for exponents with the same base. Multiplication means add the exponents together. Division means subtract one exponent from the other. Raising a power to a power means multiply the exponents: $5 - 3 = 2$ and $(2)(3) = 6$. The new exponent is 6, so the answer is q^6.

28. **(C)** Subtracting 6 from both sides makes this a quadratic equation: $x^2 + 5x - 6 = 0$. Factoring the equation gives $(x + 6)(x - 1) = 0$. Set each factor equal to 0 to find the possible values of x: $x + 6 = 0$ and $x - 1 = 0$. Therefore, $x = -6$ and $x = 1$. The only choice given is $x = -6$.

29. **(A)** This is a very common polynomial. Memorize both the factored and FOIL forms of this polynomial.

30. **(A)** Adding outside the parentheses moves the curve up. Adding 3 to the original function to form the new function moves up the original function by 3. Moving up involves the y-coordinate.

31. **(c, a, b)** Number line c shows y is less than 6. Number line a shows y is greater than -8. Number line b shows y is greater than or equal to 2.

32. **(D)** 156 is between 144 and 169. Since $(12)(12) = 144$ and $(13)(13) = 169$, $\sqrt{156}$ must be between 12 and 13.

33. **(A), (A)** Divide the coefficient of each term in the expression by the coefficient of the "divided by" term. This will produce the coefficients of the resulting expression. In this case, 24 divided by 8 is 3 and 48 divided by 8 is 6. Next, divide the exponent in each term of the expression by the exponent of the "divided by" term. Remember that the rules for dividing exponents are to subtract the exponents. In this case, x^8 divided by x^3 is x^5 (because $8 - 3 = 5$), and x^3 divided by x^3 is x^0 (because $3 - 3 = 0$). Since x^0 is equal to 1, the second term in the resulting expression is $6(1)$, or 6.

34. **(B)** Since $128 = (2)(64)$ and $\sqrt{64} = 8$, $\sqrt{128} = 8\sqrt{2}$.

35. **(B)** Multiply the decimal numbers as normal: $1.5 \times 9.3 = 13.95$. Since this is multiplication, add the exponents of 10: $(17 - 12 = 5)$. Scientific notation puts the decimal point next to the units digit. To move the decimal point one place to the left, we need one additional exponent of 10: $5 + 1 = 6$. Therefore, the answer is 1.395×10^6.

36. **(B), (A), (A)** Since angle *FBG* measures 60°, it is acute because acute angles measure less than 90°. Two angles whose sum is 180° are supplementary, like angle *FBG* and angle *AGF*. Exterior angles are outside of the parallel lines.

37. **(A), (C), (B)** The arrow symbols on lines *AB* and *CD* indicate that these lines are parallel. A transversal is a line that intersects two parallel lines. Corresponding angles are in the same position but are part of different groups of angles, like angle *FGB* and angle *GHD*.

38. **(A), (B)** Factoring a polynomial involves dividing the polynomial into the product of two binomials. To do this, you can use the FOIL method in reverse. Choose two "first" terms that will produce $3x^2$: $(3x\quad)(x\quad)$. Then choose two "last" terms that are factors of –8: $(3x\quad 4)(x\quad 2)$. Since the 8 is negative (–8), the two operation signs will be different (one positive, one negative). Choose the operation signs so that the "inner" and "outer" steps of FOIL would produce $2x$: $(x + 2)(3x - 4)$

39. **(B), (A)** Manipulate the equation into quadratic form and then factor it. Subtract 5 from both sides to get $x^2 + 2x - 15 = 0$. Factor it to get $(x + 5)(x - 3)$ by FOILing in reverse. Find values for x that will make each binomial equal to zero: $-5 + 5 = 0$ and $3 - 3 = 0$

40. **(D)** Manipulate the equation into quadratic form ($ax^2 + bx + c = 0$) by adding 5 to both sides: $4x^2 + 11x + 5 = 0$. Calculate the individual terms that are part of the quadratic formula ($-b$, b^2, $-4ac$, and $2a$) by matching the coefficients in the equation with the positions of the terms in $ax^2 + bx + c = 0$: $a = 4$, $b = 11$, $c = 5$. Substitute those values into the quadratic formula $\left(x = \dfrac{-b \pm \sqrt{b^2 - 4ac}}{2a} \right)$ and simplify.

41. **(C)** To calculate the volume of a cone, cylinder, or sphere, π (pi) must be used.

42. **(D)** The volume of the cube is $s^3 = (4)(4)(4) = 64$. The volume of the sphere is

$$\frac{4}{3}\pi r^3 = \frac{4}{3}(3.14)(4)(4)(4) = 267.95$$

SCORING YOUR MATHEMATICAL REASONING EXAM

In 2016, the GED Testing Service made some adjustments to the "Performance Levels," or score levels, that they use to evaluate GED® test scores. The new structure has three levels based on the existing 100 to 200 score range:

- Passing (145+)—This is the minimum score needed to pass a GED® test.
- College Ready (165+)—A score at or above this level indicates that the student is ready for college-level work.
- College Ready + Credit (175+)—A score at or above this level indicates that the student should qualify for college credit.

Find the number of correct answers on your practice test in the chart below to determine your performance level:

Mathematical Reasoning Exam

Score Between	Performance Level
0 and 23	Not Passing
24 and 29	Close to Passing
30 and 35	Likely to Pass
36 and 37	College Ready
38 and 42	College Ready + Credit

ANSWER SHEET
Model Test

SOCIAL STUDIES EXAM

1. Ⓐ Ⓑ Ⓒ Ⓓ

2. Ⓐ Ⓑ Ⓒ Ⓓ

3. Ⓐ Ⓑ Ⓒ Ⓓ

4. _____

5. Ⓐ Ⓑ Ⓒ Ⓓ

6. Ⓐ Ⓑ Ⓒ Ⓓ

7. Ⓐ Ⓑ Ⓒ Ⓓ

8. Ⓐ Ⓑ Ⓒ Ⓓ

9. Ⓐ Ⓑ Ⓒ Ⓓ

10. _____

11. Ⓐ Ⓑ Ⓒ Ⓓ

12. Ⓐ Ⓑ Ⓒ Ⓓ

13. Ⓐ Ⓑ Ⓒ Ⓓ

14. Ⓐ Ⓑ Ⓒ Ⓓ

15. Ⓐ Ⓑ Ⓒ Ⓓ

16. Ⓐ Ⓑ Ⓒ Ⓓ

17. Ⓐ Ⓑ Ⓒ Ⓓ

18. Ⓐ Ⓑ Ⓒ Ⓓ

19. Ⓐ Ⓑ Ⓒ Ⓓ

20. Ⓐ Ⓑ Ⓒ Ⓓ

21. Ⓐ Ⓑ Ⓒ Ⓓ

22. _____

23. _____

24. Ⓐ Ⓑ Ⓒ Ⓓ

25. Ⓐ Ⓑ Ⓒ Ⓓ

26. Ⓐ Ⓑ Ⓒ Ⓓ

27. Ⓐ Ⓑ Ⓒ Ⓓ

28. Ⓐ Ⓑ Ⓒ Ⓓ

29. _____

30. Ⓐ Ⓑ Ⓒ Ⓓ

SOCIAL STUDIES EXAM

> **DIRECTIONS:** This practice exam contains passages, maps, charts, graphs, and political cartoons, which you will need to analyze in order to answer the questions that follow. The exam has 30 questions. You will have 75 minutes to answer those questions.

QUESTIONS 1 THROUGH 3 ARE BASED ON THE FOLLOWING PASSAGE:

PRESIDENT DWIGHT D. EISENHOWER'S
FAREWELL ADDRESS (1961)

In a speech of less than 10 minutes, on January 17, 1961, President Dwight Eisenhower delivered his political farewell to the American people on national television from the Oval Office of the White House. Those who expected the military leader and hero of World War II to depart his Presidency with a nostalgic, "old soldier" speech like Gen. Douglas MacArthur's, were surprised at his strong warnings about the dangers of the "military-industrial complex." As President of the United States for two terms, Eisenhower had slowed the push for increased defense spending despite pressure to build more military equipment during the Cold War's arms race. Nonetheless, the American military services and the defense industry had expanded a great deal in the 1950s. Eisenhower thought this growth was needed to counter the Soviet Union, but it confounded him. Though he did not say so explicitly, his standing as a military leader helped give him the credibility to stand up to the pressures of this new, powerful interest group. He eventually described it as a necessary evil.

"A vital element in keeping the peace is our military establishment. Our arms must be might, ready for instant action, so that no potential aggressor may be tempted to risk his own destruction. . . . American makers of plowshares could, with time and as required, make swords as well. But now we can no longer risk emergency improvisation of national defense; we have been compelled to create a permanent armaments industry of vast proportions. . . . This conjunction of an immense military establishment and a large arms industry is new in the American experience. . . . Yet we must not fail to comprehend its grave implications. . . . In the councils of government, we must guard against the acquisition of unwarranted influence, whether sought or unsought, by the military-industrial complex. The potential for the disastrous rise of misplaced power exists and will persist."

The end of Eisenhower's term as President not only marked the end of the 1950s but also the end of an era in government. A new, younger generation was rising to national power that would set a more youthful, vigorous course. His farewell address was a warning to his successors of one of the many things they would have to be wary of in the coming years.

Source: "President Dwight D. Eisenhower's Farewell Address (1961)." *Our Documents.* Last accessed July 28, 2016. *www.ourdocuments.gov/doc.php?doc=90.*

1. What did President Eisenhower believe was essential in keeping peace?
   (A) remaining allies with as many countries as possible
   (B) maintaining capitalism
   (C) equal rights for all
   (D) a strong military

2. Based on the passage, which of the following would President Eisenhower most likely support today?
   (A) an increase in educational funding
   (B) an increase in defense spending
   (C) an expansion of the size of the armed forces
   (D) a decrease in worldwide nuclear arsenals

3. Which of the following best describes the tone of President Eisenhower's speech?
   (A) optimistic
   (B) nostalgic
   (C) cautionary
   (D) pessimistic

QUESTIONS 4 AND 5 ARE BASED ON THE FOLLOWING GRAPH AND
PASSAGE:

WITHOUT A HIGH SCHOOL EDUCATION

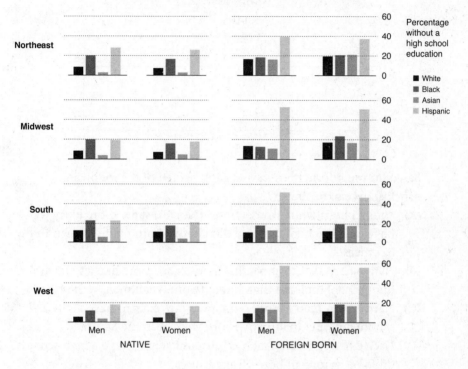

This graph explores variation in high school education attainment within
selected race and Hispanic origin groups by sex and nativity between regions.
Attainment of a high school diploma (or equivalent level of education) is
generally very high in the U.S., so this graph focuses on the percentage of the
population 25 and older who do not have that level of education. There are
notable differences between foreign-born and native population among many
groups. For example, in the West, 57 percent of Hispanic foreign-born males
had less than a high school education compared with 19 percent of Hispanic
native-born males. Nineteen percent of Asian foreign-born females had less
than a high school diploma compared with 5 percent of Asian native-born
females.

Source: "Without a High School Education." *United States Census Bureau.*
Last accessed September 16, 2016. *www.census.gov/dataviz/visualizations/035/.*

4. From the following list, choose the area where native-born black men have the highest graduation rate. Write your answer in the box below:

Northeast
Midwest
South
West

```

```

5. Based on the information in the graph, which of the following conclusions can be drawn?
   (A) Foreign-born white women in the Northeast are more likely to have a high school diploma than native-born white women in the Northeast.
   (B) Native-born black women in the West are more likely to have a high school diploma than foreign-born Asian men in the West.
   (C) Native-born men in the South are more likely to have a high school diploma than native-born women in the South.
   (D) Native-born Hispanic men are just as likely to have a high school diploma as foreign-born Hispanic men.

QUESTIONS 6 THROUGH 8 ARE BASED ON THE FOLLOWING PASSAGE:

EXECUTIVE ORDER 9066: RESULTING IN
THE RELOCATION OF JAPANESE (1942)

Between 1861 and 1940, approximately 275,000 Japanese immigrated to Hawaii and the mainland United States, the majority arriving between 1898 and 1924, when quotas were adopted that ended Asian immigration. Many worked in Hawaiian sugarcane fields as contract laborers. After their contracts expired, a small number remained and opened up shops. Other Japanese immigrants settled on the West Coast of mainland United States, cultivating marginal farmlands and fruit orchards, fishing, and operating small businesses.

Their efforts yielded impressive results. Japanese Americans controlled less than 4 percent of California's farmland in 1940, but they produced more than 10 percent of the total value of the state's farm resources.

As was the case with other immigrant groups, Japanese Americans settled in ethnic neighborhoods and established their own schools, houses of worship, and economic and cultural institutions. Ethnic concentration was further increased by real estate agents who would not sell properties to Japanese Americans outside of existing Japanese enclaves and by a 1913 act passed by the California Assembly restricting land ownership to those eligible to be citizens. In 1922 the U.S. Supreme Court, in *Ozawa v. United States*, upheld the government's right to deny U.S. citizenship to Japanese immigrants.

Envy over economic success combined with distrust over cultural separateness and long-standing anti-Asian racism turned into disaster when the Empire of Japan attacked Pearl Harbor on December 7, 1941. Lobbyists from western states, many representing competing economic interests or nativist groups, pressured Congress and the President to remove persons of Japanese descent from the west coast, both foreign born (*issei*— meaning "first generation" of Japanese in the U.S.) and American citizens (*nisei* — the second generation of Japanese in America, U.S. citizens by birthright). During Congressional committee hearings, Department of Justice representatives raised constitutional and ethical objections to the proposal, so the U.S. Army carried out the task instead. The West Coast was divided into military zones, and on February 19, 1942, President Franklin D. Roosevelt issued Executive Order 9066 authorizing exclusion. Congress then implemented the order on March 21, 1942, by passing Public Law 503.

After encouraging voluntary evacuation of the areas, the Western Defense Command began involuntary removal and detention of West Coast residents of Japanese ancestry. In the next 6 months, approximately 122,000 men, women, and children were moved to assembly centers. They were then evacuated to and confined in isolated, fenced, and guarded relocation centers, known as internment camps. The 10 relocation sites were in remote areas in 6 western states and Arkansas: Heart Mountain in Wyoming, Tule Lake and Manzanar in California, Topaz in Utah, Poston and Gila River in Arizona, Granada in Colorado, Minidoka in Idaho, and Jerome and Rowher in Arkansas.

Nearly 70,000 of the evacuees were American citizens. The government made no charges against them, nor could they appeal their incarceration. All lost personal liberties; most lost homes and property as well. Although several Japanese Americans challenged the government's actions in court cases, the

Supreme Court upheld their legality. *Nisei* were nevertheless encouraged to serve in the armed forces, and some were also drafted. Altogether, more than 30,000 Japanese Americans served with distinction during World War II in segregated units.

For many years after the war, various individuals and groups sought compensation for the internees. The speed of the evacuation forced many homeowners and businessmen to sell out quickly; total property loss is estimated at $1.3 billion, and net income loss at $2.7 billion (calculated in 1983 dollars based on the Commission investigation . . .). The Japanese American Evacuation Claims Act of 1948, with amendments in 1951 and 1965, provided token payments for some property losses. More serious efforts to make amends took place in the early 1980s, when the congressionally established Commission on Wartime Relocation and Internment of Civilians held investigations and made recommendations. As a result, several bills were introduced in Congress from 1984 until 1988, when Public Law 100-383, which acknowledged the injustice of the internment, apologized for it, and provided for restitution, was passed.

Source: "Executive Order 9066: Resulting in the Relocation of Japanese (1942)." *Our Documents*. Last accessed July 28, 2016. *www.ourdocuments.gov/doc.php?doc=74.*

6. The relocation of Japanese Americans during World War II is most similar to which of the following?
    (A) relocation of individuals in the path of a hurricane
    (B) enslavement of African Americans during the 1700s and 1800s
    (C) imprisonment of someone who has not been charged with nor committed any crime
    (D) internment of Jews in concentration camps during the 1930s and 1940s

7. In the 1980s, Public Law 100-383 was passed, which provided Japanese

Americans with   [Select   ∨] .
                    (A) reparations
                    (B) restrictions
                    (C) due process
                    (D) internment

8. What was the total amount of income and property lost by Japanese Americans?
   (A) $1.3 billion
   (B) $2.7 billion
   (C) $4 billion
   (D) $122,000

QUESTION 9 IS BASED ON THE FOLLOWING POLITICAL CARTOON:

9. What does the political cartoon above depict?
   (A) There is conflict within the Republican Party.
   (B) There is conflict between the Democratic and Republican Parties.
   (C) The Democrats oppose the Atlantic Pact.
   (D) There is bipartisan agreement on the Atlantic Pact.

QUESTIONS 10 THROUGH 12 ARE BASED ON THE FOLLOWING PASSAGE:

LOUISIANA PURCHASE TREATY (1803)

Robert Livingston and James Monroe closed on the sweetest real estate deal of the millennium when they signed the Louisiana Purchase Treaty in Paris on April 30, 1803. They were authorized to pay France up to $10 million for the port of New Orleans and the Floridas. When offered the entire territory of Louisiana—an area larger than Great Britain, France, Germany, Italy, Spain and Portugal combined—the American negotiators swiftly agreed to a price of $15 million.

Although President Thomas Jefferson was a strict interpreter of the Constitution who wondered if the U.S. Government was authorized to acquire new territory, he was also a visionary who dreamed of an "empire for liberty" that would stretch across the entire continent. As Napoleon threatened to take back the offer, Jefferson squelched whatever doubts he had and prepared to occupy a land of unimaginable riches.

The Louisiana Purchase Agreement is made up of the Treaty of Cession and the two conventions regarding the financial aspects of the transaction.

Source: "Louisiana Purchase Treaty (1803)."*Our Documents*. Last accessed July 28, 2016. *www.ourdocuments.gov/doc.php?doc=18.*

10. From the following list, choose the opportunity that the Louisiana Purchase provided to the United States. Write your answer in the box below.

> Westward expansion
> Closer proximity to enemies
> Profit by selling land
> Search for buried treasure

11. Despite President Jefferson's doubts, what does the execution of the Louisiana Purchase assume?
    (A) Napoleon would take back the land.
    (B) The United States did not have the right to acquire these lands.
    (C) The United States had the right to acquire these lands.
    (D) The United States needed the approval of Great Britain, France, Germany, Italy, Spain, and Portugal to purchase the land.

12. The Louisiana Purchase is most similar to which other acquisition by the United States?
    (A) the capture of Guam during the Spanish-American War
    (B) the United States declaring independence from Great Britain
    (C) the changing of the name New Amsterdam to New York
    (D) the purchase of Alaska for $7.2 million

QUESTIONS 13 AND 14 REFER TO THE FOLLOWING PASSAGE:

OFFICIAL PROGRAM FOR THE MARCH ON WASHINGTON (1963)

The civil rights movement in the United States during the late 1950s and 1960s was the political, legal, and social struggle to gain full citizenship rights for black Americans and to achieve racial equality. Individuals and civil rights organizations challenged segregation and discrimination using a variety of activities, including protest marches, boycotts, and refusal to abide by segregation laws.

On August 28, 1963, more than 250,000 demonstrators descended upon the nation's capital to participate in the "March on Washington for Jobs and Freedom." Not only was it the largest demonstration for human rights in United States history, but it also occasioned a rare display of unity among the various civil rights organizations. The event began with a rally at the Washington Monument featuring several celebrities and musicians. Participants then marched the mile-long National Mall to the Memorial. The three-hour long program at the Lincoln Memorial included speeches from prominent civil rights and religious leaders. The day ended with a meeting between the march leaders and President John F. Kennedy at the White House.

362 • Pass Key to the GED® Test

The idea for the 1963 March on Washington was envisioned by A. Philip Randolph, a long-time civil rights activist dedicated to improving the economic condition of black Americans. When Randolph first proposed the march in late 1962, he received little response from other civil rights leaders. He knew that cooperation would be difficult because each had his own agenda for the civil rights movement, and the leaders competed for funding and press coverage. Success of the March on Washington would depend on the involvement of the so-called "Big Six"—Randolph and the heads of the five major civil rights organizations: Roy Wilkins of the National Association for the Advancement of Colored People (NAACP); Whitney Young, Jr., of the National Urban League; Rev. Martin Luther King, Jr., of the Southern Christian Leadership Conference (SCLC); James Farmer of the Conference of Racial Equality (CORE); and John Lewis of the Student Nonviolent Coordinating Committee (SNCC).

The details and organization of the march were handled by Bayard Rustin, Randolph's trusted associate. Rustin was a veteran activist with extensive experience in putting together mass protest. With only two months to plan, Rustin established his headquarters in Harlem, NY, with a smaller office in Washington. He and his core staff of 200 volunteers quickly put together the largest peaceful demonstration in U.S. history.

Source: "Official Program for the March on Washington (1963)."
Our Documents. Last accessed July 27, 2016.
www.ourdocuments.gov/doc.php?doc=96.

13. Which of the following ideas is exemplified in protest marches?
    (A) suffrage
    (B) Jim Crow laws
    (C) natural rights
    (D) freedom of assembly

14. The "March on Washington for Jobs and Freedom" was the largest demonstration in United States history. What does this suggest about the civil rights movement?

   (A) A large number of Americans believed in the civil rights movement.

   (B) The civil rights movement represented a minority of the population.

   (C) The civil rights movement was not successful.

   (D) The civil rights movement led to equality for all.

QUESTIONS 15 THROUGH 17 ARE BASED ON THE FOLLOWING PASSAGE:

WAR DEPARTMENT GENERAL ORDER 143: CREATION OF THE U.S. COLORED TROOPS (1863)

The issues of emancipation and military service were intertwined from the onset of the Civil War. News from Fort Sumter set off a rush by free black men to enlist in U.S. military units. They were turned away, however, because a Federal law dating from 1792 barred Negroes from bearing arms for the U.S. Army. In Boston disappointed would-be volunteers met and passed a resolution requesting that the Government modify its laws to permit their enlistment.

The Lincoln administration wrestled with the idea of authorizing the recruitment of black troops, concerned that such a move would prompt the border states to secede. When Gen. John C. Frémont in Missouri and Gen. David Hunter in South Carolina issued proclamations that emancipated slaves in their military regions and permitted them to enlist, their superiors sternly revoked their orders. By mid-1862, however, the escalating number of former slaves (contrabands), the declining number of white volunteers, and the pressing personnel needs of the Union Army pushed the Government into reconsidering the ban.

As a result, on July 17, 1862, Congress passed the Second Confiscation and Militia Act, freeing slaves who had masters in the Confederate Army. Two days later, slavery was abolished in the territories of the United States, and on July 22 President Lincoln presented the preliminary draft of the Emancipation Proclamation to his Cabinet. After the Union Army turned back Lee's first invasion of the North at Antietam, MD, and the Emancipation Proclamation was subsequently announced, black recruitment was pursued in earnest. Volunteers from South Carolina, Tennessee, and Massachusetts filled the first authorized black regiments. Recruitment was slow until black leaders such as Frederick Douglass encouraged black men to become soldiers to ensure eventual full citizenship. (Two of Douglass's own sons contributed to the war effort.) Volunteers began to respond, and in May 1863 the Government established the Bureau of Colored Troops to manage the burgeoning numbers of black soldiers.

Nearly 40,000 black soldiers died over the course of the war—30,000 of infection or disease. Black soldiers served in artillery and infantry and performed all noncombat support functions that sustain an army as well. Black carpenters, chaplains, cooks, guards, laborers, nurses, scouts, spies, steamboat pilots, surgeons, and teamsters also contributed to the war cause. There were nearly 80 black commissioned officers. Black women, who could not formally join the Army, nonetheless served as nurses, spies, and scouts, the most famous being Harriet Tubman, who scouted for the 2nd South Carolina Volunteers.

Source: "War Department General Order 143: Creation of the U.S. Colored Troops (1863)." *Our Documents.* Last accessed July 28, 2016. *www.ourdocuments.gov/doc.php?doc=35.*

15. The creation of the U.S. Colored Troops most likely [Select ▾] the North in their fights against the

(A) aided
(B) impeded
(C) neutralized
(D) had no effect on

Confederate states of the South.

16. What percentage of African-American soldiers died due to infection or disease?
    (A) 40%
    (B) 50%
    (C) 75%
    (D) 85%

17. Why would border states consider seceding if African Americans were permitted to join the armed forces?
    (A) Many people who lived in the border states sided with the South.
    (B) The border states were for the freedom of African Americans but only if African Americans didn't serve in the armed forces.
    (C) The border states were being forced to stay in the Union.
    (D) The border states were staunchly against slavery.

QUESTION 18 IS BASED ON THE FOLLOWING POLITICAL CARTOON:

18. What is the central idea of the political cartoon above?
    (A) There are too many guns in Washington, D.C.
    (B) The Second Amendment enables the United States to maintain peace with other countries.
    (C) An increase in arms will help the United States maintain peace.
    (D) Peace is in jeopardy.

QUESTIONS 19 THROUGH 21 ARE BASED ON THE FOLLOWING PASSAGE:

LEND-LEASE ACT (1941)

In July 1940, after Britain had sustained the loss of 11 destroyers to the German Navy over a 10-day period, newly elected British Prime Minister Winston Churchill requested help from President Roosevelt. Roosevelt responded by exchanging 50 destroyers for 99-year leases on British bases in the Caribbean and Newfoundland. As a result, a major foreign policy debate erupted over whether the United States should aid Great Britain or maintain strict neutrality.

In the 1940 Presidential election campaign, Roosevelt promised to keep America out of the war. He stated, "I have said this before, but I shall say it again and again and again; your boys are not going to be sent into any foreign wars." Nevertheless, FDR wanted to support Britain and believed the United States should serve as a "great arsenal of democracy." Churchill pleaded, "Give us the tools and we'll finish the job." In January 1941, following up on his campaign pledge and the prime minister's appeal for arms, Roosevelt proposed to Congress a new military aid bill.

The plan proposed by FDR was to "lend-lease or otherwise dispose of arms" and other supplies needed by any country whose security was vital to the defense of the United States. In support of the bill, Secretary of War Henry L. Stimson told the Senate Foreign Relations Committee during the debate over lend-lease, "We are buying . . . not lending. We are buying our own security while we prepare. By our delay during the past six years, while Germany was preparing, we find ourselves unprepared and unarmed, facing a thoroughly prepared and armed potential enemy." Following two months of debate, Congress passed the Lend-Lease Act, meeting Great Britain's deep need for supplies and allowing the United States to prepare for war while remaining officially neutral.

Source: "Lend-Lease Act (1941)." *Our Documents*. Last accessed July 28, 2016. *www.ourdocuments.gov/doc.php?doc=71.*

19. What was the greater purpose of the Lend-Lease Act?
     (A) to provide Britain with destroyers
     (B) to gain leases on British bases
     (C) to support democracy
     (D) to align the United States with Germany

20. What argument for the bill does Secretary of War Henry L. Stimson
     make?
     (A) The United States is being proactive by making strategic moves.
     (B) The bill is inaccurate because the United States is buying, not
          lending.
     (C) Congress should be wary about passing the bill because Germany
          is a potential enemy.
     (D) The bill will enable the United States to continue to remain
          neutral and avoid war.

21. What did the United States stand to gain from the Lend-Lease Act?
     (A) destroyers
     (B) acquisition of lands in England
     (C) future military support
     (D) a place to dispose of obsolete arms

QUESTIONS 22 AND 23 ARE BASED ON THE FOLLOWING GRAPH:

POPULATION GROWTH IN THE DISTRICT OF COLUMBIA

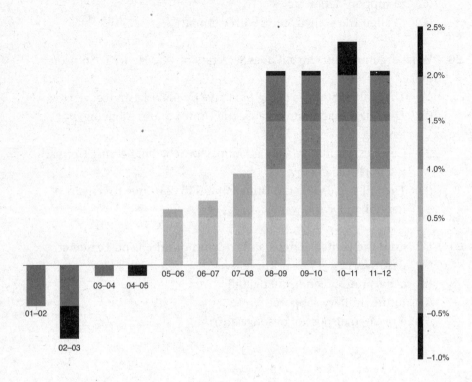

22. According to the graph, which period of time saw the greatest increase in population? Draw a dot below the correct time period in the boxes below.

●

2002–2003	2004–2005	2007–2008	2010–2011

23. Which of the following periods would have likely had the least need for an increase in educational funding? Draw a dot below the correct time period.

•   ·

2002–2003	2004–2005	2007–2008	2010–2011

QUESTIONS 24 AND 25 ARE BASED ON THE FOLLOWING GRAPH AND PASSAGE:

STATE-TO-STATE MIGRATION

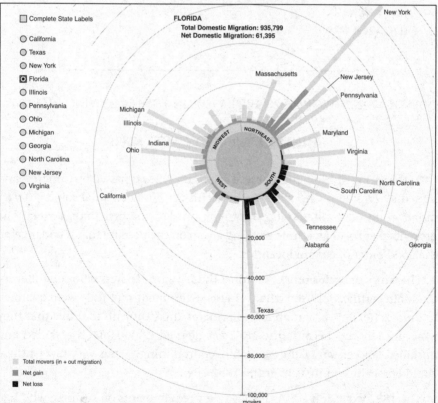

This graphic, using data from the American Community Survey, illustrates the total number of movers between states for the 12 most populous states, based on the 2010 population. While there is considerable gross domestic migration (total number of movers) between states each year, the number of movers in and the number of movers out are similar, resulting in relatively small net gains or losses.

24. According to the graph, to which state did Florida lose the most people?
    (A) Michigan
    (B) New York
    (C) Georgia
    (D) Texas

25. According to the graph, which region saw the greatest singular state-to-state migration?
    (A) Northeast
    (B) South
    (C) Midwest
    (D) West

QUESTIONS 26 THROUGH 28 ARE BASED ON THE FOLLOWING PASSAGE:

CHINESE EXCLUSION ACT (1882)

In the spring of 1882, the Chinese Exclusion Act was passed by Congress and signed by President Chester A. Arthur. This act provided an absolute 10-year moratorium on Chinese labor immigration. For the first time, Federal law proscribed entry of an ethnic working group on the premise that it endangered the good order of certain localities.

The Chinese Exclusion Act required the few non-laborers who sought entry to obtain certification from the Chinese government that they were qualified to immigrate. But this group found it increasingly difficult to prove that they were not laborers because the 1882 act defined excludables as "skilled and unskilled laborers and Chinese employed in mining." Thus very few Chinese could enter the country under the 1882 law.

The 1882 exclusion act also placed new requirements on Chinese who had already entered the country. If they left the United States, they had to obtain certifications to re-enter. Congress, moreover, refused State and Federal courts the right to grant citizenship to Chinese resident aliens, although these courts could still deport them.

When the exclusion act expired in 1892, Congress extended it for 10 years in the form of the Geary Act. This extension, made permanent in 1902, added restrictions by requiring each Chinese resident to register and obtain a certificate of residence. Without a certificate, she or he faced deportation.

The Geary Act regulated Chinese immigration until the 1920s. With increased postwar immigration, Congress adopted new means for regulation: quotas and requirements pertaining to national origin. By this time, anti-Chinese agitation had quieted. In 1943 Congress repealed all the exclusion acts, leaving a yearly limit of 105 Chinese and gave foreign-born Chinese the right to seek naturalization. The so-called national origin system, with various modifications, lasted until Congress passed the Immigration Act of 1965. Effective July 1, 1968, a limit of 170,000 immigrants from outside the Western Hemisphere could enter the United States, with a maximum of 20,000 from any one country. Skill and the need for political asylum determined admission. The Immigration Act of 1990 provided the most comprehensive change in legal immigration since 1965. The act established a "flexible" worldwide cap on family-based, employment-based, and diversity immigrant visas. The act further provides that visas for any single foreign state in these categories may not exceed 7 percent of the total available.

Source: "Chinese Exclusion Act (1882)." *Our Documents*. Last accessed July 28, 2016. *www.ourdocuments.gov/doc.php?doc=47*.

26. What was the likely catalyst for the Chinese Exclusion Act of 1882?
     (A) the Geary Act
     (B) lack of jobs for natural-born citizens
     (C) fear of overcrowding
     (D) anti-Chinese sentiment

27. After 1968, which of the following would be a legal number of Chinese immigrants?
     (A) 18,744
     (B) 20,482
     (C) 68,002
     (D) 75,000

28. What was the purpose of the Geary Act?
    (A) to extend the regulations in the Chinese Exclusion Act
    (B) to enhance the ability of Chinese people to immigrate to the United States
    (C) to grant equal immigration rights to all
    (D) to freeze all immigration

QUESTIONS 29 AND 30 ARE BASED ON THE FOLLOWING TABLE:

PERCENT OF MEN AND WOMEN WITH FIRST MARRIAGES BY AGE

Age	Men			Women		
	1970	1988	2009	1970	1988	2009
Under 20	18.4	6.9	3.6	41.8	17.7	6.9
20–24	57.0	38.7	23.5	46.0	43.3	31.5
25–29	16.2	33.9	34.3	7.7	26.1	32.9
30–34	4.1	13.6	19.5	2.0	8.5	15.3
35–39	1.8	4.4	9.0	0.9	2.8	6.3
40–44	1.0	1.4	4.3	0.6	0.8	2.9
45–49	0.6	0.5	2.8	0.4	0.3	1.9
50–54	0.3	0.3	1.4	0.2	0.2	1.0
55–59	0.2	0.2	0.9	0.1	0.1	0.6
60–64	0.1	0.1	0.3	0.1	0.1	0.4
65 and over	0.1	0.1	0.4	0.1	0.1	0.2

Source: U.S. Census Bureau, American Community Survey, 2009; National Center for Health Statistics, 1970, 1988.

29. About _____% of 50- to 54-year-old women entered into their first marriage in 1988.

30. What does the trend in data suggest?
    (A) People are getting married earlier in life.
    (B) People are getting married later in life.
    (C) People are getting married at about the same age as they always have.
    (D) Women are getting married earlier, while men are getting married later.

SOCIAL STUDIES EXAM ANSWERS EXPLAINED

1. **(D)** The passage states in several ways that keeping the peace required maintaining a strong military. Choices A, B, and C are incorrect. The passage does not indicate that these were peacekeeping factors in which Eisenhower believed.

2. **(D)** The passage makes clear that President Eisenhower recognized the dangers of an arms race but also considered it to be necessary at the time. It also states that Eisenhower was conflicted with the necessity of building up the military. These factors suggest that he would have supported a worldwide decrease in nuclear arsenals. Choice A is incorrect. Although Eisenhower may have supported an increase in educational funding, there is no evidence in the passage to support this answer. Choices B and C are incorrect. The passage indicates that although increased military spending and expanding the armed forces were necessary during Eisenhower's presidency, he would probably not support them today.

3. **(C)** The passage indicates that President Eisenhower was warning future generations. Choices A, B, and D are incorrect because they don't describe the tone of the speech.

4. **West** is the correct answer. According to the key, the graphs indicate the percentage of people *without* a high school education so look for the smallest percentage, not the highest percentage.

5. **(B)** When comparing the two bar graphs, it is clear that a smaller percentage of native-born black women in the West are without a high school education than foreign-born Asian men in the West.

6. **(C)** The Japanese Americans who were placed into internment camps had not committed any crimes nor had they been charged with any. Choice A is incorrect. Individuals who are relocated because of a hurricane are being moved for their own protection. They are free to return to their homes after the danger has passed. Choice B is incorrect. Although slavery is a form of imprisonment, the Japanese Americans were not forced to work. Choice D is incorrect because the Japanese Americans in the internment camps were not put to death.

7. **(A)** Public Law 100-383 provided Japanese Americans with reparations.

8. **(C)** Since the question asks for the total amount of income and property lost, it means you have to add $1.3 billion + $2.7 billion = $4 billion.

Choice A is incorrect because it is the total property loss. Choice B is incorrect because it is the net income loss. Choice D is incorrect.

9. **(A)** Taft and Dulles are arguing, and Vandenberg comments that it's "purely an argument between two Republicans." Choice B is incorrect because the Democrats are not involved in the argument. Choice C is incorrect because no evidence suggests the Democrats oppose the Atlantic Pact. Choice D is incorrect. No evidence shows how the Democrats feel about the Atlantic Pact, only that there is bipartisan agreement on foreign policy.

10. **Westward expansion** The Louisiana Purchase included much of the land west of the Mississippi and enabled the United States to expand westward.

11. **(C)** Despite President Jefferson's personal reservations based on his interpretation of the Constitution, the execution of the purchase assumes the United States determined that it had the right to acquire these lands. Choice B is incorrect; the fact that the United States did acquire these lands indicates the opposite. Choices A and D are incorrect because no evidence supports these answers.

12. **(D)** The Louisiana Purchase and the purchase of Alaska were both cash transactions for land. Choice A is incorrect because Guam was captured during a war. Choices B and C are incorrect because neither one has to do with the acquisition of land.

13. **(D)** Protests are a form of assembly.

14. **(A)** The number of participants indicates a broad belief in the civil rights movement.

15. **(A)** "Aided" best completes the sentence.

16. **(C)** According to the passage, of the 40,000 African Americans who died, 30,000 died from infection or disease. This constitutes 75% of the African-American soldiers who died. Choices A, B, and D are incorrect.

17. **(A)** If the concern was that the border states would secede, obviously many people who lived in those states sided with the South. Choices B, C, and D are incorrect. No evidence supports any of these answers.

18. **(D)** The depiction of a hand, labeled "peace," that is grabbing for Uncle Sam's coattails while Uncle Sam runs away with a rifle indicates that

peace is in jeopardy. Choices A, B, and C are incorrect. Although the political cartoon contains elements from each of these answer choices, none of these choices is fully supported.

19. **(C)** The third paragraph indicates that President Roosevelt suggested the federal government support any country whose security is vital to the defense of the United States. Choices A and B are incorrect. Although these were effects, neither was the greater purpose of the Lend-Lease Act.

20. **(A)** The passage indicates that passing the Lend-Lease Act would enable the United States to "[buy] our own security while we prepare." Choices B, C, and D are incorrect because no evidence supports these answers.

21. **(C)** Giving Great Britain the support it needed at the time would create a relationship where Great Britain could reciprocate in the future. Choice A is incorrect because the United States gave destroyers to Great Britain, not the other way around. Choice B is incorrect. The United States was not acquiring lands in England; it was leasing land at British bases. Choice D is incorrect because it misinterprets the phrase "dispose of arms."

22. The bar aligned with the highest percentage is the one that corresponds with **2010–2011**.

23. If the population decreases, there is less need to increase educational funding. The years **2002–2003** saw the greatest decrease in population growth.

24. **(D)** The darkest shading indicates net loss, and the bar corresponding to Texas has the largest amount of the darkest shading. Choices A, B, and C are incorrect.

25. **(A)** New York had the greatest singular state-to-state migration, and New York is in the Northeast. Choices B, C, and D are incorrect.

26. **(D)** The last paragraph states that "anti-Chinese agitation had quieted," indicating that there was, at one time, anti-Chinese sentiment. Choice A is incorrect because the Geary Act was a subsequent law. Choices B and C are incorrect. No evidence supports these answers.

27. **(A)** The last paragraph states that a maximum of 20,000 people could enter the United States from any one country. Choices B, C, and D are incorrect; they are all over 20,000.

28. **(A)** The passage clearly indicates that the Geary Act was intended to extend the provisions of the Chinese Exclusion Act. Choices B and D are incorrect. The Geary Act did not enhance or freeze immigration completely. Choice C is incorrect because the Geary Act limited immigration rights.

29. **0.2** According to the table, 0.2% of women age 50–54 entered into their first marriage in 1988.

30. **(B)** The chart indicates that fewer people are getting married early in life, while the number of people getting married later has increased. Choice A is incorrect because the table suggests the opposite. Choice C is incorrect because the table suggests there is a great change in the age when people marry. Choice D is incorrect. Although men are, in fact, getting married later, so are women.

SCORING YOUR SOCIAL STUDIES EXAM

In 2016, the GED Testing Service made some adjustments to the "Performance Levels," or score levels, that they use to evaluate GED® test scores. The new structure has three levels based on the existing 100 to 200 score range:

- Passing (145+)—This is the minimum score needed to pass a GED® test.
- College Ready (165+)—A score at or above this level indicates that the student is ready for college-level work.
- College Ready + Credit (175+)—A score at or above this level indicates that the student should qualify for college credit.

Find the number of correct answers on your practice test in the chart below to determine your performance level:

Social Studies Exam

Score Between	Performance Level
0 and 17	Not Passing
18 and 21	Close to Passing
22 and 25	Likely to Pass
26 and 28	College Ready
29 and 30	College Ready + Credit

ANSWER SHEET
Model Test

SCIENCE EXAM

1. Ⓐ Ⓑ Ⓒ Ⓓ

2. Ⓐ Ⓑ Ⓒ Ⓓ

   Ⓐ Ⓑ Ⓒ Ⓓ

   Ⓐ Ⓑ Ⓒ Ⓓ

   Ⓐ Ⓑ Ⓒ Ⓓ

3. Ⓐ Ⓑ Ⓒ Ⓓ

   Ⓐ Ⓑ Ⓒ Ⓓ

   Ⓐ Ⓑ Ⓒ Ⓓ

   Ⓐ Ⓑ Ⓒ Ⓓ

   Ⓐ Ⓑ Ⓒ Ⓓ

4. Ⓐ Ⓑ Ⓒ Ⓓ

5. Ⓐ Ⓑ Ⓒ Ⓓ

6. Ⓐ Ⓑ Ⓒ Ⓓ

7. Ⓐ Ⓑ Ⓒ Ⓓ

8. Use the lines below for your answer.

9. Ⓐ Ⓑ Ⓒ Ⓓ

10. Ⓐ Ⓑ Ⓒ Ⓓ

11. Ⓐ Ⓑ Ⓒ Ⓓ

12. Ⓐ Ⓑ Ⓒ Ⓓ

13. Ⓐ Ⓑ Ⓒ Ⓓ

14. Ⓐ Ⓑ Ⓒ Ⓓ

15. Ⓐ Ⓑ Ⓒ Ⓓ

16. Ⓐ Ⓑ Ⓒ Ⓓ

17. Ⓐ Ⓑ Ⓒ Ⓓ

18. Ⓐ Ⓑ Ⓒ Ⓓ

8. _____

_____

_____

_____

_____

ANSWER SHEET
Model Test

SCIENCE EXAM

19. Ⓐ Ⓑ Ⓒ Ⓓ

20. Ⓐ Ⓑ Ⓒ Ⓓ

21. Ⓐ Ⓑ Ⓒ Ⓓ

22. Ⓐ Ⓑ Ⓒ Ⓓ

23. Ⓐ Ⓑ Ⓒ Ⓓ

24. Ⓐ Ⓑ Ⓒ Ⓓ

25. Ⓐ Ⓑ Ⓒ Ⓓ

26. Ⓐ Ⓑ Ⓒ Ⓓ

27. Ⓐ Ⓑ Ⓒ Ⓓ

28. Ⓐ Ⓑ Ⓒ Ⓓ

    Ⓐ Ⓑ Ⓒ Ⓓ

29. Ⓐ Ⓑ Ⓒ Ⓓ

    Ⓐ Ⓑ Ⓒ Ⓓ

30. Ⓐ Ⓑ Ⓒ Ⓓ

    Ⓐ Ⓑ Ⓒ Ⓓ

31. _____

    _____

    _____

32. Ⓐ Ⓑ Ⓒ Ⓓ

33. Ⓐ Ⓑ Ⓒ Ⓓ

34. Ⓐ Ⓑ Ⓒ Ⓓ

    Ⓐ Ⓑ Ⓒ Ⓓ

    Ⓐ Ⓑ Ⓒ Ⓓ

35. _____

SCIENCE EXAM

> **DIRECTIONS:** This practice exam contains various stimuli, which you will need to analyze in order to answer the questions that follow. This exam has 35 questions. You will have 90 minutes to answer the questions.

1. When a new species becomes established in an ecosystem, it can often disrupt the existing relationships between predators and their prey (animals that predators eat). A new species may outcompete an existing predator for food sources and habitat, or an existing predator can become prey for the new species. One of the most well-documented ecological impacts of a species invasion was that of the sea lamprey in the Great Lakes, which devastated the lake trout fishery during the 1940s and 1950s. As the native predator became prey to the invasive sea lampreys, populations of prey fish like the alewife multiplied out of control.

   According to the information above, what happened in the Great Lakes during the 1940s and 1950s?
   (A) Lake trout began to feed on sea lampreys instead of alewives. This reduced the sea lamprey population, and the alewife population grew as a result.
   (B) Alewives began to feed on sea lampreys. This reduced the sea lamprey population, and the lake trout population grew as a result.
   (C) Sea lampreys began to feed on lake trout. This reduced the population of lake trout, and the alewife population grew as a result.
   (D) Alewives began to feed on lake trout. This reduced the lake trout population, and the sea lamprey population grew as a result.

QUESTIONS 2 AND 3 REFER TO THE FOLLOWING SCATTER PLOT:

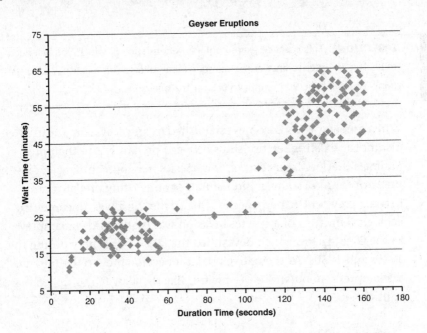

2. Select the word or phrase that correctly completes the sentence:

Most eruptions occur with either [Select ∨] durations

(A) short
(B) both long and short
(C) even
(D) equal

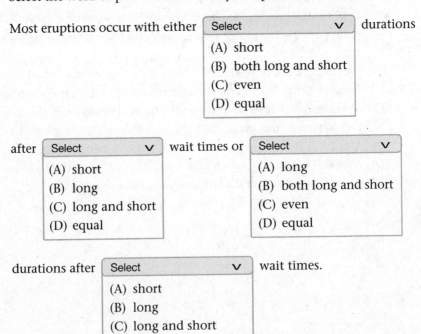

after [Select ∨] wait times or [Select ∨]

(A) short
(B) long
(C) long and short
(D) equal

(A) long
(B) both long and short
(C) even
(D) equal

durations after [Select ∨] wait times.

(A) short
(B) long
(C) long and short
(D) equal

3. Select the word or phrase that correctly completes each sentence:

Short eruptions tend to last [Select ⌄] 20 seconds

- (A) less than
- (B) between
- (C) more than
- (D) as long as

but [Select ⌄] 60 seconds. Long eruptions tend to

- (A) less than
- (B) between
- (C) more than
- (D) as long as

last [Select ⌄] 160 seconds but [Select ⌄]

- (A) less than
- (B) between
- (C) more than
- (D) as long as

- (A) less than
- (B) between
- (C) more than
- (D) as long as

120 seconds. Very few eruptions last [Select ⌄]

- (A) less than
- (B) between
- (C) more than
- (D) as long as

60 and 120 seconds.

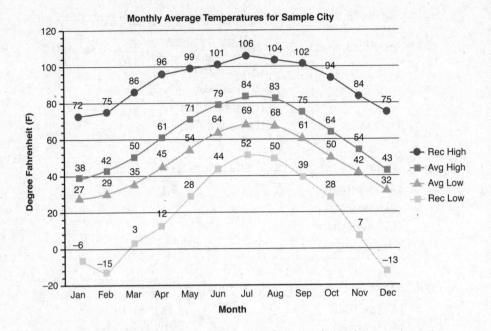

The graph above reflects temperature data gathered over a 10-year period. The "average high" and "average low" temperatures give a single 10-year average for each month. The "record high" and "record low" temperatures are the highest and lowest temperatures recorded for each month during the 10-year period.

4. Which month has the greatest range between record low and record high temperatures?
   (A) January
   (B) February
   (C) November
   (D) December

QUESTIONS 5 THROUGH 8 REFER TO THE FOLLOWING INFORMATION:

The temperature of the Earth is regulated by a relationship between the Sun, the surface of the Earth, and the Earth's atmosphere. Energy in the form of solar radiation (sunlight) travels from the Sun to the Earth. A portion of this energy is reflected away, either by the Earth's atmosphere or surface, but roughly half of this energy is absorbed by the surface of the Earth and converted to infrared (heat) energy. This heat is then released back into the atmosphere.

A large portion of the infrared energy emitted passes through the atmosphere and into space. A smaller portion of this energy is absorbed by chemicals in the atmosphere known as "greenhouse gases." As these gases absorb heat, they cause an increase in atmospheric temperature. Without greenhouse gases, the Earth would be significantly colder and unable to support many of its current forms of life, including human life. Greenhouse gases include water vapor (H_2O), carbon dioxide (CO_2), methane (CH_4), and ozone (O_3).

The most significant greenhouse gas in terms of warming effect is water vapor (H_2O). Water vapor absorbs the majority of the global heat emissions absorbed by the atmosphere. Research data suggest that the absorption capacity of water vapor in the atmosphere increases as atmospheric temperature increases. The second most significant greenhouse gas in terms of warming effect is carbon dioxide (CO_2). As the average concentration of atmospheric carbon dioxide increases, it absorbs increasing amounts of heat, contributing to an increase in atmospheric temperature.

The carbon cycle is a process by which carbon in the atmosphere is absorbed, stored, and released by the biosphere (land, oceans, and living things). On land, plants absorb carbon for use in photosynthesis, and most of this carbon is converted to biomass (leaves, stems, and roots) or transmitted into the soil. Living plants return unconverted carbon into the atmosphere during respiration. Biomass carbon is returned to the atmosphere during decomposition. Carbon in the soil is released during the respiration of microbes and other living things in the soil.

A small amount of carbon absorbed and stored by the biosphere is not released back into the atmosphere. Instead, it is retained in the soil. This retention of carbon is called *biosequestration*. The highest levels of carbon biosequestration in soil are found in regions at high latitudes with colder climates. For example, large amounts of carbon are stored in the *permafrost* (frozen soil) found in cold climates like *tundra* and *boreal forests*. Most of the carbon captured in permafrost remains sequestered unless the permafrost melts or is otherwise affected by increasing temperatures.

5. According to the passage, which of the following is NOT a greenhouse gas?
   (A) carbon dioxide
   (B) water vapor
   (C) carbon monoxide
   (D) ozone

6. Based on the passage, all of the following are true EXCEPT
   (A) Water vapor is a more significant factor in warming than carbon dioxide.
   (B) Methane is a less significant factor in warming than carbon dioxide.
   (C) Carbon dioxide is a more significant factor in warming than ozone.
   (D) Methane is a more significant factor in warming than ozone.

7. What is the most likely effect of an increase in the concentration of CO_2 in the atmosphere?
   (A) an increase in the concentration of water vapor in the atmosphere
   (B) an increase in the concentration of methane in the atmosphere
   (C) an increase in the absorption capacity of water vapor in the atmosphere
   (D) an increase in the absorption capacity of ozone in the atmosphere

8. In recent decades, global temperatures have been trending higher, with greater rates of change near the North and South Poles. Explain how warming could interfere with carbon biosequestration in soil, including both the cause of the interference and the potential effect on the atmosphere. Include multiple pieces of evidence from the passage to support your answer. (This could take approximately 10 minutes to complete.)

9. An element's atomic number describes the number of protons in the atomic nucleus of the element. The number of particles in the nucleus of an atom is positively correlated to its atomic weight. A portion of the Periodic Table of the Elements is shown here.

Atomic number →	7	8	9	10
Symbol →	N	O	F	Ne
Element name →	Nitrogen	Oxygen	Fluorine	Neon
	15	16	17	18
	P	S	Cl	Ar
	Phosphorous	Sulphur	Chlorine	Argon

Which element has the smallest atomic weight?
(A) nitrogen
(B) neon
(C) phosphorous
(D) argon

QUESTIONS 10 THROUGH 13 REFER TO THE FOLLOWING INFORMATION:

G	Dominant Allele
g	Recessive Allele
GG	Homozygous (shows dominant trait)
Gg	Heterozygous (shows dominant trait)
gg	Homozygous (shows recessive trait)

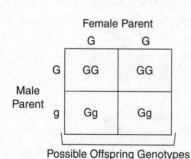

Possible Offspring Genotypes

10. The Punnett square shows a genetic cross. If the cross produces 20 offspring, how many will likely be homozygous?

    (A) 0
    (B) 5
    (C) 10
    (D) 20

11. According to the diagram, what is the probability that an offspring will show the recessive trait (g)?

    (A) 100%
    (B) 50%
    (C) 25%
    (D) 0%

12. Which of the following is the most likely distribution of offspring from a cross between a Gg parent and a Gg parent?

    (A) All will be heterozygous.
    (B) All will be homozygous.
    (C) Half will be heterozygous, and half will be homozygous.
    (D) One-quarter will be heterozygous, and three-quarters will be homozygous.

13. An organisms's *phenotype* describes the outward appearance of a genetic trait. If the dominant allele G carries the trait for yellow color in pea plants, what percentage of the offspring from a $GG \times gg$ cross will display the yellow phenotype?

    (A) 0%
    (B) 25%
    (C) 50%
    (D) 100%

THE EINSTEIN THEORY OF RELATIVITY

As summarized by an American astronomer, Professor Henry Norris Russell, of Princeton, in the *Scientific American* for November 29, Einstein's contribution amounts to this:

> "The central fact which has been proved—and which is of great interest and importance—is that the natural phenomena involving gravitation and inertia (such as the motions of the planets) and the phenomena involving electricity and magnetism (including the motion of light) are not independent of one another, but are intimately related, so that both sets of phenomena should be regarded as parts of one vast system, embracing all Nature. The relation of the two is, however, of such a character that it is perceptible only in a very few instances, and then only to refined observations."

Source: Lorentz, H. A. Excerpt from "The Einstein Theory of Relativity."
Reprint of the 1920 Edition, *Project Gutenberg*, 2004.
www.gutenberg.org/ebooks/11335.

14. Which characteristic of a scientific theory is demonstrated by Einstein's theory as described in the passage above?
    (A) It predicted and explained scientific findings that took place after the theory was first expressed.
    (B) It identified a relation that is very difficult to perceive.
    (C) It involved a lot of refined observation.
    (D) It provided a broad explanation that applies to many large subjects related to the natural world.

QUESTIONS 15 THROUGH 19 REFER TO THE FOLLOWING INFORMATION:

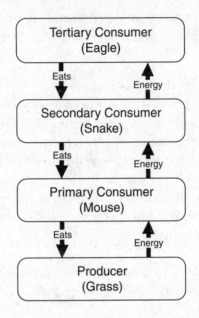

All living things require energy to survive, and this energy is usually contained in the food that a living thing eats. The simple food chain above shows the relationship between producers and consumers as well as the flow of energy between different members of the chain. Light energy from the sun is captured by plants through photosynthesis and is transferred up the chain: primary consumers eat producers, secondary consumers eat primary consumers, and tertiary consumers eat secondary consumers. Consumers are often referred to as "predators" and producers as "prey," although some predators (secondary consumers) are prey for (eaten by) other predators (tertiary consumers).

Since the size of a population is closely related to the size of its food supply, the relationships between the levels in a food chain serve to keep the populations of each group in balance. For example, an increase in the population of mice would reduce the amount of grass since more mice will need to eat more grass to survive. That same increase in the mouse population would likely lead to an increase in the population of snakes since more mice means more food for more snakes. By comparison, a decrease in the population of mice would probably have the opposite effect. There would be more grass since fewer mice exist to eat it and also fewer snakes since they would have less food available.

The top predator in a food chain refers to the consumer that has no natural predator. In the example on the previous page, the eagle is the top predator. An invasive species is a species that enters an ecosystem and competes for food with the species that are already present, disrupting the existing food chains. Invasive species are often new top predators because they have no natural predators in the new ecosystem. This can have a negative effect on the existing top predators since competition for their sources of food will increase. For example, if a new species of bird was introduced that fed primarily on snakes, the population of eagles would likely decrease as the eagles faced new competition for their food source (snakes). In some cases, the formerly top predator becomes prey to the new predator, which will also reduce the population of the previous top predator.

15. Which of the following would most negatively affect the total population of all groups in the food chain described in the passage?
    (A) a disease that kills grass and other edible green plants
    (B) a disease that paralyzes mice
    (C) a disease that prevents snakes from digesting meat
    (D) a disease that causes blindness in eagles

16. Which invasive species would be the least disruptive to this food chain?
    (A) a nonnative rodent that eats grass
    (B) a nonnative owl that eats mice
    (C) a nonnative weasel that eats snakes
    (D) a nonnative bird of prey that eats eagles

17. Herbivores are animals that eat plants. Carnivores are animals that eat other animals. Based on the information in the passage, which of the following is true?
    (A) All consumers are carnivores.
    (B) Some consumers are carnivores, and some are plants.
    (C) Some producers are plants, and some are carnivores.
    (D) Some consumers are herbivores, and some are carnivores.

18. The energy that flows up through a food chain begins with producers (plants). According to the information in the passage, how does the producer acquire the energy it supplies to this food chain?
    (A) The grass absorbs fossil fuels in the soil through its roots.
    (B) The grass absorbs heat in the air through its blades (leaves).
    (C) The grass creates energy in its cells through asexual reproduction.
    (D) The grass blades (leaves) absorb light from the sun.

19. Many people argue that humans are the top predator in virtually all food chains. Based on the information in the passage, which of the following statements best supports this view?
    (A) Some predators, like bears, wolves, and sharks, eat humans.
    (B) Technology enables humans to use almost any existing top predator as a food source.
    (C) Humans consume large amounts of grains, fruits, and vegetables.
    (D) Humans raise animals like cows and chickens to provide food like eggs and milk.

---

20. Which two siblings from the third generation are NOT affected by the inheritable trait?

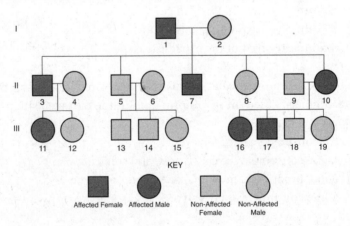

KEY

Affected Female   Affected Male   Non-Affected Female   Non-Affected Male

    (A) 11 and 16
    (B) 5 and 6
    (C) 14 and 19
    (D) 13 and 15

QUESTIONS 21 THROUGH 26 REFER TO THE FOLLOWING INFORMATION:

Month	Day of Month	Avg Daily Sunlight (kJ/m²)	Avg Daily Precipitation (mm)
April	1	7390.33	8.62
April	2	22834.31	0.5
April	3	23344.83	0
April	4	5846.87	22.11
April	5	13870.4	2
April	6	15799.67	0.2
April	7	18173.74	0
April	8	23357.81	0
April	9	20661.87	0
April	10	22936.32	0.91
April	11	10553.78	1.32
April	12	16167.93	9.09
April	13	11822.81	0.54
April	14	20765.47	0
April	15	25218.16	0

Source: North America Land Data Assimilation System (NLDAS)

21. What was the mean daily precipitation for the entire 15-day period? (Round to the nearest mm.)
    (A) 3
    (B) 4
    (C) 5
    (D) 6

22. What was the median daily precipitation for the entire 15-day period? (Round to the nearest mm.)
    (A) 0.2
    (B) 0.5
    (C) 0.91
    (D) 1.32

23. What is the mode of the set of 15 daily precipitation measurements?
    (A) 0
    (B) 0.5
    (C) 2
    (D) 22.11

24. What is the approximate range of the set of 15 daily sunlight measurements?
    (A) 25,000
    (B) 22,000
    (C) 20,000
    (D) 19,000

25. Which of the following best describes the correlation between daily precipitation and daily sunlight?
    (A) positive correlation
    (B) negative correlation
    (C) no correlation
    (D) variable correlation

26. A kilojoule (kJ) is equal to 1,000 joules. Which of the following correctly represents the average daily sunlight on April 5 in joules?
    (A) 1.579967×10^7
    (B) 1.38704×10^7
    (C) 1.579967×10^4
    (D) 1.38704×10^4

27. A botanist wanted to study the effects of variations in sunlight hours on the rate of the growth of oranges. He planted an orange tree in each of three greenhouses that are adjacent to each other on a large, open lot. He set the greenhouse skylights so that one tree got 12 hours of sunlight per day, one tree got 8 hours of sunlight per day, and one tree got 4 hours of sunlight per day. He measured the diameters of each orange on each tree once per week and recorded the measurements. He repeated this process for two years.

In the study above, what is the independent variable?
(A) the location of the greenhouses
(B) the amount of sunlight
(C) the species of orange tree
(D) the growth rate of the oranges

QUESTIONS 28 THROUGH 31 REFER TO THE FOLLOWING INFORMATION AND TABLE:

Atoms consist of three types of particles: protons, neutrons, and electrons. Protons carry a positive (+) electrical charge, and electrons carry a negative (–) electrical charge. Neutrons are neutral, meaning that they carry neither a positive nor a negative charge. When the number of protons in an atom is equal to the number of electrons, there is a balance between the positive and negative charges, making the atom neutral.

When the number of protons in an atom is not equal to the number of electrons, the atom is called an ion and carries an electrical charge. When the number of protons is greater than the number of electrons, the atom is a positive (+) ion. When the number of electrons is greater, the atom is a negative (–) ion. Ions of opposing charges tend to attract one another into ionic bonds. These bonds are formed when an electron is transferred from one atom to another, giving the two atoms opposing electrical charges. Ions with similar charges (+ and +, – and –) tend to repel one another.

The table below lists the numbers of protons and electrons for five different atoms.

Atom	Protons	Electrons
1	1	1
2	11	10
3	14	15
4	17	18
5	19	19

28. Select the word or phrase that correctly completes the sentence:

Atoms 3 and 4 are [Select ⌄] to form an ionic bond

(A) not able
(B) able
(C) sometimes able
(D) designed

because they have [Select ⌄] electrical charges.

(A) the same
(B) opposing
(C) no
(D) negative

29. Select the word or phrase that correctly completes the sentence:

Atom 2 is [Select ⌄] ion because it has [Select ⌄]

(A) a neutral
(B) a negative
(C) not an
(D) a positive

(A) a greater
(B) a smaller
(C) the same
(D) a nonexistent

number of protons compared to the number of electrons.

30. Select the word or phrase that correctly completes the sentence:

Atoms [Select ⌄] are able to form an ionic bond because

    (A) 1 and 5
    (B) 2 and 4
    (C) 3 and 4
    (D) 1 and 4

they have [Select ⌄] electrical charges.

    (A) the same
    (B) opposing
    (C) no
    (D) similar

31. Write the numbers for atoms 1, 2, 3, 4, and 5 in the appropriate box according to electrical charge.

Negative Charge	Neutral Charge	Positive Charge

QUESTIONS 32 THROUGH 35 REFER TO THE FOLLOWING TABLE AND INFORMATION:

Number of Valence Electrons

		1	2	3	4	5	6	7	8
	1	1 H Hydrogen	2 ← Atomic Number He ← Symbol and Helium Element Name						
Periods	2	3 Li Lithium	4 Be Beryllium	5 B Boron	6 C Carbon	7 N Nitrogen	8 O Oxygen	9 F Fluorine	10 Ne Neon
	3	11 Na Sodium	12 Mg Magnesium	13 Al Aluminum	14 Si Silicon	15 P Phosphorous	16 S Sulfur	17 Cl Chlorine	18 Ar Argon
		S1	S2	P1	P2	P3	P4	P5	P6
		S-Block		P-Block					

Position in Electron Configuration

In the table above, selected information is presented from the Periodic Table of the Elements. Valence electrons are electrons in an atom's outermost electron shell, called a valence shell. Periods refer to the number of electron shells present in an atom of a given type. The first electron shell in an atom can hold a maximum of 2 electrons. For atoms with more than one electron shell, the valence shell can hold a maximum of 8 electrons. All information shown assumes that the elements are neutral, meaning that the number of electrons in each element equals its atomic number.

32. All of the following statements about boron (B) are true EXCEPT
    (A) boron's first electron shell can hold a maximum of 2 electrons.
    (B) boron's atomic number is less than 18.
    (C) boron has 5 electrons.
    (D) boron has 3 electron shells.

33. Which of the following is true about phosphorous (P)?
    (A) It has 5 electrons.
    (B) It has fewer valence electrons than does chlorine.
    (C) It has more electron shells than does chlorine.
    (D) It has 2 electron shells.

20. **(D)** Choice D is correct because only 13 and 15 are from the third generation (III), are siblings (parents are 5 and 6), and are unaffected by the inheritable trait (light gray).

21. **(A)** Add the precipitation amounts and divide by 15. Then round 3.019 down to 3.

22. **(B)** After ordering the values from smallest to largest, the middle value (the 8th value) is 0.5.

23. **(A)** The most commonly appearing value is 0.

24. **(D)** The difference between the highest and lowest values is approximately 19,371, which is closest to 19,000.

25. **(B)** On days when the precipitation is high, the sunlight is low. On days when the precipitation is low, the sunlight is high.

26. **(B)** A kilojoule is 1,000 joules = 10^3 joules. The average daily sunlight on April 5 in joules is $13,870.4 \times 1,000 = 13,870,400$. Converting to scientific notation moves the decimal point 7 places to the left, making the product 1.38704×10^7.

27. **(B)** The independent variable is the one that another variable (called the dependent variable) "depends" on (i.e., is affected by). In this case, the growth rate of the oranges "depends" on the amount of sunlight, and the amount of sunlight does not "depend" on any other element of the experiment.

28. **(A), (A)** The second paragraph of the passage states that ions with similar charges tend to repel one another, which prevents them from forming an ionic bond. Atoms 3 and 4 both have more electrons than protons, giving them both a negative charge.

29. **(D), (A)** Atom 2 has 11 protons and 10 electrons, giving it a net positive charge.

30. **(B), (B)** Atom 2 is a positive ion, and atom 4 is a negative ion. These opposing charges are the basis for the ionic bond because objects with opposing charges attract each other.

31. **3 and 4 are negative, 1 and 5 are neutral, 2 is positive** Atoms with more electrons than protons are negative ions, atoms with more protons than electrons are positive ions, and atoms with the same number of each have a neutral electrical charge (i.e., no charge).

32. **(D)** Boron's atomic number is 5. This means it has a total of 5 electrons. Boron is in the second period, which means that it has two electron

shells. This is because the first electron shell of any element can hold a maximum of two electrons, so an additional shell is needed to hold the other 3 electrons.

33. **(B)** Phosphorus's atomic number is 15, which means it has a total of 15 electrons, not 5. It has 5 valence electrons, which refers to the number of electrons in the outermost electron shell. Chlorine has 7 valence electrons. Both phosphorus and chlorine are in the third period, which means that they both have 3 electron shells.

34. **(A), (B), (D)** Silicon is in the third period, which means it has 3 electron shells, while oxygen is in the second period, which means it has 2 electron shells. Silicon has 4 valence electrons, compared to sulfur's 6 valence electrons. Hydrogen and helium are in the first period, which means that they both have 1 electron shell. Hydrogen has 1 electron and 1 valence electron, while helium has 2 electrons and 2 valence electrons.

35. **Carbon** Carbon is in the second period, which means it has two electron shells, and it has 4 valence electrons.

SCORING YOUR SCIENCE EXAM

In 2016, the GED Testing Service made some adjustments to the "Performance Levels," or score levels, that they use to evaluate GED® test scores. The new structure has three levels based on the existing 100 to 200 score range:

- Passing (145+)—This is the minimum score needed to pass a GED® test.
- College Ready (165+)—A score at or above this level indicates that the student is ready for college-level work.
- College Ready + Credit (175+)—A score at or above this level indicates that the student should qualify for college credit.

Find the number of correct answers on your practice test in the chart below to determine your performance level:

Science Exam

Score Between	Performance Level
0 and 19	Not Passing
20 and 24	Close to Passing
25 and 29	Likely to Pass
30 and 31	College Ready
32 and 35	College Ready + Credit